BEYOND Strongholds

INFILTRATION BY THE GLORY OF GOD

CHRISTINE MEIER

CREATION HOUSE PRESS

BEYOND STRONGHOLDS by Christine Meier
Published by Creation House Press
A part of Strang Communications Company
600 Rinehart Road
Lake Mary, Florida 32746
www.creationhouse.com

This book or parts thereof may not be reproduced in any form, stored in a retrieval system or transmitted in any form by any means electronic, mechanical, photocopy, recording or otherwise without prior written permission of the publisher, except as provided by United States of America copyright law.

Unless otherwise noted, all Scripture quotations are from the Holy Bible, New International Version. Copyright © 1973, 1978, 1984, International Bible Society. Used by permission.

Scripture quotations marked NKJV are from the Holy Bible, the New King James Version. Copyright © 1979, 1980, 1982 by Thomas Nelson, Inc., publishers. Used by permission.

Scripture quotations marked KJV are from the King James Version of the Bible.

Scripture quotations marked AMP are from the Amplified Bible. Old Testament copyright © 1965, 1987 by the Zondervan Corporation. The Amplified New Testament copyright © 1954, 1958, 1987 by the Lockman Foundation. Used by permission.

Copyright 2002 by Christine C. Meier
All rights reserved

Library of Congress Catalog Card Number: 2002103143
International Standard Book Number: 0-88419-874-X

02 03 04 05 06 87654321
Printed in the United States of America

To contact the author:
Christine Meier
8688 A. D. McCall Rd.
Milton, FL 32583
whirlwindworship@aol.com

In memory of my Uncle Chet who, much to the chagrin of my mother and grandmother, at the age of three nicknamed me Tiger.

And in memory of Pastor and Sister Nunzio Leggio, our first pastors who taught us what it was to have the heart, love and sacrifice of spiritual tigers while we ascended to the heights on hinds' feet.

Special Thanks

My first and foremost is an offering of thanksgiving and dedication to Jesus. My prayer for the families, believers and individuals who read this book is that their dedication to Jesus will be stirred to overwhelming heights and they will be infused with the glory of our Father.

Some specific words of thanks are due:

To the members of the Hendrickson family who put up with me hogging their computers as they helped type a good portion of this book; to Jens and Kerstin Uhder, who used their professional expertise at translating books into English in order to help me translate "my English" into an English everybody else can understand.

To my family and other co-workers—without their support, this book would not have been finished.

While I may say "thank you" to my husband Bill last, he is truly the first one I should thank, outside of our Lord. My heart wells with gratitude for the covering he has been for every aspect of my life. He has shown forth Christ to me through more than twenty-two years of marriage like no mere mortal on earth could ever have done. Because of his Christ-like leadership, I could flourish. It goes without saying that if he were not my husband, I do not believe this book would ever have been written. I am eternally grateful to Jesus that He has prepared us as mates for life.

A Vision

As I turned to look, I saw a magnificient crown that became a splendid warrior's helmet, which turned into a breathtaking rose. I never lost sight of all three, but as I turned to look, one would become more pronounced than the other.

The crown had gems that shone forth with abundant light. Shaped like a princess tiara, it was not dainty, but bold and elegant. When I turned again I could see this helmet of war. It shown with a brilliant light that was almost blinding. It had an aspect of God in it that could kill off anything that did not belong to God. As I looked closer I saw this stunning rose. It was not frail as roses are in this world. It was made of a material that could not decay. It was unbreakable–indestructible. There were drops of dew that came from this rose that looked like liquid diamonds.

I never lost sight of these three items in the vision. As I was looking, I realized I was staring at the book you are now holding in your hand. But I was also seeing a call from God that was mine but wasn't mine at all; it belonged to *Him*. Jesus wanted to give this call and mantle to His bride, the church, as she travels from glory to glory–from earthly to the heavenly.

God Bless you as you journey in Christ.

1 Cor. 2:9
1 John 3:1
1 Cor. 13:12, 13

Disclaimer by Way of Explanation

This book was written between 1993 and 1997. It was typed and edited in 1998 and 1999 with various revisions being made at the suggestion of different editors from 2000 to the first part of 2002. The editing was primarily for structural flow, grammar and some content.

The goal of this book is to look at how our human strongholds can prevent God in glory from abiding upon us and then provide some positive suggestions for removing those strongholds. While some of the issues raised in this book may be similar to some current teachings by other authors, this was totally unintentional. All subject matter was researched first-hand from the Scriptures and from the book sources listed. All book sources used are footnoted.

My problem has always been that I'm too soon to the table. God always speaks to me years before I can even fathom what He's saying, because it seems to me that He's not saying the same thing to anyone else. I have this annoying habit, especially for those who have to live with me, of always looking at the future but living in the present. For those who don't know me, this can be quite challenging. In 1993, when I started the research for this book, neither my husband nor I had any idea that we would be living in Florida in 1997. Even as late as 1996, I had never heard of Brownsville Assembly of God. We moved to the area due to my husband's business, not really knowing where God would have us go to church. In 1997 we became members at Brownsville and have been blessed by this wonderful church and the special anointing that God has so graciously deposited in her midst. It would be a shame for anyone reading this book to make any connection between our membership there and any subject matter discussed here. In fact, just the opposite is true. It was a blessing for me to discover in 1998 that God spoke to the leadership at this church to implement programs that would keep some of the issues discussed in this book from taking place. At least for me, personally, this gave me confirmation and comfort that what the Lord showed me so many years before was "on target." We are still members and pray to remain faithful members for many years to come.

Throughout this book, I capitalize some things that normally would not be, and place in lower case some things that most authors capitalize. One of those obvious places is the name "satan." I'm sorry, but I refuse to capitalize his name. I pray you, the reader, can get accustomed to seeing it in smaller case.

Whenever names are mentioned, testimony releases are on file with the publisher, and/or the individual or individuals so mentioned are fictional. Any similarities to living persons is purely coincidental.

Many blessings in Christ as you go from glory to glory!

–Christine C. Meier

Contents

	Introduction ix
1	Beyond Strongholds 1
2	Recognizing the Time of Our Visitation ..19
3	The Word 37
4	The Word in His Prophets 53
5	His Knowledge 95
6	His Presence 117
7	The Name 151
8	His Image in His People 183
9	His People in His Image 215
10	Where Do We Go From Here? 249

Introduction

This work began one day in August of 1993. Father began speaking to me of His glory and how the church was intertwined and connected with that glory. I began spouting Scripture and blurted out, "Yeah, but You said You would not give your glory to another." (See Isaiah 42:8.) Immediately I sensed the Holy Spirit's rebuke, "Research the glory, starting with Genesis through the Word to John 1:1." He also instructed me to listen to a tape from a former pastor of ours who had preached on the subject many years before. As quickly as God spoke He became silent. As any child does when corrected, I did as instructed and started the research. I started to notice how often God's glorious presence was connected with *theophanies* throughout the Scriptures. *Theophanies* are the "manifestations or appearances of God to a person in a form that they can understand." With my research on His glorious presence nearly complete, I listened to a tape on the subject by a previous pastor of ours. I was quite surprised because He preached a good portion of what I had been learning from my personal research in a sermon five to ten years before. I thought it was nice of the Holy Spirit to give me such a confirmation. Frankly, I just thought this must have been a personal learning experience the Lord wanted to take me through in the Scriptures. Little did I realize that I was merely at the beginning, and the next few years would prove to be quite a learning experience!

Never the Same

This book was birthed as a result of my being arrested by the manifest presence of God during personal times with the Lord at home and as His glory fell upon the congregation of the church we attended. Although the experience was wonderful, I found that I felt troubled, as well. I began to see patterns of resistance in people. I realized from my study that there are various aspects of God's glory manifested during a visitation from God. I began to notice certain degrees of resistance to some of these expressions of God when He showed up in glory. Feeling somewhat confused—not with the manifestations of God's glory, but by these resistances—I turned to the Lord. He had already taken me through a study of His glory in the Scriptures, especially in the book of Ezekiel. When I realized that the resistances I had seen in the Scriptures were the same ones I was witnessing in His people, I marveled at the intricacy of God and His Word. When God Almighty shows up in His manifested glory no one is ever the same. Nevertheless, human attitudes of resistance to the Word of God can remain, even in the presence of God's glory. There are resistant attitudes toward diversifying leadership roles with the introduction of women and those of different nationalities and people of color. These attitudes can hinder the broader movement of God. While these attitudes may start on an individual basis, they can become corporate attitudes. These are strongholds of the mind. Those who hold them can seem impossible to dissuade from their opinions.

If we are honest and look at ourselves as God's people corporately and at ourselves as individuals, we will realize that if Christ is coming back for a church without spot or wrinkle, we're not it! (See Ephesians 5:27.) So, while the Holy Spirit—together with cleansing by the Word—will maintain us and make us spotless and wrinkle free, we need to be responsible for doing all we can to facilitate that process. I am not here to point out what's wrong with the Church of Jesus Christ. That would be like picking out a speck of dust in someone else's eye while a splinter (or worse, a beam) blinds me. I've developed a deep respect for the Old Testament practice of ripping one's clothes and putting on sackcloth and ashes. Thank God we now have redemption of sins through Jesus' blood. Yet a deep stirring in my spirit keeps reminding me that, unless we as God's people pay attention to some of these areas of personal bondage, we will be bound to repeat the mistakes made by our spiritual ancestors in Israel and

Introduction

by those during the more modern moves of God.

In each chapter I examine a particular aspect of God in His glory. I look at the specific human stronghold of resistance to God that often accompanies that aspect of glory. I then look at positive and scriptural steps to overcome these issues in our lives. Chapter 1 lays a foundation for the types of strongholds we will be discussing, while presenting an overview for teachings on the glory of God, as well. Chapter 2 provides an overview of the different expressions that we see when He comes in glory, along with the two main strongholds which resist Him when He comes. The remaining chapters address the strongholds specifically. I should also mention that I do not intend to address controversial matters concerning creation theology and eschatology, or end-times teachings. Such teachings have little impact upon whether or not an individual has a stronghold. When we as a people discover that we have a stronghold, our only concern should be to remove it through repentance and obedience. Israel of Christ's time exercised lively debates on different theological issues. And while Jesus may have rained on some of their parades concerning these issues, His main focus was getting them to understand their sinful strongholds, to repent and to believe in Him. In like fashion, my desire in presenting this material is to encourage people to look fully at the cross, repent of our strongholds and be restored by the blood, the Spirit and the totally cleansing power of Father God in glory.

Seeing His Glory

One day, to help me better understand all of this, the Holy Ghost called me into the sanctuary of the church I was attending. I sat quietly, slightly elevated from the ground on steps leading up to a small alcove area. After quietly worshiping in prayer-song before the Lord, the Holy Spirit directed my attention toward the altar. As in previous times, I could see the glory of the Lord shimmering over that place. What a beautiful sight! Then He spoke, "This is the last time you shall see the glory in this place."

BEYOND STRONGHOLDS

Stunned, I asked no questions. Somehow I just knew why. My heart waited for the Lord to confirm this word. (See 2 Corinthians 13:1.) He did so within three weeks. While I never did see the *Shechinah* in that place again, the manifestations and the practices of the people stayed the same, just as if the Lord in *Shechinah* glory was still there.

This reminded me of a passage found in Alfred Edersheim's book, *The Temple: Its Ministry and Services*.[1]

> **Thus far the Rabbis: All the more impressive is their own admission and their lament—so significant as viewed in the light of the Gospel: "For three years and a half abode the Shechinah" (or visible Divine presence) "on the Mount of Olives,"—waiting whether Israel would repent—"and calling upon them, 'Seek ye the Lord while He may be found, call upon Him while He is near.' And when all was in vain, then the Shechinah returned to its own place!"**

This book is not meant to be all-inclusive. This book is not meant to talk about all strongholds. It is not meant to talk about all aspects of God in glory. Broken down in simplest terms, strongholds are sin, and God in glory is His presence. God's presence cannot reside with sin. Edersheim quotes the old rabbis as testifying that God gave them three and half years to deal with the issues He was making known to them. Knowing God is a growth process. We know some things about God that Israel of old did not know. There are some today that are farther along in God's growth process than others. For those farther along than this book can go, bear with me in Christ. What this book is meant to be is an encouragement to all saints, both those who work in ministry full time as salaried workers and those who work for our Lord without stipend. It's not meant to be a how-to book either. It's simply meant to expose some aspects of our own stubbornness and how our adversary will use that stubbornness to try and trap us. Our adversary never was and never will be a problem for God. During Jesus' time on earth the devil and his

Introduction

crew were never a problem for our Lord. Much of Jesus' trouble came from the religious crowd and the worldly government of His day. What this book is meant to do is to encourage all of us to experience God's multifaceted glory in this day and age and be changed by His all-encompassing presence. As we present ourselves as living sacrifices, we become incense housed in His whirlwind worship. (See Romans 12:1–3.) We will become so transformed that the world and religious crowd will want more of Jesus. If we refuse and resist Him now, we stand the chance of repeating their mistakes.

I quote Edersheim again:

> The Shechinah has withdrawn to its own place! Both the city and the temple have been laid "even with the ground," because Jerusalem knew not the time of her visitation (Luke 19:44). "They have laid Jerusalem on heaps" (Ps. 79:1). "The stones of the sanctuary are poured out in the top of every street" (Lam. 4:1). All this, and much more, did the Savior, the rightful king of Israel, see in the near future, when "He beheld the city, and wept over it." And now we must search very deep down, sinking the shaft from 60 to over 125 feet through the rubbish of accumulated ruins, before reaching at last the ancient foundations. And there, close by where once the royal bridge spanned the deep chasm and led from the City of David into the royal porch of the Temple, is "the Jews' wailing place," where the mourning heirs to all this desolation reverently embrace the fallen stones, and weep unavailing tears—unavailing because the present is as the past, and because what brought that judgment and sorrow is unrecognized, unrepented, unremoved. Yet, "Watchman, what of the night? Watchman, what of the night? The watchman said, The morning cometh, and also the night. If ye will inquire, inquire! Return, come!"[2]

Then I heard a loud voice in heaven say: "Now have come the salvation and the power and the kingdom of our God, and the authority of his Christ. For the accuser of our brothers, who accuses them before our God day and night, has been hurled down. They overcame him by the blood of the Lamb and by the word of their testimony; they did not love their lives so much as to shrink from death. Therefore rejoice, you heavens and you who dwell in them! But woe to the earth and the sea because the devil has gone down to you! He is filled with fury, because he knows that his time is short."

—Revelation 12:10–12

Chapter One

BEYOND STRONGHOLDS

While we wait for our Lord's return, we sometimes view His coming as an invasion. The Scriptures make it clear that our Lord will come to some as a thief in the night, similar to a surprise invasion. But what leads up to this invasion? Jesus told us to occupy until He comes. (See 1 Thessalonians 5:2.) In occupying, we take up the territory or space that usurping demon forces have stolen. But how? Who helps us do this? First and foremost we have the blood of Jesus and the testimony of Jesus Christ that make us overcomers. (See Revelation 12:11.) Then the Holy Spirit establishes communication lines and gives us spiritual gifts as blessings to renew our brethren and as weaponry against our adversary.

What has Father God given us? The Father has given us Himself in glory. The Bible says that the whole earth is full of His glory. (See Isaiah 6:3.) During certain times of revival and reformation, He allows His glory to fill us, even with our resistance and sin. But these resistances prevent God in glory from abiding and remaining upon us forever. (See Isaiah 42:8.) This creates the need for infiltration. It's as if God must fill us in increasing increments. As God in glory infiltrates our strongholds and saturates us individually, we become an occupying force for Jesus when He does return. Infiltrating our strongholds is subtler, taking more time, but it is also more complete. When an invasion takes place, pockets of resistance can remain. When you infiltrate you wipe out resistance.

One would think that, as we submit more and more to the will of God—because of the blood of Jesus and the indwelling Holy Spirit—our hidden resistances would be swept away when God in glory shows up. Remember that we work out our salvation with fear and trembling as we are taken from glory to glory. (See Philemon 2:12; 2 Cor. 3:18.) We must work as God does His good work in us.

By way of example, the *Shechinah* glory rested upon the temple in Israel in a manifested way to a far greater extent than anything we've experienced. Still, their resistances are cataloged in the Scriptures over and over until they finally resisted the Lord of Glory Himself.

When our resistant strongholds have been made into fortresses and we lull ourselves into believing that the manifestations of God's glory are a sign that we have no resistant human attitudes, we deceive ourselves. (See 1 John 1:8–10.) Sooner or later God in His glory moves on. We cannot suppose that, because God in glory is among us, we have no strongholds or hidden issues to address.

Israel acted as if they had no issues to deal with while the Lord of Glory Himself, Jesus Christ, walked among them for three years. For three years many resisted the Lord of Glory, and they ultimately crucified Him. This precipitated judgment from God, which took many of our Jewish brethren down the hard road of persecution and tribulation. John the Baptist tried to warn them ahead of time to repent. Thankfully many did. But by comparison, only a small number got to experience God in abiding glory on their lives following Christ's ascension.

Abiding Glory

I believe that now is the time that God desires to abide upon us continuously in a manifested way. He wants to do this in order to draw thousands to Christ and to bring judgment upon the satanic world system. If we wish to see Him abide in glory, we will have to pull down patterns of resistant human attitudes. These attitudes resist different expressions of God as He manifests Himself to us in glory through His Word, His knowledge, His presence, His name and through His people.

The church generation that has gone before us has, to some extent, ignored this issue. I believe that God is currently sending a transitional generation that will review these issues and usher God in glory to earth in a manifested way. This generation is being trained and prepared by the Holy Ghost to speak to a generation of children.

When Jesus came to earth the first time, He needed the prophet John the Baptist—a relative from His own family—to prepare His way. How much more shall we, covered and partaking of that same blood, prepare the way for our Elder Brother as He comes to earth the second time. If we can recognize the times of our visitations and succeed in making the crooked paths straight, we could prepare the way for the Lord with a generation of young people. As God in glory comes upon all creation—literally changing the atmosphere we inhabit—the lion will be able to lay down with the lamb, and a child would surely lead them. (See Habakkuk 2:14; Isaiah 11: 1-9.)

What Is the Glory?

While our hope and faith remain unshaken in Christ's efficacious blood, let's study the problems of these resistances. Whenever God manifests His person on earth in a form in which we humans can understand, we as Bible students have come to call these appearances *theophanies*. We see Him coming by fire or a cloud, speaking to Moses or Abraham or a number of other Old Testament saints.

When God shows up His glory comes with Him. You can no more separate Him from His glory than you can separate Christ from the Word. The Bible teaches us that God is light. (See 1

BEYOND STRONGHOLDS

John. 1:5.) It's impossible to separate Father God from light or to separate light from the Holy Spirit. This is because God the Father, God the Son and God the Holy Spirit are One. Christ is the Word, and Jesus is the Only Begotten Son of the Father. It's important to realize that we can never separate any part of God from who or what He is.

Nevertheless, we can study the different aspects of who God is. In order to do that, sometimes a line is drawn, or an illustration is given to help us understand how awesome God is. That is why God appears in *theophany* form. He appears in order to reveal Himself to us. When God invades our time and space to reveal Himself to us so that we might understand Him, His glory always accompanies Him. The difficulty for me in attempting to define the glory of God is that it is like trying to define God. What words can one find to describe Him? But for the purpose of better understanding His glory, I will make an attempt.

God's glory is the weighty presence that surrounds Him. The Hebrew word for glory is *kabod*. It includes the weighty splendor and lavish magnificence of His honor. God's glory is weighty simply because it surrounds Him. The other word our Jewish brethren had for this manifestation of God's presence was the word *Shecaniah*. It can also be spelled in our English language as *Shechinah*. This word is translated as "YAH has dwelt." We understand it as the visible divine presence of God. We understand this more as the atmosphere around Him as He invades our time and space. As a result, He allows us to see or feel "something."

Howd is another Hebrew word that refers to the glory of God. This is the word that's used when God's glory is displayed in the heavenlies, as we read about in Habakkuk 3:3: "God came from Teman, the Holy One from Mount Paran. Selah. His glory covered the heavens and His praise filled the earth." It is through this passage that we understand that when God shows up, His glory is present as an outward extension of His person. In this verse of Scripture we can see that when He shows up His glory literally covers the heavens. I suppose this is why we use the terms "the glory has *fallen* on us." Because God covers the heavens in glory and because He—and by extension His glory—is so weighty, we feel as if He has *fallen* on us, when, in fact, all He probably did was say "hello." Mount Sinai shook when He showed up. It would make sense that as a result of His covering the heavens in glory, the earth would fill with His praises. (See Habakkuk 3:3.)

His Glorious Purposes

God reveals Himself in glory. He reveals His grandeur in beauty, excellence, honor and majesty. So it is He—His presence. God is light. God is a spirit. When He comes His glory rises upon us. God is a consuming fire, and our God is love. By allowing Himself to be represented by glory, light, fire and love, he defines these things rather than these defining Him. Nevertheless, I suppose we, as human beings, need some word to describe Him. This is why He reveals Himself. This is why we need *theophanies*, appearances and manifestations of His glorious presence.

Over the centuries, great revivals, renewals and restorations have taken place, which resulted in different kinds of manifestations of God in glory. All have produced the same outcome—God showed up in glory, and no one was ever the same. Sometimes such appearances changed widely held church practices and/or theology. They also reached beyond the church and dramatically impacted the secular world.[1]

God's glory always showed up as a part of a larger purpose and plan. Often it appears that once His purpose was complete, the glory lifted and God's manifested presence left. But did God in manifested glory really want to leave? If so, why create Adam and Eve with the privilege of unbroken fellowship with God? In fact, we know His purpose was to continue that fellowship for all eternity, and so He will! But what if His constant appearance to make a change in us meets with the same problem Adam and Eve fell into in the Garden—namely, sin? The Bible warns us that His Spirit will not always strive with us. (See Genesis 6:3.) When God has poured Himself out gloriously and some change has taken place, but we are not ready to continue changing, His glory departs and all looks the same as it did before. God desires to abide in us with a passion that we cannot comprehend. Nevertheless, He will not abide with man's willful resistances to the total purposes that He has desired to accomplish by manifesting His all glorious presence. It is for this reason that this book endeavors to reveal these resistances so that we might pull them down from the lofty places we put them. Such resistances are called strongholds or fortresses in the Scriptures.

Three Major Types of Strongholds

The Bible speaks of three different categories of fortresses or strongholds. They are:

- human strongholds (Gen. 11: 4; Judg. 6:2; Jer. 6:27, KJV)

- godly strongholds (2 Sam. 22:2,3; Ps. 61:3; Prov. 18:10)

- satanic strongholds (Isa.14: 5,13; Ezek. 28:18; Matt. 12:24–29)

While the Old Testament often refers to physical fortresses or strongholds that represent spiritual ones, New Testament teachings are more explicit. The apostle Paul clearly states in 2 Corinthians 10:4, 5 that strongholds are arguments, ideas (thoughts) or pretensions that set themselves up against what God thinks or knows. He is writing to believers and referring to human thoughts and ideas, not demonic ones. While devils are not beyond attempting to institute thoughts or ideas in our minds to thwart all that God does, Paul's primary concern is human thoughts and arguments—especially those within the church, where subtle resistances to God-knowledge affect the corporate Bride of Christ.[2]

It might help us to see these strongholds from a different angle. Not to state the obvious, but a stronghold is a place of strength. We have developed areas in our characters from which we draw

Beyond Strongholds

strength. When these areas, habits or attitudes become places where we are so strong that we don't need God or so strong that we think we know better than He does, they are now human strongholds that have become ungodly. God's character will no longer be evident in those parts of our lives.

A hypothetical example might help. Suppose you have a pastor that is a strong leader. This individual was raised in a home where order kept the family running smoothly. There were no surprises. This was a source of strength and stability for the children. But it also left a subtle attitude that anything out of the ordinary was to be viewed with suspicion. This pastor unknowingly grew up with the attitude that, in order for there to be stability, everything had to be controlled so that there were no surprises. You can see from our hypothetical example that this pastor is in for a surprise when God decides to use people or circumstances to effectuate His plans.

While order for any church can be an excellent source of godly strength, this attitude can go too far. This pastor and the church that he leads must bring their particular stronghold to the cross so that God may bring this source of human strength that has gone awry in line with His plans. If they do not, they may miss a time of glorious visitation from the Holy Ghost.

Conversely, you can have just the opposite stronghold. You may have a pastor who was raised in a home where Mom and Dad were spontaneous. Nothing was regulated. Growing up was so much fun in this household that any controls were viewed with suspicion. The children were encouraged to be very individualistic. Any challenge to their individuality was taboo. You can see from this hypothetical situation what kind of pastor this person will become. This pastor and the church she leads in this manner are in for a huge surprise when God comes in glory because He does so on His prescribed order. If they do not institute God's prescribed order and discipline, the glory cannot be shouldered properly.

In both these hypothetical situations, an active desire to repent of long held attitudes was necessary. These attitudes were not necessarily bad from a human viewpoint, but they needed adjustment by the Holy Spirit so He can be comfortable and can rest. In each instance a source of human strength needed to be brought to the cross and crucified so that God could resurrect a source of godly strength or a godly stronghold.

We see this same theme in Psalm 89:40. Here it says that God has established David's line, covenant and throne. Yet in verse 40 we realize that God has broken through and reduced David's strongholds—his line, covenant and throne—to ruins. In other words, God took away everything that was a source of human strength so that the only source of strength David had left was God. We all know from David's life that, when he repents, God always restores him.

The other difficulty with our strongholds is that they tend to be reproduced in the people we have some authority over. You can see from our two hypothetical examples that these pastors will preach and teach from two totally different childhood experiences. Without even realizing it, many in the congregation will begin to view God's Word from the same strongholds these pastors have if they, themselves, are not in a right relationship with God and His Word. Thank God that our Lord knows we are but flesh. He keeps and protects His churches so that in many churches the good is passed onto us instead of the negative.

He is so gracious and longsuffering. He gives us time to mature and grow in the Holy Ghost, and we learn that repentance is a daily act, not just a first time event. But suppose we never come to realize that one of our strongholds needs to be brought to the cross? Whether we like it or not it is still our responsibility to bring our own sin to the cross. It is only at the cross that we can find grace and mercy overflowing.

Only we as individuals can pull down our own high-minded ideas from the lofty places we put them. Once we take these stronghold resistances seriously and deal with them in godly ways, Christ will cause all other disobedience to be brought under His subjection, including heavenly demonic strongholds. (See 2 Corinthians 10:6, AMP.)

Beyond Strongholds

Since the church is made up of individual believers, these resistances start within us individually. It is when we do not recognize them as resistant strongholds that they can become corporate strongholds. These strongholds are nothing more than our own fleshly desires wanting it our own way, especially in the house of the Lord. Flesh reproduces flesh and it provides demons a place or fortress in which to either hide or attack people, or from which to oppress them. The enemy can use these attitudes as well, particularly if we refuse to repent of them and search out their roots.

The purpose of this book is not to research different types of human strongholds but to review those specific human strongholds that resist God when He comes in glory. If we truly desire for God's glory to abide in our churches and in us in a manifested way, we will need to deal with our strongholds. When God has continually poured out His glory over His people through the centuries and these same patterns of resistance exist, judgment is at hand. (See Isaiah 28: 9–22.) I'm not being a doomsayer here, nor do I believe bad things are in store for God's people. On the contrary, I believe we win! If we really believe what we preach and we really expect God to show up forever, we need to provide a place for Him in our hearts and our churches where He is as comfortable as He is in heaven. When we don't provide such a place for God, we are close to instituting two Old Testament concepts that can lead to judgment.

Tamei and Shaatnez

God stirs up controversy every time He sends prophets or comes to earth Himself. Frankly, I think He does this just to show us our strongholds. Biblical history has shown us that instead of dealing with our issues we shoot the messengers. Without exception, every Old Testament prophet, including Jesus, came on the scene to break up what scholars have called "priest craft."

Priest craft, as a stronghold, is similar in its negative connotation to witchcraft, but it is different. Priest craft is a result

BEYOND STRONGHOLDS

of our debate with God's desire to do things His way when He arrives on the scene. When we, as priests, function by Jesus Christ, who is the Word, through the Holy Spirit we function as holy vessels. When we confuse our fleshly understanding with God's holy desires, or when we substitute a portion of what He says for what we desire in our carnality, then we function in priest craft.

Two Old Testament words better explain this concept. When you tell Christian people not to sin, often their attitude sounds like this: "I don't smoke or chew or go with those who do. So I don't sin." It is hard to convince some people that spiritual sin is the same as physical sin. Strongholds are those attitudes that we use as shields of faith to protect us instead of God. Only His Word and His Spirit can be our shield of faith. When we substitute our own systems of protection for His Word and mix our own desires with the Holy Spirit's commands, we function in two different Hebrew words. They are *tamei* and *shaatnez*.

Tamei is most often translated as "tainted or polluted." More modern scholars believe that the word *tamei* is best translated through the modern word radioactivity.[3] In other words, the environment around us becomes so charged by the radioactive toxicity of our sin that God leaves.

Here's the subtlety of radioactivity. In and of itself it is not toxic. What makes it toxic is that it fools you, causing you to exchange the real for the fake. Radioactive chemicals such as Strontium 90 mimic calcium, Cesium 137 mimics potassium and Carbon 14 mimics nitrogen. Our bodies depend upon calcium and potassium for good health. Every plant that grows on our planet needs nitrogen. When the real calcium, potassium or nitrogen is not present, in order to survive, our bodies will substitute whatever counterfeit they find that mimics the real. Plants do the same thing.

In fact, this acceptance of counterfeit minerals is so dangerous that even after a small amount of exposure, our bodies can begin preferring the substitute counterfeit instead of the real even when the real is available, because the counterfeit becomes easier to assimilate.

Beyond Strongholds

Now think of this in spiritual terms; how easy it is for us to get ideas, thoughts and pretensions (2 Cor. 10:4, 5) that can exalt themselves over and above what God thinks or knows. Satan will always try to substitute his ways instead of what God wants. Isn't this what the antichrist is—an attempt at substitution for Jesus Christ?

Shaatnez has to do with mixing things in matters in which only God is allowed to mix things. Under the Old Covenant, fields, crops, clothing and animals fell into this category. While the word *tamei* dealt more with the pollution of the sanctuary, vessels and people, *shaatnez* encompassed how people survived outside the temple. Mixing could only be accomplished as God deemed fit, not according to their individual human judgment.

The Old Testament leaders and priests worked hard to keep up the appearance of following these laws (they didn't smoke or chew or go with those who do). But the very attitudes that these words and laws would have prevented had they been obeyed in the priests' hearts were attitudes they functioned in every day. They had so twisted Scripture by substituting their own interpretations of the law that they found it easy to crucify Christ, thus creating a *tamei*, or polluted spiritual environment. They so mixed God with their own desires that for forty more years they didn't miss a heart beat, but kept the temple going as if Christ had never been there. They mixed what they thought God wanted with what He was actually doing on earth.

Defilement in Our Temples

Christ comes to change our attitudes and how we do things. Jesus came to change the programs, rules and regulations of the priests in the temple and to change the hearts of the Jewish people in general. 1 Corinthians 10 mentions the rich history that God has laid down for us through our Jewish brethren as an example.

Paul speaks about our ignorantly partaking and fellowshipping with demons. He is speaking about eating foods offered as a sacrifice to Greek or Roman deities. Most of us as Christians would say we never partake in any of those practices. Yet we never notice our own patterns of resistance that we set up as protections for God and the Bible. These patterns of resistance are attitudes, rules, programs and regulations. They are based upon our own motives, attitudes and plans. When we fail to recognize them as fleshly motives—not plans ordained by God—we then institute our own programs, rules, regulations and ideas to support our plans. These rules, regulations, ideas and attitudes are set up, I believe, out of good intentions, even though they may be misguided in their applications. (See 2 Corinthians 10: 4–5.) We then become subject to pride and grow increasingly unwilling to change or correct these patterns and practices.

These rules, attitudes and ideas can create a structure or stronghold all by themselves. Sometimes they aren't even spoken out loud, but everybody knows they exist. Unfortunately, if these things are not God ordained, nothing but human flesh covers them. They are protective shields of behavior that humans have set up. Demons need places of protection or structure. These hidden places can become coverings for them. (See Matthew 12:43; Ezekiel 8:5.) For principalities and powers that have taken a region captive, a perfect place to hide in order to oppress people is in a church or over a group of individuals with attitudes, rules or ideas that have an unhealthy effect on those around them. They become unhealthy because they are human instituted, not God ordained. You might say that God's anointing would not be on such endeavors.

We fail to realize that each individual and church is given gifts from God, saved or unsaved (Rom. 11:29). Saved folks get more gifts from God over a period of time than unsaved people. Since these gifts and callings are irrevocable, we are going to function in them no matter what we do. We can use God's gifts to get what we want, and it can look very good and feel anointed because it is. It's His anointing, and He doesn't take it back just because we decide He should. Remember how the Lord told Samuel that it grieved Him that He had made Saul king? (See 1 Samuel 15:10, 11.) He's God; why didn't he take Saul out immediately instead

Beyond Strongholds

of wait 21 more years? Our Lord's gifts and callings are irrevocable. If He took the kingship back from Saul immediately He would violate His own Word. Instead He gave Saul all those years to repent. Of course, this also gave David time to learn how to be a better king than Saul. Time is getting closer and closer to our Lord's Second Coming. I believe He is challenging His people to act more responsibly with His anointing while under His glory. As God's time schedule moves along whenever He shows up, His presence will begin to draw a very distinct line in the sand. He is God, and only His will and His plans and purposes can stand.

Three Purposes of God

God has done all He has done on the earth to fulfill three goals or purposes.

1 First, to redeem a chosen people called out from before the foundation of the earth. (See Ephesians 1:4; Hebrews 4:3b; 1 Peter 1:20.)

2 Second, to establish a bride for Christ who learns how to rule and reign over the usurping enemy force that has occupied God's earth. (See Ephesians 1:20–23; 2:6.)

3 Third, as Christ's bride functions in Christ through the Holy Spirit in occupying until He comes, we prepare the earth for Father to rest and for His glory to cover the earth as the waters cover the seas. (See Isaiah 6:3; Habakkuk 2:14.)

When we lose sight of this bigger picture of God coming in glory, we lose sight of our resistances to that glory and the complicities those resistances have with demons, principalities and powers. Satan does not want God in glory to infiltrate those on earth, including sinners. If God does, satan's time is up–and we win. If he can seduce us into building up stronghold resistances when God arrives in glory, making us believe that what we're doing is totally "God," then he thinks he can forestall the inevitable. When our church practices or ideas have gained us many victories, and they become a source of strength, God may come to break them. (See 2 Chronicles 16:7–9.) God alone must be our source of strength. If we fail to change these practices or ideas, they become resistant strongholds.

The sad reality is that we mix (*shaatnez*) God's glory, which is upon us with our resistant strongholds. In so doing, we function as Paul exhorted us not to in 1 Corinthians 10, by "eating" something that demons can find comfort and rest in, and so we become partakers with them. Paul gives the readers the benefit of the doubt when we do such things in ignorance. Repentance and submission to God through Christ's blood wipes our sins away. But when God in glory shows up in a manifested way, very few of us can claim ignorance.

The enemy's tactics have, unfortunately, increased over the last few decades. (See Revelation 12:12, 17.) The lie has been his primary weapon. When we believe his lies he is then able to steal, kill and destroy. (See John 10:10.) Death by any means is his favorite tool because it is his final and most effective tool.

Plainly speaking, when God in glory shows up, it's His way of doing things—His will be done on earth as it is in heaven. When we, in our own limited wisdom, mix our plans with God's plans and our ways of doing things with His ways, we enter into the dangerous realm of control and manipulation. When we substitute our limited knowledge for God's limitless knowledge, we create a *tamei*, or polluted, environment that stunts our growth in Christ and negatively impacts those around us.

Believing a Lie

In the next few chapters, we will get into specific causes and effects, but nearly all start with believing a lie and conditioning our minds to walk in that direction. When our thoughts exalt themselves against God's desires, His ways of doing things or His

Beyond Strongholds

revealed Word, and we refuse to submit to Him, rebellion takes over. It's this rebellion that gives entrance to the enemy into our lives. While rebellion usually starts in small ways, it can end with whole nations being stolen by territorial spirits who set up princes and rulers. (See Song of Solomon 2:15.) Satan is then given reign to steal, kill and destroy. Thank God Ephesians chapters 1 and 2 tell us we are seated with Christ far above their rule. It is a sad thought that many acknowledge this by word but their prayers and actions deny this truth.[4]

Christ mentions these issues when He speaks to the church in Pergamum and talks about satan's rule in that city and what strongholds were evident in the hearts and minds of the believers, with the resultant sins accompanying those thoughts. (See Revelation 2:12, NIV.) In fact, to almost every first century church mentioned there, He points out the strongholds or thoughts and teachings and what they were producing in the people. This is why there was a common exhortation to overcome. Because Christ has called us to be overcomers, the apostle Paul spoke often of our need to renew our minds, especially in connection with God's gifts. (See Romans 12:1–2.) It is by the blood of Christ and His testimony that we overcome. (See Revelation 12:11.) It is by God washing us with the Word and both baptisms that our minds are renewed. (See Ephesians 5:26–27; Hebrews 6:1–3.) And it is through His wonderful gifts and by prayer and faith that we have weaponry for the battle so we can overcome.

Revival and Restoration

God makes no mistakes when He sends renewal or revival. Each one has restored some foundational truth of God back into practice, whether it was the gifts of the Holy Spirit, the fivefold ministry or the motivational gifts. (See 1 Corinthians 12, 13, 14; Ephesians 4; Romans 12.) We need all that God has so we can live in the Spirit His way in order to be overcomers.

It is also no coincidence that every revival or renewal was preceded by prayer, intercession and spiritual warfare, along with the truths God was imparting for those gifts. For example, intercession and teaching took place by John Hus as much as one hundred years prior to the Protestant Reformation. In the case of the Charismatic Renewal, intercession and teaching took place by Rees Howells forty years before.[5]

Paul writes, "The weapons of our warfare are not carnal, but mighty through God to the pulling down of strongholds; Casting down imaginations, and every high thing that exalteth itself against the knowledge of God, and bringing into captivity every thought to the obedience of Christ" (2 Cor. 10:4,5, KJV). These strongholds are within us—in our thoughts, imaginations and high-minded ideas. Therefore, repentant actions of humility through group prayer, along with intercession, deliverance, inner healing and worship teams become valuable weapons in the hands of any church. Churches with fivefold ministries overseeing these teams can see countless souls saved and reap the benefits of the kingdom of God expanded within their sphere of influence.

But what happens once we take back a city or region for God? Our victory can only be maintained by the Almighty, Himself, filling us with all that He is so that His glory quickens us and everything around us. Apostles, prophets, pastors, teachers and evangelists cannot maintain a region or city for Christ if they fail to recognize God and the purposes He wishes to accomplish by manifesting Himself in glory. Israel failed to do so and met with disaster after Solomon's dedication of the temple. (See 2 Chronicles 5:14; 12:1, 8; 24: 18, 19.) The Israelites failed to repent before God so their land might be healed. The resultant confiscation of their land by territorial spirits and demons caused famine, death and destruction. The Israelites exchanged God's way of doing things for faith in a king. (See 1 Samuel 8: 6-9.) It took time for them to reap the harvest, but reap they did! God mercifully ordained the prophet Daniel to humble himself before the Almighty, confessing the sin of the people and asking forgiveness for a nation. One prophet understanding a time of visitation produced an entire nation who could understand God's timing regarding the rebuilding of Jerusalem and the

Beyond Strongholds

appearance of Messiah! Yet to this day there are still some Jewish leaders who do not recognize Daniel as a prophet, which is why the book of Daniel is not placed with the other prophetic books in Jewish Bibles.

If the people of Israel could not maintain the portion of land entrusted to them by God, and if the early church with all its gifts has needed to be restored, what makes us think we can take back earthly territories stolen with anything less than full armor, weaponry and the infiltrating power of God's manifest presence in glory?

In the sixth year, in the sixth month on the fifth day, while I was sitting in my house and the elders of Judah were sitting before me, the hand of the Sovereign Lord came upon me there. I looked, and I saw a figure like that of a man. From what appeared to be his waist down he was like fire, and from there up his appearance was as bright as glowing metal. He stretched out what looked like a hand and took me by the hair of my head. The Spirit lifted me up between earth and heaven and in visions of God he took me to Jerusalem, to the entrance to the north gate of the inner court, where the idol that provokes to jealousy stood. And there before me was the glory of the God of Israel, as in the vision I had seen in the plain. Then he said to me, "Son of man, look toward the north." So I looked, and in the entrance north of the gate of the altar I saw this idol of jealousy. And he said to me, "Son of man, do you see what they are doing—the utterly detestable things the house of Israel is doing here, things that will drive me far from my sanctuary? But you will see things that are even more detestable."

—Ezekiel 8:1–6

Chapter Two

RECOGNIZING THE TIME OF OUR VISITATION

The word *sanctuary* can convey the meaning of a place of godly strength for safety—in other words, a stronghold. In Proverbs it says that the name of the Lord is a strong tower. (See Proverbs 18:10.) The word *kedesh* means "a sanctum," which is a strong place of safety. The word *kodesh* means a "holy sanctuary." The word *kadesh* means a "male prostitute or idolater." They all stem from the same root, only the vowels change. We see from Ezekiel 8:1–6 that Israel was doing things that would chase God from His sanctuary. Later on in the chapter the Bible quotes the elders as saying, "The Lord does not see us; the Lord has forsaken the land." As a result of this attitude they continue on in their sin. God says to Ezekiel,

> Have you seen this, son of man? Is it a trivial matter for the house of Judah to do the detestable things they are doing here? Must they also fill the land with violence and continually provoke me to anger?...Therefore, I will deal with them in anger; I will not look on them with pity or spare them. Although they shout in my ears, I will not listen to them.
>
> —Ezekiel 8:17, 18

BEYOND STRONGHOLDS

The attitudes of these elders showed that they thought God did not see what they were doing. They defiled a place of godly strength and prostituted themselves there. As a result they were not able to shoulder Him in glory; they had not prepared the temple. Jesus told many parables of people not being ready when the son of man appeared, and He admonished us to be ready. (See Matthew 24: 36–51, 25:1–13; Revelation 16:15, 19:7.)

Under both Old and New Covenants God appears when He feels comfortable or at home. There are certain expressions of God that are highlighted to us when He comes. He comes as the **Word**. His **presence** and **knowledge** accompany Him. He comes in His own **Name** and on His **people**, who should express His very nature and character.

Every time God determined to appear throughout the Bible it was called a *coming* or *parousia*. He is the One who was and is and is to come. (See Revelation 4:8.) There are many "comings" spoken of in the Bible, including our Lord's Second Coming. Each time God came He accomplished a predetermined outcome. Each Old Testament visitation was cloaked in symbolism and mystery. We've called them *theophanies*. Unfortunately, we humans take thousands of years to understand the manifold purposes in just one of His appearances. Every time He comes it's glorious.

Let's look at God appearing to the prophet Ezekiel by the Kebar River in Babylon. (See Ezekiel 1 and 2.) One thing I notice when I read these two chapters is that it's difficult to determine whether Ezekiel was ushered into the glory or God in glory moved to totally encompass Ezekiel—or both! Ezekiel means "God strengthens." As a priest and prophet, Ezekiel's ministry was encompassed by the sanctuary, where the glory is. (See Ezekiel 1:3.) God's sanctuary, or God's stronghold, was Ezekiel's strength. God embraces Ezekiel and ushers him into His heavenly sanctuary. It is only in God's sanctuary—as it becomes the inner sanctuary of our hearts and minds—that God strengthens us.

Look at the prophet's response to being ushered into this appearance of the Lord in glory in Ezekiel 1:28. He falls face

Recognizing the Time of our Visitation

down! But God's response in Chapter 2:1-2 is, "Stand Up." God speaks and the Spirit raises or strengthens Ezekiel, both calling and commissioning him at the same time. This is called a *theophany* because God appeared in a form that Ezekiel could understand.

Incubated And Enveloped In Glory

So in human terms, God explains different aspects of Himself through His appearances in glory. First the prophet saw a windstorm, a cloud, flashing light and, finally, lightning. Does that sound familiar? In Genesis 1, the Holy Spirit hovered or brooded over the earth much like a cloud. The Hebrew term gives the sense of hovering like a bird of prey does in the air and brooding as in incubation, like a chicken does with her eggs. In Genesis we see light brought forth, and the expanse separated to create clouds and water. Later in Exodus, we see the cloud and the light (fire) guiding Israel. In Genesis the Word and the Spirit bring forth. In Exodus they are following God's commandment (Word). But in our passage here in Ezekiel, it's in the midst of Ezekiel's *theophany* experience (before, during and after) that the **Word** of the Lord came and was *coming* to Ezekiel. Ezekiel was enveloped with God's **presence**, for Ezekiel 1:4 says he was "surrounded by brilliant light." He saw something else in the center of that fire, enveloped or surrounded by the presence: the four living creatures. In Ezekiel 1:24, when the creatures moved, they produced sound. In Ezekiel 3:12-14, as we read about the same experience, now we understand that in the presence of His glorious appearance (verse 12), it is the Holy Spirit working all in all through Ezekiel and these "creatures."

So now we see different expressions of God in glory. This produces a change in Ezekiel. It's after the Spirit lifts Ezekiel up and takes him away that he is able to return to his people with a different **knowledge**. He is filled with bitterness and anger of spirit, overwhelmed by the knowledge of their sin and rebellion. In order for Ezekiel to fulfill his mission he had to receive

knowledge from the Holy Spirit so he could call his people to repentance. He was a transitional prophet, preaching about a change in worship and how Israel would function. In like fashion, Jesus prophesied that Israel would experience a change in worship after He ascended. This is because the Holy Spirit could now abide in us. Jesus said He would not leave us comfortless but send the Comforter who would lead, guide and remind us of all things.[1]

In this way the Counselor gives us the knowledge we need to go through all of God's preordained transitions. Now that's knowledge—God knowledge!

In His glory is the Word, and when His Word is preached it brings His presence. In His presence we are known and we know. But whom do we know? We know HIM. Look at Ezekiel 1:24. Ezekiel heard the voice of the Almighty. The Hebrew name used in this passage in Ezekiel for Almighty is *Shaddai*. What's in a name? In this case it means the self-sufficient God who nourishes, supplies and satisfies. Jesus said in John 14:26, "But the Counselor, the Holy Spirit, whom the Father will send in My **Name,** will teach you all things and will remind you of everything I have said to you." It's in the **Name** of Jesus that we have the victory. It's in the name of Jesus that demons must flee. It is only in the name of our Lord that we can stand. Jesus nourishes, supplies and satisfies.[2]

While we're looking at different aspects of God in glory, there is one in the book of Ezekiel that we usually pass over. We see God and angels and God's throne room scene much like a scene from the book of Revelation. But one real element that we sometimes overlook is mankind infused with God's glory. To say it differently, it is the **people** of God, His redeemed, infused and reflecting the glory of God. Who did Ezekiel represent? He was a remnant or a called-out one from among his people. Not only was he present, seeing and hearing all of these wondrous sights, he was very much a participant. But here's the catch when you're in God's glorious presence: "But you, son of man, listen to what I say to you. Do not rebel like that rebellious house; open your mouth and eat what I give you." (See Ezekiel 2:8.)

Recognizing the Time of our Visitation

Resistance

Whether we want to admit it or not, God in glory meets resistance. His **Word** meets resistance. His **knowledge** meets resistance. His **presence** meets resistance. His **name** meets resistance and His **people** meet resistance. Resistance from the world? Well, yes. But if that were the only source of resistance then Jesus would have returned long ago. In the same manner that Ezekiel was called to preach a transitional change, so our time of visitation of God in glory is meant to prepare us for a change, as well. God desires to change the way in which we "do church." His Word, His knowledge, His presence, His name and His people face just as much resistance from within ourselves as God in glory does from the unsaved world.

Control and Manipulation

In the next seven chapters we will look at specific resistances to God coming in glory. They are strongholds built up against His word, His knowledge, His presence, His name and His coming in glory upon His people. But for now, let's take a look at two classic Biblical human strongholds. They are control and manipulation. You might be asking how it is that two very modern words could be seen in something as old as the Bible. We've already mentioned God's three purposes on the face of the earth, but they deserve review.

1 One is to redeem a kingdom of priests, a chosen people or called-out ones unto Himself (Rom. 10:9–13; 1 Pet. 2:4–5, 9–10).

2 The second is to establish a bride for Christ who rules and reigns with Him (Eph. 1:3–4, 18–23; 2:6–7; 5:31–32).

3 The third is for His glory to cover the earth as the waters cover the seas (Isa. 6:3, 1:9; Hab. 2:14, 3:3).

BEYOND STRONGHOLDS

When Christ came to seek and save what was lost He accomplished these three purposes. (See Luke 19:10.) The fullness of His accomplishment is also awaiting an appointed time. You might ask the question, "what has control and manipulation got to do with all of this?" When God in glory abides over you in all consuming power, who is in control? Not you or I! If you have ever experienced this, you know what I mean. Because of His awesome presence all you can do is sit in awe. (See Genesis 15:12.)

When God orchestrates things and tells you His purposes and plans and begins to implement them, He may move immediately or He may wait. We don't always perceive which is which, either in our own lives or in the church. So what happens? All too often we try to control the situation and manipulate circumstances. When we do we subtly enter into rebellion (control) and stubbornness (manipulation), which is witchcraft and idolatry. There is a vast difference between godly authority and responsibility and control and manipulation. Control is an elusive thing. It looks good on the surface as we institute plans and programs. But like anything else that's done in the flesh, it won't be tested until that last day when it will show itself as hay, wood or stubble.

Control and manipulation are heart conditions. Faith is a crucible that tests what is really in our hearts. Do we believe God can actually take care of His planet? If we do, then it's easy to be responsible for that which God calls us to be responsible for and leave alone what is not our business. When we can function that way, He conveys His authority to us. We've passed the test, and He can trust us with His business.

Authority and Responsibility

To understand this better let's look at 1 Samuel 15. God gave Saul authority, and with that authority came responsibility. It easily can be said that God gives responsibility first and tests and builds us there before He confers authority. Nevertheless, Saul was in authority. In 1 Samuel 15:3, God's instructions were given from

Recognizing the Time of our Visitation

the mouth of the prophet Samuel. He said to take the stronghold and utterly destroy all—leave nothing spared.[3]

It was Saul's responsibility to carry out the Word. As we live and work, God's Word comes. We don't always perceive it, and certainly we're blinded many times to our hearts' motives. In verse 9, God reveals Saul's heart—"They were unwilling to destroy completely." Why? Because in their eyes this plunder was valuable, even though God said it wasn't valuable enough to Him to keep it alive a minute longer than it needed to be. To the casual observer, Saul's argument to the prophet in 1 Samuel 15:20-21 seems legitimate—they killed with the sword and brought back the best to be sacrificed. After all, in verse 24 Saul implies the people outnumbered him, and they started taking the spoil. So Saul gave in.

But a closer look at Saul's response in verses 20 and 21 will show that he knew better. The Hebrew word Samuel uses in his instructions to Saul is *charam*. It conveys the meaning of separating something for total destruction as incense to be consecrated to the Lord. In other words, destroy it swiftly and immediately so that you never see it again. By Saul repeating the same word used by Samuel in his instruction in 1 Samuel 15:3 (he repeats it in 1 Sam. 15:15, 20-21 also), it shows that he understood the full implication of the word. Saul desired to control the situation and manipulate the outcome. The Lord looks on this as arrogance. The Hebrew literally translates like this: "Indeed, (like) a sin of diviners is rebellion, (like) the iniquity of terafim (household idols) a display of arrogance."[4]

Samuel declares that rebellion is as witchcraft and stubbornness is as idolatry. Let's put it in modern terms. When you think what God has given you isn't good enough, or you feel you've got a better way, that's control. When God attempts to reveal your heart to you, but you've got theology behind a list of excuses for not obeying God, that's manipulation and a display of arrogance in God's eyes. In 900 B.C. Israeli terms, Samuel calls it witchcraft and idolatry (rebellion and stubbornness). Look, if you will, at Isaiah 5:18-23 and Isaiah 42:8. You will see that God refuses to compete with our rebellion and stubbornness. They are witchcraft and idolatry to Him. And yet, the amazing part of Saul's story is that God gave Saul twenty-one years to repent after pronouncing judgment in 1 Samuel 15: 26–29. Some argue that this reprieve gave David time to learn how to be king, but God's plans are as multifaceted as He is in glory.

Defensiveness Leads to Impoverishment

During the next twenty-one years Saul tries to kill David. This strife within Saul does not benefit the nation of Israel. In fact it carries through to David's kingship. (See 2 Samuel 16: 3–8; 19: 24–30.) David has his own control and manipulation issues to address that produce strife for the nation, as well. (See 2 Samuel 11–19.)

These strongholds produce strife because we are literally warring against the Lord. We see the same pattern today. After we have experienced hurt and wounding at the hands of other people we raise up attitudes that we think will protect us from being hurt again. Many times abused people or people who have been wronged go for counseling. The counselors urge them to assume responsibility and take authority over their lives and actions. Counselors warn against crossing the line and trying to control and manipulate all those around them as a way to protect themselves from being hurt again. Using hurt Christians to beat up their brothers and sisters is the devil's handiwork. This is why it's so important to study these strongholds. If we try to defend our positions and say the issues do not exist, the devil will surely use them.

Look at 2 Samuel 24:1 and 1 Chronicles 21:1. In one book it says the Lord incited David to number Israel, and in the other it says that satan incited him. Which is it? I think it's both. I think the Lord was tired of their strongholds and allowed the enemy to have his way—for a season. I'll make a statement here: defensiveness always leads to impoverishment. In this portion of Scripture we see that the nation suffers the loss of 70,000 lives because of this stronghold of arrogance. It isn't until David repents from counting his "defenses" that the plague is stopped. There is good news in this story. It's in the exact place that David

Recognizing the Time of our Visitation

offers a sacrifice of repentance that God has Solomon build the temple in which God later appears in glory. (See 1 Chronicles 21:27–22:1 and 2 Chronicles 5:13,14.)

These two strongholds can also cause us to miss some aspect of God even if we do repent. Remember Moses on Mount Horeb with the fire (light) and smoke (cloud) surrounding the Mount? What did the people do? Out of defensiveness and fear they told Moses to go and talk to God. The Egyptians had abused them, and now all they could see was an abusive God whom they feared. As a defense they sent Moses. But this attitude produced impoverishment even though they feared God correctly. Psalm 103:7 says, "He made known his ways to Moses, his deeds to the people of Israel." That's a shame. If you know His ways you will always see His deeds. It seems if we do not deal with these issues all we will see are His manifestations. We will never know Him intimately.

When God shows up, when He is in control, all of Him shows up with Him. All that He is, all His presence, all His knowledge, all His Word and all His name. This can be too much of an all consuming experience. We retreat from Him because we fear losing the control. We act defensively and can't trust Him, either because of childhood experiences, recent hurts or both. Unfortunately, we fear Him and shun Him because we don't want certain areas of our personalities exposed. These are stronghold resistances to God's manifest presence when God in glory has come in a place or on a person.

Out of Order?

I need to ask two important questions. Why control and manipulation? And why is this issue important for us today? After all, if God in glory has manifested Himself in a church or on a person there must not be any control issues there, right? Wrong! Just because the glory is being manifested, this is not proof there are no strongholds, especially the main strongholds to the glory of God, which are control and manipulation. When we use the manifestations of God to imply that we have no strongholds or sin, we are denying the Lord of glory. The universe is made of positive controlling forces—gravity being one of them. There is an order that is godly. Unfortunately all of us, including many church leaders, have a perception of godly order that may not be completely from God.

In this false perception of godly order and authority, control and manipulation follow if we are not willing to be changed by the Holy Ghost. I'm not talking about obvious orderly conduct. Swinging from chandeliers and jumping on top of elderly people, all under the guise of "the spirit fell on me," is a church that is out of order.

The kind of control I'm talking about is trying to control what godly people say, how they pray for one another or trying to control how people think. I emphasize the word godly here. Obviously, we must act in a godly and holy way. All church leaders have the burden to exhort God's people to behave in a godly and moral fashion—to be holy as He is Holy. But we are not the Holy Spirit. He may use us to preach a convicting message about our unholy speech. He may use us to teach people intercession or godly ministry when we pray for other people. He may use us to speak apologetically concerning aspects of our day and age in an attempt to open human minds up to godly change, or He may ask us simply to *be* a witness or example of proper Christ-like thinking. But in no way can we make demands on people and expect them to fulfill our own ideas of godliness.

Scripture is explicit enough as to what God's demands are. The Pharisees expected Jesus and the disciples to wash their hands before they ate. That fulfilled some of their ideas of holiness. Jesus told them clearly that it wasn't what went into their mouths that defined holiness but what came out of them. (See Matthew 15: 1–11.) From Genesis onward, each aspect of God manifested in glory teaches us how God responds. Once sin was conceived, God Almighty did not demand that iniquity not be found in Lucifer. After iniquity was found, God took action by sending Christ as a ransom to prevent satan from causing more harm.

Recognizing the Time of our Visitation

God did not control Adam and Eve so they would not see the fruit or hear the serpent. God assumed responsibility and exercised His authority by cutting off their access to the tree of life. If we would learn from our first parents' mistake and from God's example, we would realize there's no fear of missing God. After all, isn't that the lie the serpent tried to feed our first parents? He made them feel that in some way they weren't like God and needed a certain fruit so they wouldn't miss Him. He got them to act defensively and get out of godly order. When we're accepting appropriate, God-ordained responsibility, we are functioning just as He would want us to. Control and manipulation take us out of godly order. This is always satan's first trick. If Adam and Eve had tended that garden responsibly, no vegetable-eating pest would have been allowed to distract them from the job. And if it did show up they should have assumed authority and said, "Hey, wait a minute! You're not allowed in here because God said so. You need to go eat fruit elsewhere because we're not allowed to eat this particular fruit anyway."

Understanding the Motives of Control and Manipulation

We must begin to understand our motives for control and assume responsibility in a balanced way with the guidance of the Holy Spirit. We never "arrive" because God always gives us new challenges and learning experiences. But we can begin somewhere. I asked the question, "why control and manipulation?" Besides getting us out of godly order, control and manipulation stamp out hope. This is one of a series of fundamental strikes or weapons the enemy uses against us. This is why 1 Corinthians 13 is so important. It says, "These three remain: faith, hope and love. But the greatest of these is love." When we lose hope we lose sight of God and who He is and what He is like. I've seen many homeless people who have lost hope. If we cannot show them Jesus and allow the knowledge of Him to birth hope within them then all the money in the world will not help them. Without Christ's hope they will wind up homeless again. Christians can get themselves into situations where their hope is subtly drained from them by their own desires for control and manipulation and by those who control and manipulate them. This is why control and manipulation are so dangerous. They stamp out hope.

This is why we must forsake our own desires to control and manipulate. We must learn instead how to assume Christ-like responsibility and allow room for God's authority. Some people are strong enough to leave a situation because they refuse to be controlled. Other folks have been so duped by control that when they finally look around all hope seems gone. The good news is this: the reason they are able to look around is because of the Holy Spirit. He never leaves us comfortless or hopeless.

Control Through Lies

Satan can wipe out the hope of God's people in each succeeding generation when he uses the lie to control them. But we have hope in God and we marvel at how He works—Christ in you, the hope of glory. (See Colossians 1:27.) God's Word exposes the lie and the truth can prevail throughout each succeeding generation.

This brings us to the second question that was asked: "Why now?" What is it about the time in which we are living that God is bringing these issues to our attention in a more pronounced way? With God closer in abiding glory than ever before we must be prepared for His imminent return. When we lay down our control and assume godly responsibility for His planet, we give the devil no place to rest. As satan sees God in abiding glory fill us to overflowing, He realizes his time is short. So he must continue to control us or get us involved in controlling each other.

Our particular generation has seen privacy laws taken away in a diabolical way under the guise of protecting us from fraud. The fact remains that while we can set up protections from fraud, it is possible to cross the line with some of these regulations. Drivers' license numbers are sometimes required as information to confirm who we are. Many companies require our Social Security numbers to identify us, which is stated as illegal right on the back of our Social Security cards! Yet these practices make it easier to obtain these numbers and steal our identities. The desire to control us and know exactly who we are so that information can be manipulated is frightening.

There is talk of some hospitals now identifying babies by DNA or genetic blood samples in an effort to "protect" them from foul play. Privacy-rights groups are in a tizzy over the implications of demanding that every baby born be DNA-typed at birth, with that information kept on file for whatever later purpose it might serve.[5]

A Need-to-Know Spirit

The church must guard against pollution by this need-to-know spirit. (See Daniel 12: 4.)

How has this spirit been able to gain such a foothold? Because we have forsaken knowing as God knows and discerning the body of Christ through the gifts given by the Holy Spirit. Paul told the Corinthians that many of them became weak and slept because they had taken the Lord's communion unworthily, not discerning the body. (See 1 Corinthians 11: 17–34.) This is not just limited to having an unholy party at communion. It deals with attitudes concerning one another and more particularly who each one of us is in Christ. This knowledge is given by God to help the body grow and mature, not to be used against one another or to be consumed with prideful attitudes.

We've instituted our own knowledge, our own control and our own way of doing things.[6] How is satan able to deceive us when God in glory appears so we can't recognize one another in Christ and we must resort to manmade methods? We have not allowed God in glory to have His way totally.

We fear so we control. Afraid that one thing or another will get out of control and people will begin to be in the flesh we, with the flesh, order and manipulate the situation for our own self-suited outcomes. This comes from fear. We fear missing God. Fear cannot trust God. When we're acting responsibly there is no need to control. When God in glory falls on those acting in faith with true Christ-like responsibility, His ways and plans become obvious. But when we're in the flesh, we're in fear. We can't see the invisible *Shechinah* Glory or see the angels or hear the sounds of heaven. We've lost the perception of heaven because of our strongholds. (See Isaiah 42:8; Genesis 6:3.) When this happens, we fear so we control and manipulate.

After many generations in this kind of environment we become conditioned to think that it's normal not to see God in glory and the heavenly realm. With each succeeding generation it's politics and business as usual. This happened to our Jewish brethren more than 2000 years ago. This is what *tamei* and *shaatnez* look like after many generations. It's not evident immediately, but sooner or later the overriding word or prophetic anointing on us as God's people becomes dull or is outright silenced. What may not be evident immediately is His presence eventually begins to fade or not be received with the same intensity. The knowledge of knowing as He knows, which is gracefully conveyed to us because of the blood of Jesus by the precious Holy Spirit, is substituted for head knowledge. His name no longer meets with shouts of praise. Soon the accomplishments of men supercede the fame of God. And His people, who were controlled in the beginning, become controlled also at the end. They are never raised up as one bride, one body with one multifaceted diamond of glory upon her to expose and destroy the works of the devil and bring restoration to the earth. Instead of glory, we are left with a one-man show, with sheep demanding to be spoon fed instead of being raised up as Holy Spirit-anointed saints of Jesus Christ, the Word. What has really been deposited in them is the same fear with the same need to control and manipulate.

What Would Happen If...

What would happen if we did not fear, but in faith we confronted

Recognizing the Time of our Visitation

the challenges by bringing together the fivefold ministry on its knees to ask, "What shall we do, Father?" What if we waited upon God for His understanding and wisdom and did not submit to someone's personal ideas of domination and control. We don't respond in this way because we have not built church structure upon the fivefold ministry. We listen to somebody's doctrine that says the apostle is not functioning today. Or someone tells us the prophet should have no input in these all-important everyday matters. Or the shepherd or shepherdess is somewhat imperfect and needs our "protection." Or, God forbid, the teacher teaches in areas hard to understand and we don't like it. Maybe the evangelist is offending too many good Christians by calling all sinners to repentance. Like Adam and Eve of old, we are in disobedience to the Word of God. We have not done things His way totally. As a result we're hiding or trying to cover up what we're doing under the mask of a particular rule or somebody's theology. Sometimes we don't even recognize that we're doing these things.

The good news is, when we repent, God forgives. When we allow God in glory to show up, the enemies within and without are exposed. When we repent strongholds are shattered. When His Word is preached, He shows up in glory. When His people are released, the glory overshadows them. (See Isaiah 28:5.) In His presence is fullness of joy, and at His name every knee bows. His glory and knowledge shall cover the earth (See Habakkuk 2:14.) When His knowledge abounds, His glory is manifested. (See Habakkuk 3:3.) Smoke and fire accompany Him, and many become afraid. If we refuse to change, we give the devil a foothold or stronghold and, as the glory on Moses' face dimmed, the glory on us diminishes. But let's take heed to the words of the apostle Paul who says in Ephesians 4:27, "Do not give the devil a foothold." Instead, let's go on in encouragement and repentance to his words in 2 Corinthians 4:6, "For God, who said 'let light shine out of darkness,' made his light shine in our hearts to give us the light of the knowledge of the glory of God in the face of Christ" (2 Cor. 4:7, 13, 14).

Moses' face was veiled so the Israelites could not see that that glory was not an abiding glory but a diminishing one. So Paul says the gospel is "veiled to those who are perishing. The god of this age has blinded the minds of unbelievers, so that they cannot see the light of the gospel of the glory of Christ, who is the image of God" (2 Cor. 4: 3–4). Infiltration by God in glory is how we are raised to resurrection and how we are changed, both in spiritual things and at the end of the ages. It is the very light of Christ and the illumination of His glory that the world will see upon us. If we refuse to move with the Holy Ghost in glory with His transitions, we will be like unbelievers. We will become blinded by the god of this age so we cannot see the light of the glory of Christ and follow it by night as God gave Israel the fire to follow. Instead, some of us may stay in the wilderness.

If we repent and return, He will lead and guide us. We may yet see the *Shechinah* return and abide upon us like a multifaceted diamond. As we gaze into His face, we can see a different color or brilliance with every shimmer of light, like a diamond. Let's study the awesome splendor of God in glory and look at different facets of Him together.

To whom can I speak and give warning? Who will listen to me? Their ears are closed so they cannot hear. The word of the Lord is offensive to them; they find no pleasure in it.

—Jeremiah 6:10

Chapter Three

THE WORD

Unlike other aspects of God in glory, including His presence, His knowledge, His name and His people, the Word is a Person. In other words, when you enter a room your presence does too, as does your knowledge and your name. These are all aspects of *who* you are, but they may not necessarily be the *you* we should see. You may speak words that represent who you are, but you may just as easily speak things that don't truly represent you. We put up facades quite easily.

But in the case of God, the Almighty, John 1 tells us that the Word was (is) God. The Word came in the form of flesh, and we beheld His glory—the glory of the only Begotten of the Father—full of grace and truth. When the Word is preached, His glory shows up, and yet when His glory is present, so is His Word. We know the Word to be God—a person—our Lord and Savior, Jesus Christ. (See John 1:1–14, Colossians 2:8, 9.) You cannot separate God from His presence, His name, His knowledge or His glory. You can't separate the Word from God, for the Word is God. Ultimately, nothing can separate God from His people. (See Rom. 8:38–39.) With this understanding as a foundation for our study of God's glory, let's look at Genesis 1.

Through His Word, God's glory is revealed in His creation, and we see it all around us today. (See Romans 1:20.) Genesis 1 is where we get our first glimpse of God going forth in glory. As in

BEYOND STRONGHOLDS

all other divine visitations or *theophany* appearances, God came to transform. The Word says, "The earth was formless and empty." (See Genesis 1:2.) The Hebrew word *tohuw* means a desolate waste. It's used here and in Deuteronomy 32:10, where it's translated "howling waste."[1]

Out of this picture of the Word of God going forth we see that "Darkness was over the surface of the deep, and the Spirit of God was hovering over the waters." (See Genesis 1:2.) The word *rachaph* means literally "to hover or brood." It conveys the meaning "to flutter [as a bird's wings]," and the concept of resting or being relaxed is also inferred. (See Deuteronomy 32:11; Naham 1:3; Luke 1:35, 3:22; Hebrews 1:1–3; 4:1.)

The Hebrew word for the word of the Lord is *davar*.[2] This word has the dual meaning of "being a driving force [which has the potential to be destructive] that creates something out of nothing [which is creative]." From this we can see that throughout Scripture and history, including church history, God's pattern is to allow death or destruction and then send new life or redemption. I'm reminded of God's other appearances in the Old Testament when He came in a consuming fire and a soothing cloud, both giving life and growth through charred earth. I'm reminded of the flood of Noah that brought destructive water and water necessary for life. The Bible tells of Abraham's three visitors who were sent to convey blessing and then judgment upon Sodom and Gomorrah. Then there is Joshua's experience with the Captain of the Lord of Hosts who must have been a fearsome sight with sword drawn. But as Joshua humbles himself, bowing and exposing the back of his neck to the drawn sword, he sees Jericho delivered into Israel's hands. We could go on and on with these examples. The most profound example is Christ's sacrifice on the cross, which, in one moment, dealt with both loving redemption and the cruel judgment of sin. And of course, the example of His final coming in harvest, which will bring both final redemption and final judgment.

While it might be far easier for God to create anew, His way is to redeem. Therefore, it shouldn't shock or surprise us when satan

The Word

comes to attack every aspect of God's Word. Imagine the power of the Word spoken forth in faith. When Christ spoke, He turned the world right-side up. When the early church spoke God's Word, they were accused of turning the world upside down! We have become familiar with demonic and worldly resistances to God's Word. But what happens when those strongholds reside within the church? For example, most of Israel's enemies who lived in the land she was commanded to possess were related to her by blood–Canaanites, Moabites, Ammonites, Edomites, Ishmaelites, Hittites and Amorites. I call them her enemies within. It was only when she totally disobeyed God's Word that outsiders, or foreign enemies, were sent against her. Some of these were Philistia, Egypt, Assyria, Babylonia and Greco-Roman. So we, like Israel of old, have "enemies within" us that will not obey God's Word. I've called them strongholds, because we have made these attitudes fortresses. We have a tendency to sugarcoat the disobedience. God is gracious and merciful, wooing us to obedience. (See Romans 2:4.) It is only after our disobedience has been made into strong fortresses that God must send His Word and break them up. He loves us too much to leave us as we are. When this takes place and we remain in disobedience, we give outside forces (the devil and the world) a right to attack us.

Spirit, Soul and Body

When God in glory shows up it is to establish His rule as King and kick out the foreign enemies that our ungodly human strongholds have fostered. But almost without fail, God's visitation is met with subtle and not so subtle resistance to God's Word. That same Word churns soil when spoken through the mouth of a prophet, and that same creative Word (or *davar*) of the Lord is a driving force, bringing order out of chaos. (See Jeremiah 1:9–10.)

The resistances I've observed personally and through Bible study are based on two conditions that produce attitudes or strongholds, both godly and human. If the resistances produce human strongholds and we refuse to dismantle them, they have the potential to invite or hide demonic strongholds. When both of the conditions reside together in a place or a person you will surely see resistances to the Word in glory. They are as follows:

The first condition: an improper understanding of spirit, soul and body.

This is not a lack of understanding regarding what our souls and spirits do or how they develop. These are important questions that all new believers ask. This condition involves the misalignment of spirit, soul and body. At that point the order would be soul, body and spirit; or body, soul and spirit. As baby Christians, our pastor taught us that the Word and Spirit feed our spirits, and, in turn, our spirits feed our souls. Our souls feed our bodies. This is why it's so important to speak and think the thoughts that God has for us. (See Jeremiah 29: 11, KJV.) Ultimately whatever you feed your spirit man will feed your body. This made sense to me as my own pastor explained what parts of our beings our spirits, souls and bodies occupied, how they developed and the doctrine of salvation and how God's Word ministers to us in spirit, soul and body. C. Peter Wagner makes the observation in his book, *Churches That Pray*, that warfare prayer, or binding and loosing, in and of itself, never saved a soul.[3] He then goes on to describe scripturally that it's only the preaching of the gospel of Jesus Christ that saves souls.

On several occasions, while ministering Jesus to people, we have had trouble getting them to understand what Christ did for them so that they may be set free. The Holy Spirit would reveal that a demon was attempting to block God's plan for salvation in those peoples' lives. At that point we have the total right to bind the enemy because he is attempting to thwart one of God's purposes on earth.

On one such occasion, while we were ministering to a man, he agreed with us of his need for salvation. We would actually get to the point of praying the sinner's prayer, and he would stop and go off on another subject. After thirty minutes of this, the Holy Spirit let me know that a demon was blocking the man's

The Word

salvation. Under my breath so the man couldn't hear me, I bound satan in Jesus' name and invited the Holy Spirit to release this man's understanding. Within three minutes he was saved and receiving deliverance. We were then able to minister Jesus effectively in other areas of his life.

Satan sets up hindrances against people truly hearing the Word and believing. (See Romans 10; 2 Corinthians 4:4.) The enemy is able to do this because man's unregenerate spirit is dead to the things of God. (See Romans 7:5, 6; 8:5-7; 1 Corinthians 2:14, KJV.) They cannot hear or discern the Word of God. Therefore, the proper order of an individual's being, which should be spirit, soul and body, gets mixed up. Either his soul becomes preeminent over his body and spirit or his body rules over his soul and spirit.

Unregenerate man feeds the flesh through the mind or emotions with television, radio, alcohol, drugs—you name it. Satan is then able to prevent him from hearing God's Word fully and being saved. Unbelievers have all the same emotional baggage that Christians have; the difference is their spirits are dead unto God. (See 1 Peter 4:5-6, KJV.) If they get saved, their spirits are made alive. (See Ephesians 2:1-6; Colossians 2:13, KJV.) They eat, live and drink in God's Word and Spirit. That Word feeds their human spirits, and their minds become renewed. (See Romans 12:2; Ephesians 5:14, KJV.) Little by little, or in big chunks, the baggage starts to fall off. Praise God! That's when we begin our journey of walking out our salvation with fear and trembling, and we are sanctified by the washing of the Word. (See Philemon 2:12; Ephesians 5:26.)

Salvation and sanctification are instant, but they are also processes that are walked out by faith. I don't mean to suggest that emotions are bad or that when God's presence falls upon you or His Word comes to you that you shouldn't respond emotionally. Praise God that He touches us emotionally. Experiencing God can be an emotional experience. It's unfortunate that some cults today feed off of old gnostic teachings that believe the soul and body are not blessed by God or ordained for His service. Paul says our bodies are to be temples

BEYOND STRONGHOLDS

of the Holy Ghost. (See 1 Corinthians 3:16, 17; 6:19.)

Hebrews 4 is a great passage of Scripture to read for understanding the working of the Word of God in our lives. What the joint is to two connecting bones, the soul is as a connector to the spirit and the body. (See Hebrews 4:12.) When our spirit man is in fellowship with God and His Word, it has the same effect as the marrow has in reproducing life's blood to our bodies. No wonder we can enter into rest and fellowship by not hardening our hearts in unbelief when we hear Him. (See Hebrews 4: 1–3a.) His very Word does all the work as it judges our thoughts and intents and exposes them by the Holy Spirit to lead us to repentance and wholeness throughout our spirits, souls and bodies. (See Hebrews 4:12, 13; 1 Jonah 1:1, 5–10.)

Believers With No Foundation

But what happens to the Christian who has never had a foundation laid with God's Word regarding an understanding of spirit, soul and body? He or she never had Hebrews 4 made alive to them by the Holy Spirit. Or worse, he or she functions by emotional feelings, and then sets about to support and justify those emotions through the Bible or good Christian books or other sources of learning. As a result, these people never quite learn how to live totally by and through the Word and the Holy Spirit. Their souls are still stronger in mind, will and emotions as they teach themselves how to preach, teach, sing and talk all the good language of a Christian. What happens when those believers have some minimal training and are given papers to become ministers, and then they start to gather a church together and begin preaching? You say this can't happen. Well, it does. Sunday after Sunday, sermons are preached concerning how those pastors feel with just enough Word smattered throughout to give their emotions Biblical credibility. The good news is this: if hearts are in the right place, that Word smattered throughout will do the work God sent it out to do, because His Word never returns void. (See Isaiah 55:11.) Sooner or later, more balanced teaching

The Word

becomes available, and the ministers seek God for more training and for help from other leaders trained by the Holy Spirit. The Holy Spirit will help their infirmities as they pray, while He reveals to them that the soul is still in charge of some areas it should not be. (See Romans 8:26-27.)

While this scenario can have a happy ending, because the Word is God, I've left out one small and unfortunately very real element—the liar, our adversary, the devil. His only weapon is the lie. For some reason he seems to know when our spirit man is being made strong in Jesus and our lives are being made right and put in order by the Holy Spirit. When this is the case, He is not able to steal, kill and destroy as long as the truth—God's Word—is being revealed in our lives. (See John 10:10.) With our spirits, souls and bodies coming in line with the Holy Spirit, a key source for the weakness that causes us to believe his lies is taken away. He must do something quickly. The good news is found in James 4:7, which says that if we're submitting to God and resisting the devil he must flee—it's the Word. We can stand on it! But what happens when we don't recognize our true enemy? What happens if he masquerades under the guise of an offense? Remember this is done to thwart or hinder God's Word. Here comes the second domino in a succeeding line of the devil's antics to get us to resist the Word of the Lord as God comes in glory.

The second condition for resisting the Word in glory: Offenses

When these two conditions are present to some extent, and God in glory has come, chances are there are strongholds present in our understanding of some aspects of His Word. Remember that God comes in glory for the purpose of evicting usurping spirits and establishing godly rule—whether over individuals for salvation or the church as His Bride. (See Habakkuk 2:14; Isaiah 6:3.)

There are several Greek words for our one word "offense." The primary two are *proskomma*, and *skandalon*. *Proskomma* is used to describe an occasion for stumbling or apostasy, which comes from the word *proskopto*. It means "to strike against or beat, to stumble or trip up." The second word, *skandalon*, is where we get our English word *scandal* from. I've been told that this word derives its literal meaning from our modern concept of a mousetrap. Everyone who baits a mousetrap uses his or her own favorite bait. My husband swears by Swiss cheese, fat and peanut butter. The little hook that you secure the bait to that trips the trap is a perfect example of the Greek concept behind the word *skandalon*. This is why satan uses his own favorite bait because he's observed that it's your own "favorite" problem.

This is the word that Jesus uses in Matthew 18:7 when he says, "Woe to the world because of the things that cause people to sin!" Christ had been speaking about the kingdom of heaven in the past several chapters since Matthew 4:17. He challenged the earthly understanding of His disciples by walking on water in chapter 14 and earthly teachings of the Word by the Pharisees in chapter 15. He's back to challenging traditional concepts of cultural divisions, faith and bread when He heals the Canaanite woman's daughter and feeds the four thousand. By chapter 16, we see Him again confronting the earthly traditions of the Pharisees and the thoughts of the disciples. Overall, His continuing theme is the difference between God's understanding of His kingdom versus various earthly or manmade understandings. In other words, it involves how we perceive God and heaven to be one way, when it's really something else. Jesus came to reveal their misconceptions and institute His Father's thoughts and plans.

It's no wonder we get a glimpse of the transfigured Christ in chapter 17. After all, that's what God in glory does: He changes us from the earthly to the heavenly. But in Matthew 16:23, Jesus rebukes satan, who was speaking through Peter's stronghold ideas of who Messiah was and what He should do. The Lord tells Peter that he is an offense to Him. In Matthew 17:27, Jesus instructs Peter to pay a two-drachma tax so they won't offend the resident tax collectors. In these passages we see two very different types of offense: one where we offend God, the other where we offend man.

The Word

By Matthew 18, Jesus starts to discuss offenses in greater detail. Many preachers relegate Matthew 18 to a discourse on forgiveness. Some use it to support the concept of binding and loosing. And still others use the chapter as a discourse on children's ministry.

While all these issues are valuable and certainly worthy of study, I'd like to put forth another thought. The chapter starts off with the disciples asking, "Who is the greatest in the kingdom?" I can imagine that even asking this question offended some. Actually, their question is not so very off. Christ had been revealing what the kingdom of God is like and its antithetical characteristics with earth for quite some time leading up to this point. Jesus continues with the concept of what the kingdom is like after they leave Galilee through to chapter 20. The disciples' question revealed that they were grasping at something. His answer is mind-boggling. He takes a child and begins to teach. Now, remember, the overall theme is the difference between God's kingdom (the kingdom of the skies, as the literal Greek says) and what we perceive as rulership here on earth. Christ uses the example of the purity of a child, juxtaposing it with the *skandalon* or the offense—the trap or hook-bait of the enemy.

It is also interesting to note that Jesus uses the term "a millstone about the neck." Edersheim states that because of the burden of financially providing for a wife and children, the Rabbis referred to this care as a proverbial expression, "a millstone about the neck." It amazes me how Jesus uses their everyday expressions (expressions which have lost their full meanings) to fly in the face of their lousy attitudes. The Law made it very clear that a man was to marry and bear children. God viewed it as an honor bestowed by Him. In fact, the Law, the Mishnah and the Talmud provided so much for the wife that the Rabbis coined the disdainful phrase "millstone about the neck," attesting to their rebellion to the letter and Spirit of the Law.[4] Today we might hear people call this slang idiom a "ball and chain."

BEYOND STRONGHOLDS

Satan's Trap of Offense

Jesus' words flew in the face of the Jewish leadership's conventional attitudes and expressions. We could say that He offended them. The Scriptures tell us that Christ is a stone of stumbling, and a rock of offense. (See 1 Peter 2:8, KJV.) This is because Jesus spoke as a Spirit-led man, not a man led by His soul. Satan used the Jewish leadership's lack of godly understanding to offend them. When satan sets a trap or offense, you can easily wind up feeling hurt. In fact, that's the idea. Hurt feelings lead to unforgiveness and bitterness. Jesus speaks in Matthew 17 and 19 of different areas in which offenses can take place. These three specific areas are the same offenses that have lead to every war the world has ever known. They include:

- religious offenses
- husband-wife offenses (or the battle between the sexes)
- the offense of riches, or more explicitly, the deception of power

This is why Jesus exhorted us to forgive seventy times seven. (See Matthew 18:22.) If we are bound in the trap of unforgiveness, we can't loose the power of the Holy Ghost over us, and we bind the move of God on our own lives. (See Ephesians 4:26, 27; Hebrews 12:15.) When we live in forgiveness, one towards another, we loose God's working power and bind satan's ability to deceive. When we live this way, we become like the little child whom Jesus brought into the midst of the disciples to teach them heaven's concept of who was the greatest, as opposed to their stronghold ideas. Think of all the wars we could avoid when we walk in forgiveness toward one another, always willing to release others of their offenses against us. When we remain in a state of repentance before our Heavenly Father as His children, we bind the devil's authority here on earth. Father looks on us as His children, hears our cries and comes down to that "air" level that the devil is in and looses satan's legal right to

The Word

offend us further. Only repentance does this, not shouting at the devil, not trying to "pull" him down. He is already a defeated foe. All we need are the keys to forgiveness to unlock satan's stranglehold on earth.

Offenses and Revival

About this time you might be wondering what this has to do with God in glory falling and his people resisting the Word. Let's use a hypothetical example of a church working out of these issues. They are a wonderful group of people with a heart towards God. Behind the scenes, the Holy Spirit has been working through their imbalances in spirit-soul-body issues, corporately.

They start to pray for God to fall in their midst; crying out for revival, renewal, refreshing or just more of Jesus. He shows up. They may be only part of the way through the Holy Spirit's school to correct their imbalances, and they may or may not have received enough sound theology about maintaining an open heaven over their lives individually or corporately. Hypothetically, let's just suppose that the Spirit of God falls in glory upon a church that doesn't believe in the baptism of the Holy Ghost with the evidence of speaking in tongues. Or, He decides to fall on a church that doesn't believe in intercessory prayer, prophetic ministry, the healing ministries, women in leadership or one that doesn't believe in fivefold ministry—or you pick your own particular issue. It is always easier to say we have no problem with these issues, but our actions speak louder than our words. If you feel that those ministries are fine in someone else's church, but not in yours, then a stronghold is in place. But whatever the issue is, eventually the enemy will use someone or something to offend you personally or corporately. In fact, many times it seems like a legitimate offense. In other words, you feel you have a right to be offended concerning how someone functioned or acted or whatever. Combine this with a slight, or not so slight, imbalance in spirit, soul and body—compounded with the God of glory falling sovereignly—and I'd say you have been set up by the Holy Spirit to make a choice. You can overcome your personal resistance or stronghold, or dig your heels in and refuse to budge! Perhaps you believe that everything must be perfect in an individual or church for God in glory to fall, so they will never have to deal with these issues. Let's look at some places where God came in glory and see if there is a pattern.

Obedience Can Overcome

The creation is the first example that we see. God shows up on the earth as Ruler. There were no usurpers or resistances there—yet. He turns the title deed over to Adam and Eve by His Word. (See Genesis 1:26, 28–30.) God blessed them and commanded them. Neither Adam or Eve were unbalanced in any area; they couldn't be, for there was no sin. They were in communion with God in glorious fellowship. Satan had nothing but the subtle lie, "Did God really say…" (Gen. 3:1) and "You will not surely die" (v. 4). What this lying trap did was cause Eve to look toward the tree as the source to feed her body and soul. So a substitution took place (*tamei*). She substituted literal food for God's Word to feed her soul. Then the Scripture says she saw it was "good for food and pleasing to the eye, and also desirable for gaining wisdom" (Gen. 3:6). Once the bait had been set in the trap (*skandalon*), the stumbling or apostasy (*proskomma*) was not far behind. The Word says in verse 7, "Then the eyes of both of them were opened, and they realized they were naked." With the bait taken, the trap was sprung and mankind has suffered the loss. The Word of the Lord to Adam was clear. (See Genesis 3:17.) Adam resisted the command of that word because of his soul's desire to remain with Eve. He substituted and mixed His desires with God's Word (*tamei* and *shaatnez*). As a result he put into motion the curse placed upon the serpent and the ground. Because they handed over the dominion of the earth to decay, the earth and its creatures now suffer. Thanks be to God for Christ's sacrificial death in ransoming us all from the curse and its judgments.

The Word

The Cloud and Fire

Another appearance of God in glory is seen through Moses and God's deliverance of Israel. God shows up by fire at night and a cloud by day. But the man Moses is a good example of how God brings us through carnality to a place where we are the salt of the earth. It's not hard to imagine that living in Egypt in the lap of luxury as a son of Pharaoh's daughter did not cause Moses to start life as a spiritually balanced person. People have been just as offended as Moses was when he saw the oppression of the Israelities, but those people did not resort to killing. It didn't take satan much time to incite Moses into disobeying the command of God concerning murder. But God in glory had not appeared to Moses yet. The offense drove Moses to flee to the backside of the Sinai desert. Nowhere do we have an account of Moses repenting. Maybe he did; maybe he did not. In any event, the very offense that drove him away from Egypt drove him to a confrontation with the God of glory, by a bush that burned but was not consumed. After that experience, God starts to prophesy to Moses. (See Exodus 3 and 4.) In other words, He reveals His promises to him and commands him. Now, when God does that it's called His Word. So, God shows up by His Word in glory to Moses.

To read these two chapters is to read God, the Almighty, dialoging with an extremely resistant man. I am not criticizing Moses, but it's amazing to see how, in two chapters, he tries five times to convince God this is not a good idea. (See Exodus 3:11, 13; 4:1, 10, 13.) In fact, Moses hides his face when the Lord first reveals Himself because he is afraid—sounds like Adam and Eve. (See Exodus 3:6.) I'd say this is a resistant man, especially with all the proof that God needed to provide to Moses. We've already seen that Moses is not exactly spirit-soul balanced when God appears. But what about the offense? Well, it's already been in the making. It's on his way back to Egypt that we see it. Exodus 4:24 says, "The Lord met Moses and was about to kill him." Moses had not circumcised his son. The Scriptures do not indicate his reasons. That he knew he should is obvious by his wife,

BEYOND STRONGHOLDS

Zipporah's, response. Moses was a son of Abraham and thus circumcised. Zipporah was a daughter of Midian, also a son of Abraham through his second wife Keturah. These facts made circumcision mandatory. As with Adam, Eve and Cain, sin was at the door. Unlike them, Zipporah followed God's Word. The story might have ended here except that we know that a people need to be delivered, and God in glory will lead them in the form of fire and a cloud. We'll discuss this later. For now, the good news is that when we repent and we don't resist, the strongholds of our minds can be pulled down. In obedience we can be overcomers. Like Moses, we can become the deliverers God intends for us to be.

Have faith in the Lord your God and you will be upheld; have faith in His prophets and you will be successful.
—2 Chronicles 20:20

Do not touch my anointed ones; do my prophets no harm.
—1 Chronicles 16:22; Psalm 105:15

Chapter Four

THE WORD IN HIS PROPHETS

God chooses to put His words in people's mouths. When He does, and there are resistances to His Word in the spiritual realm, you will see a resistance to the prophets. It masquerades itself in subtle ways, sometimes even as an offense. We are speaking about God coming to rest on earth in glory, both in our lives individually, and in our churches corporately. The devil has set up two interesting demonic strongholds in this specific area to try to prevent God from remaining on us for extended periods of time. But it is our human strongholds, when they come in agreement with these demon attackers, which give the enemy strength. The devil is a copycat. If our prayer of agreement in holiness is so powerful that Jesus comes into our midst, the devil will surely attempt to get us to agree with him instead. If he can get people, saved or unsaved, to be offended and attack God's messengers, he can attempt to institute an atmosphere or environment of defilement.

The one characteristic that separated the temple of Jehovah from the heathen temples of its day was the absence of homage paid to demons—either by sacrifices, statues or by the priests cutting themselves. A word that can be used to understand the Old Testament concept of defilement of the temple was the

BEYOND STRONGHOLDS

Hebrew word *tamei*. We talked about this in Chapter One. It has the meaning of radioactivity. In other words, the atmosphere becomes so toxic God leaves. There were several sacrifices for different defilements in order to purge articles and people. One source of defilement was bearing false witness. The remedy was serious. (See Deuteronomy 19:16–19.) Thank God, Christ's blood cleanses us from all sin when we ask for forgiveness. Nevertheless, there is little remedy for people that believe they are doing God a favor by purging a true prophet, having been convinced by the devil that he's false. This is, in effect, bearing false witness.

God always uses the number two as an example of a prophetic witness—"the testimony of two or three witnesses" (Deut. 19:15; 2 Cor 13:1); pairs like Adam and Eve, Moses and Aaron, the Father and the Holy Spirit, and the Spirit and the Bride. So the enemy, the copycat, sends two specialized attackers. God sends people called prophets who thwart the enemy's plans in this area. We see them in both the Old and New Testaments. We see both male and female. In the New Testament, we see them out of every tribe and nation as well as both genders. One of the best examples of a prophet used by God against these satanic attackers is Elijah. Except for Enoch, Elijah was the only prophet caught up in glory and translated. Elijah moved in power and glory. He offered the evening sacrifice as a priest, and confronted the priests of Baal. Jesus states that symbolic Elijah, in the form of John the Baptist, had to first come before His appearing. (See Matthew 11:14.) As God raises up an end-time prophetic people, they will have to deal with these specialized attackers. We will look at Elijah as a symbolic type of prophet that God raises up and Ahab and Jezebel as the examples of the two demonic specialists satan uses to work with our own strongholds. In Ahab and Jezebel's case, you couldn't find better examples of unbalanced souls with offenses oozing from them. In the New Testament we will look at fivefold ministry, especially the prophets as people God raises up and Jezebel and Babylon as satanic attackers.

During the early 1980's, when prophetic ministry was being restored to large portions of the body of Christ, satan used one

The Word in His Prophets

of the nastiest accusations—especially against female prophets—he could think of. He called them Jezebels. It's a shame how we repeat things we never research. Let's look at this modern day offense. It was usually used to refer to someone suspected of trying to control the pastor. Of course, immature or improperly educated prophetic voices can make mistakes and thus cause concern in a church. And pastors do experience resistances from people who try to control them, although rarely from a prophetic minister. Control usually takes place in the form of a board member or other elder. It is the job of the shepherd or shepherdess to guard against satanic attacks. While I have yet to be called a "Jezebel," I have seen other people butchered by this accusation. I have watched as outright lies were levied against them (with this I have some personal experience). Thank God we gain experience in walking in forgiveness, pulling up any bitter root the enemy of our souls tries to plant. Before we label someone, let's look to see if they fit the bill.

History Repeats Itself

When we study the example of Ahab and Jezebel, we are looking at spirits of two different categories—principalities and powers. When we speak about the Word of the Lord in glory, and our disobedience in not obeying His Word, we are looking at substitution or mixing (*shaatnez*). Nowhere is this more hellish than with prophetic gifts and with prophets. This is what these attackers want us to do. They want us to mix our hurts or our own understanding of the Word of God. In this way we then function defiled. The early apostles and other fivefold ministers always exposed the ability of principalities and powers to deceive and defile God's leadership and God's people. Once defiled, mixing of God's plans and our own plans is done. This gives demons the legal right to come to earth and oppress us. We see Paul talk about dismantling arguments and ideas, both human and satanic. (See 2 Corinthians 10:4–5.) And that's the point: fivefold ministry has a mantle that dismantles this defilement and the arguments attached to it. If satan can, he will surely try to defile fivefold ministry, because the gifts therein are God's hierarchical gifts that expose his own hierarchical leadership.

As I studied this issue I realized how history just keeps repeating itself when we refuse to change. These two spirits are seen throughout the Old and New Testaments. Ahab is representative of a religious spirit, called Babylon in the New Testament, and Jezebel we see in both Testaments. The Old Testament is a shadow for our understanding of reality in the New Testament. While we study the New Testament to understand what perfection is, we always profit from looking at both the Old and New Testaments together in context, especially when we speak of spiritual forces. (See Hebrews 10:1; Colossians 2:17.) I believe these two spirits have sought to unite over God's people for a very long time.

To understand the connection between a Jezebel spirit and a religious spirit, or Babylon, a look at natural history might help us see a spiritual connection. I don't believe a Jezebel spirit, in and of itself, is strong enough to affect a church that understands its own human sins of control and manipulation. A church that helps people work through wounds and exposes the dynamics of those offenses can cut off Jezebel's source of strength. But once this spirit hooks up with Babylon, or a religious spirit, it gains power through our own spiritual mantle, and we become totally blind, as God's people, to see its influence in a church.

If we can take our eyes off the natural realm and see the pattern of satanic influence to defile God's people while they substitute their ways, the connection between these two demonic spirits and our own strongholds becomes obvious. Instead of going on a hunting expedition after wounded sheep with demons attached to those wounds, or purging prophets by insinuating that they are Jezebels, we can see that the real principality can only function and make change with those in leadership positions already.

Babylon and Israel Mix

Jezebel was a daughter of Ethbaal, king of the Sidonians (ancient

The Word in His Prophets

Phoenicia). The Phoenicians were a powerful people, having founded their own nation close to Israel. Ancient Phoenicia was roughly situated in what is now modern day Lebanon. Their first settlements in 2500 B.C. were developed under the influence of ancient Babylon, along with all of Babylon's gods (demons).[1] Even if they did not keep the exact name of the deities intact throughout the centuries, the legends and concepts of them stayed the same.

The ancient Phoenicians were related by blood to the Canaanites who were, like most others in the region, Semites. Semites descended from Shem, Shem from Noah, Noah back to Seth and Seth back to Adam. Loosely speaking they make up the people groups of Hebrews, Arabs, Assyrians, Phoenicians and Babylonians. The Babylonians (Sumeria/Chaldea/Akkadia) were founded first, then the Phoenicians and then the Assyrians. These are the sons of Ham. The Arabs (Ishmaelites) and the Hebrews descended from Shem. Subsequently, the Ishmaelites intermarried with others and became Arabs, but the Hebrews remained relatively pure blooded Semites until the time of Christ. One might wonder why the Babylonians, Phoenicians and Assyrians would be considered Semites, since they really trace back to Ham. I believe it's due to Noah's prophecy over his sons. (See Genesis 9:24–27.) He curses Ham and says he will be a slave to his brothers. And while he blesses Japhath, Japhath is still prophesied to dwell in Shem's tents. So both brothers are technically prophesied to come under the lineage in name of Shem. This is why I believe scholars don't call these people Hamites or Japhathites, but Semites. There was intermarriage between them to some extent also. And while some lines remained pure back to Shem, like Abraham did, there was definitely movement, travel and dispersal of the people geographically, which is why we find Abraham in Ur of the Chaldees (Babylon/ancient Sumeria).

When God tells the serpent that one is coming from Eve that will crush him, the devil seeks either to destroy the seed by separation and violence or to defile Eve's seed so he can't be crushed by it. So he tempts Cain to kill Abel. But God gives Eve a son, Seth, and the lineage goes on. At a crossroad in the generations, satan again uses the sin card to attempt to defile Noah's sons. Ham is disgraced. God's lineage is still pure through Shem. Jezebel (Babylon) and Ahab (Israel) marry. Because of so much defilement God wipes out their seed. Now the Semite bloodline continues pure straight through to Messiah. Of course, it's not like satan didn't try again throughout the centuries to defile or kill Messiah before He could walk. But God always kept Messiah's line pure so that, physically speaking, the Word (Christ) or the next generation remained pure. Spiritually speaking, what we are looking at is a desire by satan to pollute the Word. Eve has no seed except that conceived by the Word of God and the Spirit of God. So it is with us in the New Testament. We are not pure because of our bloodlines, but pure because of the desire to keep His Word pure in our hearts. The Word purifies us. The other Good News for us today is that even if we somehow become defiled by these spirits, we can repent and Christ's blood can wash us clean.

Effects of Mixing God's Word

We know these spirits are around when there is the total polluting of God's Word as a prophet speaks. It's one thing not to understand what someone is saying, but it's another matter to take that word and twist it. The most pronounced historical evidence of this is from the sixth century, B.C. During that period of time, there was a great wave of world religions that came on the scene, six in all, not including Judaism. Let me quote from *Eerdman's* as to the possible reason for this:

The first causes of this great movement are probably as complex as the Renaissance and Reformation in Europe 2,000 years later. One obvious possible source is the preaching of Isaiah (about 740 B.C. onwards) and the other eighth-century prophets of Israel, with the refrain from Jeremiah and Ezekiel a century or so later. Certainly we can find most of the ethical emphases of Zoroaster, Buddha (about 563–483 B.C.), Mahavira (599–527 B.C.)

The Word in His Prophets

and Confucius (551–479 B.C.) in the great prophets. It is hard to believe that no one else but Israel and Judah heard the prophets. Isaiah's language was intelligible without translation in cities all over the Fertile Crescent. The transmission of religious ideas, especially when they were so revolutionary, would be exceedingly rapid. In the time it takes us to write and publish a book, the ancient world would have gossiped the ideas far more extensively. The number of major cities from Athens to China was comparatively few, and all were cosmopolitan, with several languages spoken by the various national groups who lived there. Religious teachers and their disciples traveled constantly and, most important of all, people had the time and interest to listen to them.[2]

So it was the actual polluting of the written, as well as the spoken word of God from the mouth of God's prophets—Isaiah, Ezekiel and Jeremiah—that these religious spirits used to twist God's Word in order to reproduce these different world religions that have trapped people and damned so many souls to hell for eternity.

New Testament Mixing

With repentance through Christ's blood keeping us from defilement (*tamei*) and the spiritual hierarchy of fivefold ministry keeping us from mixing (*shaatnez*) our human soulish ideas with God's plan, satan knows he is in trouble. So what does he do? He continues to attack through offenses. This is why so many in the earlier church age have been martyred. Death is always his favorite tool. But God keeps raising up new believers. So satan infiltrated the early church with heresy. But fivefold ministry, especially the gifts of the apostles and prophets, catch him and expose his lies. So what does he do next? He wipes out the spiritual leadership authority of fivefold ministry, telling God's people these gifts aren't necessary to be in a place of prominence. Then he goes about convincing people that the prophets are heretics or Jezebels. Once he's got fivefold ministry—especially the prophets—neutered so they can't reproduce God's Word in people's lives, he then goes about to take the Bible out of the hands of the lay people. In this way, no input from God ever takes place.

This war has been going on for quite some time in our past church age and even continues today.[3] It was when the church mixed with the Roman state that a spiritual weakening took place. Rome required leadership to be Rome's way and not God's way.[4] Over the centuries many became offended and hurt by the decadence of this pollution, so they withdrew to cloisters and the monastic way of life. Unfortunately, this life shunned female input, so women could no longer influence the church, and it enclosed the Word of God behind human walls.[5] Now only the bishops had any say in anything. The spiritual leadership of fivefold ministry was lost. The elders and deacons were minimized in their own God-given gifts because man's order was now substituted for God's order and half of the army of the Lord (the women) were left with no voice. From the bishops emerged the popes.[6] This form of government was not always honorable.[7] This encouraged more wounding, offenses and suspicions. As the centuries passed, these conditions only encouraged the strongholds we see evidenced in our churches as well as our world today, namely, the idea that you can't trust authority, and women must be controlled and viewed with suspicion because they will only lead us into sin. Now that our wounded ideas have been mixed with God's Word the devil is able to enjoy wreaking havoc in the church as well as the world.

Satan's Motive in Controlling the Prophets

Satan's motive is simple: control the Word of the Lord so it never reproduces. He then tries to kill off everything and everyone that represents that Word honorably. In our modern time he does this in two ways. First he infiltrates how prophets are taught. We will look at that shortly. If he can't remove a fivefold ministry prophet, he will do anything he can to substitute his choice

The Word in His Prophets

instead of God's choice. Before we look at the specifics of this sabotage, let's look at one common misconception that allows us to attack prophets and ignore our own soul issues so we ignore solid teaching practices.

Jezebel never could have been Jezebel without Ahab, and Ahab couldn't have been Ahab without Jezebel. They were two peas in a pod. Sometimes marriage is not always for better; sometimes it's for worse. Let's make another plain observation: the kings and queens of Israel were never a type of prophetic ministry. The prophets were always the prophets, never the kings. The kings were supposed to be godly examples of shepherds leading the flock of God's people. (See 1 Chronicles 17:3, 6.) Who was Jezebel really trying to control? Not Ahab. She had him in her back pocket, and he had her in his. Even though they did it for evil, they both did everything in their power to protect the other and establish the other—even though it was for their own selfish gain. Just read the stories. Ahab gives her control over the priests. Jezebel consoles him and counsels him to do what's already in his heart by taking Naboth's field (taking the Lord's inheritance for his own selfish use). These are only two examples. There are more. Never did it occur to either one of them to obey the Word of the Lord at the mouth of the prophet. Many churches today do the same thing. Real Biblical behavior is a shepherd's understanding of prophetic intercession, prophetic worship and praise and prophesying like David did many times in the Psalms. But it never occurred to David to usurp the role of the prophet and control that ministry. Why else would he have repented at Nathan's word? (See 2 Samuel 12:13.)

Both Ahab and Jezebel tried to control and kill Elijah on many different occasions. These spirits are affecting those who try to control the prophetic ministry and its actions, taking the prophetic word and using it or the Lord's inheritance for their own self-promotion. These spirits must move through those in religious power. They must move through people who are functioning in their godly calls but are still wounded and living in offenses and unforgiveness. These folks mistake their soul issues for the Word of the Lord. They feel if they can control the situation, they or the church won't be hurt. Unfortunately, this is done by pastors and leaders as well as by sheep.

How do you overcome the devices of these spirits in your own heart? By plenty of practice. God will place you in a situation, either with a prophet or someone else, to show you your heart's true motive. Our tools with which to overcome are the Word of the Lord and faith in Him to accomplish all He has promised. Remember also that these are spirits that can affect both genders equally. Satan is an equal-opportunity devil. I have observed just as many men with these spirits as women. The only preference I've observed is that satan prefers to use husband and wife teams. But it matters very little to him who he hurts and destroys, as long as he gets the job done. Also, when these spirits move over an area or church, many innocent people can be wounded, not only those individuals that they specifically use.

Conditions These Spirits Use to Get a Foothold on a Church

There are several conditions that can enable these spirits to get a foothold. On an individual level, when our souls are running the show and we refuse to let go of our offenses concerning people, these spirits can have a party. When we subtly desire to control and be in charge, we crowd God out of the situation. But there are some other conditions or missteps that can take place in churches that further the plans of these enemy attackers. The church was established by the apostles and prophets. (See Ephesians 2:19–21.) When we do not lay out a Bible based foundation on which they can function, we have built a house on quicksand. (See Matthew 7:26.) If we do not teach people how prophets speak, many offenses can take place. Quite frequently, prophets speak of future events in symbolic language, not in literal language. This can be confusing for the spiritually immature to understand, especially if they want God's Word to fulfill some aspect of what they want to talk about. So someone

The Word in His Prophets

may accuse a prophet of falsity just because they don't hear what they want to hear or understand what they hear. One prophet may prophesy what *will* happen while another may prophesy God's desire. This happened frequently in the Bible. Wasn't it God's desire that Israel repent and not be carried away by Babylon? So He has Isaiah prophesy restoration, while Jeremiah prophesies captivity because that's exactly what will happen. Did Israel accuse both of them of falsity? They did.

A true prophet reveals the total desires and plans of the Lord—His purposes. False prophets tell fortunes. They can prophesy what will happen. Many times what will happen is not the Lord's desire, but because of our stubbornness. A true prophet that is forced to prophesy what will happen will reveal a people's sin to them while pointing them toward the road of restoration and in the direction of God's total plans and purposes. (See Isaiah 57, 58 and 59 and Jeremiah 29, 30 and 31.) True prophets prepare God's people for what is ahead—God's specific way, not man's way. This is what can cause controversy for some in our churches.

Additionally, a prophecy may be spoken in a timeframe, but it may take weeks, months or even years to fulfill. God may speak concerning an issue that may occur immediately, but the total fulfillment of that word may not take place for many, many years. This happened with the prophets in the Old Testament. One of the more well known of these prophecies was Isaiah's. He says a virgin will conceive and bear a son. (See Isaiah 7:14.) This, of course, took place some 700 years later. But for Isaiah not to be considered a false prophet something had to take place immediately, and it did. Within a year or so his wife gave birth. (See Isaiah 8:1.) Again, the confusion for many in the church as well as our Jewish brethren is the use of the Hebrew word for virgin. In the Hebrew language, life is broken up into stages, and different words are used for those stages. The word Isaiah uses could have also applied to his "damsel, maid or virgin," as well as Mary, the virgin mother of our Lord.

Prophecy from God is multifaceted. This is why we can read our Bible today and know it applies to us now. Not every modern day prophet functions in this type of a word, and not every Word from God is designed to convey multiple thoughts. Some prophets function this way and some don't. But when they do, their language is usually symbolic and not always well understood, initially, unless God confirms some aspect of it quickly.

We should also be clear and state that the true Word of the Lord exposes when sin is in the camp. I'm not excusing rudeness. The spiritual attitude of a person who claims to speak for God must always be pure, without an ongoing attitude of bitterness, unforgiveness or some other spiritual sin. What I am referring to is the fact that many church leaders are not so willing for God to use His Word from another's mouth so that some things are exposed. This, of course should be done with as much maturity and orderliness as possible. My experience in this has been that the person so used by God will have no idea of what is going on in the natural. This has happened to me on many occasions. People will swear I knew what I was talking about because the situation that later took place was exactly the word that was shared. I have had people refuse to believe that I did not know what was going on. It has made me realize that the prophets of old were not killed because they prophesied peace, new Cadillacs and bigger ministries.

No matter what level of inspiration a person claims, his or her attitude must always be holy. I have seen people with accurate words, but something is spiritually wrong with them. They may want people to come to them for a word instead of encouraging an environment where God speaks spontaneously or speaks directly to people Himself. This is pride and selfishness. This may be one aspect of what Ezekiel is referring to in Ezekiel 14. Obviously, the prophet's words were accurate since God persuaded him to prophesy, but some aspect of wanting to see his own desires must have been at work also. We must understand that functioning in the Word of the Lord is not a toy or a gift for us to do with whatever we please, no matter how good it looks.

Not laying a scriptural foundation for the many ministry gifts Jesus graces His church with before we implement them can also

The Word in His Prophets

cause problems. If we laid a firm foundation, many of the misunderstandings and improper practices would become obvious to us. It would be much easier to clear up innocent or human stronghold mistakes, and much easier to spot problems when real demons are attempting to ensnare. Just because someone can function in the gifts of the Spirit does not make him a fivefold ministry prophet. In the same way, accurately functioning in signs, healings, wonders, prophecy and casting out devils is never an indicator that the individual functioning in these gifts is right. These gifts are to confirm the preaching of the gospel of our Lord Jesus Christ and our belief in Him. (See Mark 13:22, 23; 16:15-18; Luke 24:45-49; Acts 1:2-5, 8; Matthew 7:21-23; 24:24.) Many churches do not begin on a foundation that is Bible based. And if they do, as new members or young converts are added to the church, no one sits down with them to find out what their foundational theology is based upon. Everyone wants to learn about spiritual gifts, but they become offended when you want to talk to them about repentance from dead works, faith toward God, baptisms (especially the one of fire), laying on of hands, resurrection of the dead and eternal judgment. (See Hebrews 6:1-3.)

Another problem, connected to not laying out a scriptural foundation before people move in spiritual gifts, can be the effect of traveling ministers. I've often wondered why traveling ministers come to a church and very seldom, if ever, talk about the overriding word or testimony that that particular church was called to accomplish by Jesus (a quick look at Revelation 2 and 3 will show us they all had one). And where in the building process have they gone awry, or where they are on target? Often these folks come in and share the new fad, or what I call the book of the month. I understand many traveling ministers only want to share the word God has given them for a congregation. But many Christians are substituting the reading of God's Word with listening to preachers and reading Christian books. They just do not have a strong enough Biblical foundation in place to handle some of these books or preaching. And God forbid if the shepherd decides to take the whole church down the road of that new book fad–they will shipwreck in no time. I am not being critical of using a minister to teach a congregation something God has birthed in them or may be calling them to, or of the benefit and blessing that Christian books can give. Many times this is exactly how God will speak to people. But we need to be careful, and exercise caution with prayer and fasting, before we move a whole church in a new direction. If we would lay out a solid Biblical teaching foundation explaining God's order and the different ministry gifts and how people can function in them, quite a few problems could be averted.

There are also different customs concerning prophetic release in the congregation. Some churches forbid all spontaneous gifts of prophecy during worship as interrupting worship. In my opinion this is a shame. For it is during a quiet and appropriate time in worship that prophetic release comes forward. (See Psalm 29.) Someone may come into a congregation who does not understand this custom of silence and be called a Jezebel, witch or other unholy accusation, simply because they have not understood the customs. In other churches, prophecy may only come forward at the end of worship and only by those known to the pastor. While this custom seems safe and has as much scriptural backing as the custom of prophetic release during an appropriate time in worship, a congregation may call someone an unkind name simply because he or she doesn't know that particular church's custom.

One form of release that I find no Scripture for, but is still practiced by some congregations, is release during the pastor's sermon. On the contrary, I find Scripture advising against this. If a person from a congregation which allows this visits a congregation where this practice is considered out of order, and he moves in this manner by interrupting the message, he risks being hauled out of the building. While the congregation may approve of that person's removal, I feel we should do everything to remain and move in Christian love, for love covers a multitude of sins. (See Proverbs 10:11, 12.)

The Word in His Prophets

Fivefold Ministry

When God is calling a church to implement fivefold ministry along with the fivefold ministry gift of a prophet, and no Biblical guidelines are implemented for their release, it sets an easy stage for these enemy attackers. Fivefold ministry is an amazing weapon in God's hands and a devastating mess in the hands of mankind and the devil. I believe God is using this transition time of our church generation to implement and restore these people who are given as gifts to a particular church, to a nation, and even on a global level. In less populated locales, one pastor doing everything might still work. But in other places, fivefold ministry will be the only way to function. Why? The answer is found in a reading of Ephesians 4.

These five gifts of apostle, prophet, pastor, teacher and evangelist function very similarly, but with different applications. They are all called to be bond-slaves or *doulos* to the body of Christ. They all can preach, teach, prophesy, evangelize and care for the sheep, but the way they each accomplish the tasks set out for them is quite different. Each one of them is a spiritual gift specializing in one particular area. What prevents us from truly functioning in plurality of leadership are our carnal egos and our career minded mentalities of the ministry of the Lord.

When we study Ephesians, we study what and who Paul was. When we study Paul, we can see what the attitude of people called to one of these five ministry gifts should be. If there ever was an apostle that threw a monkey wrench into the my-ministry-my-career theory, it was the apostle Paul. He worked part time supporting himself and received offerings for God's work from God's people. He was able to work with local leadership for short and longer periods of time. You may say, aren't you describing the call of an apostle, or "sent-out one," anyway? Yes. But I am also describing the attitude of someone who wouldn't allow his own offenses or attitudes to butcher the sheep. I am describing someone who would be willing to die rather than fulfill his own motives and desires for position and gain—someone who would give himself to see God's people move in faith and in understanding God's Word. Just because the apostle, prophet and evangelist tend to travel more than the teacher and the pastor, doesn't mean that sometimes they don't stay in an area for years at a time. The reason Paul was able to work with local leadership was because the carnality in his life was always being crucified with Christ. It wasn't "my" ministry; it was "I, Paul, a bondservant and slave of the Lord Jesus Christ."

When God does call a fivefold ministry prophet to a church, he or she will not only challenge and stretch God's people, but will also help maintain an open heaven to the throne so nothing hinders God's destiny on a people's lives. This can only be done by a desire for holiness and obedience to God's Word. In fact, this should not be a hindrance to the shepherd or shepherdess, but a blessing. I am speaking about true prophetic ministry, not flakiness or quacks, self-proclaimed prophets or people with an axe to grind. And frankly, when I speak about self-proclamation, this can also affect people with little or no prophetic call, as well as people with some revelatory gifts. I am also not speaking about those prophetic ministries that travel full time. The fivefold ministry gift of the prophet is no different than the rest of the bondservants in laying down his life for the sheep. This means humbly obeying the shepherding gift and loving God's people while living with them. Everyone tries so hard to build his own little kingdom (ministry), while using the Word of the Lord. I think we forget it's God's house that's supposed to be built. Many regional, national and international fivefold ministry gifts are called by God to travel and bless many churches. But a hand must be attached to a body to work properly. While many prophets travel, working alongside other fivefold ministers is, in my opinion, the most effective way the prophetic ministry can be used. It is also the most effective way the rest of fivefold ministry can function. In this way, prophetic ministry, as well as the rest of fivefold ministry, remains balanced so it can be used as the lethal weapons against the enemy God designed them to be, and the blessing they are meant to be for His Body.

The Word in His Prophets

Ephesus

Fivefold ministry is the very hand of Jesus (the Word) extended here on earth. All five must be used together by God, not just individually. You could function well with two or three fingers. But you function perfectly with all five. The goal or finish line is God in glory covering the earth. We see fivefold ministry explained by Paul in the epistle to the Ephesians. Whenever we see the various spiritual gifts explained, we should look at the theme of the book in which they were mentioned. (See Romans 12, 1 Corinthians 12, Ephesians 4.) Was seeing God in glory covering the earth Paul's goal also when he wrote to the Ephesians? Yes. The city of Ephesus was the capitol of Asia and was a gateway that opened Asia up to the rest of the world. It was also considered the head or birthplace of emperor worship. Located at the mouth of the Aegean Sea on a river that served as a caravan route from Palestine and Syria, Ephesus was the worldwide center for the cult worship of the goddess Diana, also called Artemis. As Christians, this is what they were warring against in an effort to rid the world of demonic influence so God in glory could rest and infiltrate. They were warring against principalities and powers, and the fivefold ministry gift of the prophet sees these spirits and their motives quite clearly.

In Ephesians 1, Paul explains that Christ is far above the arena of demonic attack in the heavenlies, having conquered them totally. In chapter two, Paul lets them know that, because of Christ's victory, they are in the same arena with Christ, far above demonic rule, as a result of being seated with Christ. In chapter three, he tells them that, as a result of Christ having conquered in the heavenly arena and in the arena on earth that they, as believers, must live in, the gospel may be preached to all the nations. It is in chapter four that he shows them the five spiritual leadership gifts God has given them for this battle. Chapter five talks about submission because the lack of it, rebellion, will give these spirits an excuse to remain entrenched. This is why I feel so strongly concerning submission to pastoral or apostolic authority, no matter what your calling is. And chapter six is where we find the classic discourse on the armor of God. Was this written to remove one entrenched satanic ruler in the city of Ephesus alone? Or was it written as an example for all generations of Christians so they can be prepared for warfare on Christ's terms and not on the devil's terms? I believe this is one of the reasons why it was written. Another is to show us how important fivefold ministry is, as well as the fivefold ministry gift of the prophet.

If and when God calls those in prophetic ministry to a church, they will be foundational. They will be foundational in birthing new converts, in raising the babies, in maintaining that particular church's health (repentance, deliverance and inner healing), in warfare practices (repentance, intercession, worship and spiritual gifts) and they will be foundational in putting on the roof (leadership placement and spiritual health). While there, God may have them speak about an issue concerning the construction process. But the foundation and the building process will always be paramount to them. Many times we mistake a person's gifts of the Holy Spirit as a sign that he is a fivefold ministry prophet. (See 1 Corinthians 12.) Many times a person moves in prophetic words as an intercessor or in a leadership position and we also mistake him for a fivefold ministry prophet.

Mantles Shoulder The Glory: Dangerous Substitution

When these spirits are attacking a church, I have also seen a different situation arise. These religious spirits will convince leadership to shun the prophet called to minister and refuse any right standing relationship. This can be done obviously or in more subtle ways, as we saw by our previous historical review. If a religious spirit (Ahab and Jezebel) is afflicting God's people and they are called to oversee a prophet, it is possible that a twisting of that prophet's words can occur. (See Matthew 26:3, 4, 14–16, 59–65.) There can be a misrepresentation of how that prophet functions or a distortion of these leaders' personal relationship

The Word in His Prophets

with that prophet. (See 1 Kings 18:17-18; 2 Corinthians 6:5-10; Acts 24:5-9, 27; 26:4-6.) It will be very difficult for some in the congregation to know what the truth is because of the smoke screen these religious spirits use in order to blind all of God's people. I have often felt sadness for those prophets because what satan has done is use their brothers and sisters to nullify their gift ability for that church. Satan knows a mantle when he sees one. (See Zechariah 3.) He would much rather substitute a person with no mantle or the wrong mantle than allow a saint with the right mantle in the right place.

The mantle of God shoulders the glory. It covers and becomes part of our armor. (See Genesis 37 and 41; Numbers 20:28; Leviticus 21:10; 2 Samuel 13; 2 Kings 2:14-15; John 19:23-24.) A look at Jesus' life will reveal He birthed and functioned in all 5 ministry gifts. His garments were separated 5 ways. (See Revelation 16:15.) The reason why Elijah's mantle fell to earth was because he no longer needed it. He would be in translated glory!

If we miss the purpose of God for these individuals to shoulder the glory, we will miss God in glory. Fivefold ministry prophets are not substitutes for a pastor's spouse or intercessor or inner healing minister or for any other minister. They are uniquely gifted to discern the purposes of God in glory for the sanctuary, and they are uniquely gifted to see the attacks from the enemy that defile God's people, which will cause God to leave His sanctuary. In the past we have gotten away with functioning as a partial army. I don't believe we can do this too much longer. (See Revelation 12:12; 22:12.) Jesus said the devil would do things in the last days that would attempt to fool even the elect, if it was possible (See Mark 13:22.) As a result, we will need every man, woman and child watching their "post." (See Revelation 3:2, KJV.)

Another difficulty for a church when God calls a fivefold ministry prophet is the clash that can ensue between other ministries in a church that move in revelatory gifts. Intercessors, worship and music ministers, deliverance and inner healing teams must all move in the Holy Spirit's gifts of words of knowledge, wisdom and prophecy. A fivefold ministry prophet will have been trained and tested by God in all these different ministry areas. They will be able to see where these teams or individuals are off track, right on or where trouble is coming in from the enemy. A fivefold ministry prophet will be able to counsel them in ways that a pastor might not be able to. Some have questioned whether a prophet should have that kind of influence. My response has always been, "what kind of influence did prophets have in the Scriptures?" When we look at the answer to that question we see that a key foundation stone for orderly function and worship in the Old Testament Temple was the Tabernacle of David. While David is credited with instituting this structure of prayer, worship and priestly functioning, it was always done by the Word of the Lord that was in the mouths of the prophets and in many cases implemented by them. (See Exodus 7:1; Deuteronomy 18:18; 2 Chronicles 29:25; Ezra 5:1-2, 6:14; Ephesians 2:19-22.) Again, however God is leading a church to function is how it should function. But in those churches where God is moving this way, a pastor may put a prophet over these teams as a helper—and I mean helper, not boss. In churches where these teams are immature or untested with no mantles, I've seen a pastor place a prophet as a temporary overseer to disciple them in shouldering the glory; in that way they receive a mantle. When a pastor does this it can elicit responses of Jezebel or witch (if that person is a woman), usurper or controlling authority (if that person is a man). Many times this is because a firm foundation has not been laid out defining fivefold ministry and how it—especially the prophetic gift—functions.

In years gone by these ministers have been called assistant or associate pastor because we didn't know what else to call them. In that way no one feels blocked from the shepherd. The sheep must always have free access to the pastors. To me, it makes little or no difference what you call someone. People will function in whatever gift God has given them no matter what you call them. But once you use the term prophet instead of assistant pastor, if in fact that's what the person is, hell will raise its ugly head. Why? Because the church is implementing God's hierarchy through

The Word in His Prophets

proper channels of authority. In fact, this must be done through proper channels of authority. When that takes place, God can come and rest because His order has been instituted. And when that takes place, the devil knows he's in for trouble. So he has to cause smoke screens through offenses, slander, gossip, misunderstandings and missteps.

Fivefold ministry gifts are spiritual first. It is after we receive them as gifts of God to a church that we see those gifts manifest on earth. We must put them in the place God is requiring. If we do not, I don't care how many other talented people a church has, they are in disobedience to God. So satan will do anything he can to either discredit fivefold ministry or have a church substitute one gift for another or one person for another. This is in an effort to circumvent the total plan of God for that church. I used to think it was safer to just call these people associate or assistant. In this way you don't incite demons. But I've learned that if they are true fivefold ministry prophets, hell will always retaliate. In fact, no matter how perfectly we function, hell will always try to attack. I'm of the opinion that we don't hold up under the attack because we have not implemented the Lord's vision of these ministry gifts and have not sown a sound foundation for how they should function.

Most fivefold ministry prophets do not want operational authority over the in-house church ministries they oversee or help. Sometimes God may call them in that capacity. But my experience has been that they do not seek it. Until they have to prophesy, preach or teach—especially if they must expose an attitude of sin—their desire is to make everyone else look good by helping things run smoothly and lifting up and encouraging everybody else. I wish I could say that even with that kind of attitude these spirits cannot attack. But that has not been my experience. Jealousy, strife and outright lies can still be levied against them. This is what makes many prophets travel. It is also why churches can suffer blindness. (See Matthew 15:14.) It also sets a stage where true prophets have the potential to become false prophets, as a result of many inflicted wounds festering in an environment where they receive money as they travel. All of the above habits, unfortunately, also make it easier for the spirit called Jezebel and a religious spirit (Babylon) to infect us.

Again, each church will have a different call from God to her neighborhood and sphere of influence. Not every church's fivefold ministry team will look the same. The evangelist may be the one everyone calls pastor while the pastor's spouse may actually be more pastoral. The prophet may actually be an elder. I have found, though, in those instances where God has come in glory, change takes place. More people will be added to that church and God will most often require them to implement His hierarchy. God did this extensively with the nation of Israel as they went from judge (priest) hierarchy to prophet (priest) hierarchy and then to king-prophet-priest hierarchy.

How Ahab and Jezebel Work

When we study the New Testament Scriptures of these two spirits, we come away with a much better understanding of how a religious spirit and a Jezebel spirit must work together or in tandem. Trying to control any one else is immoral enough for me. But Jesus Himself makes the reference to sexual immorality in Revelation 2:20. Is He referring only to the act of physical sin or is He speaking of a spiritual condition? It would seem both. We will speak more about a religious spirit in Chapters 8 and 9. But for our purposes of looking at a Jezebel spirit, we should understand how it works with a religious spirit and how the two become one. This turns sexual immorality into spiritual immorality and vice-versa, from our Lord's point of view.

I define a religious spirit simply as one that claims protection or covering from some source of godliness or godly appointment but does whatever is in its own mind to do, not what is in the heart and mind of the Lord. In that context, the whole human race can fall subject to these spirits—not only the ruling counsel of old (Pharisees, Sadducees and scribes); not only Muslims, New Agers or some other cult, but Christians also. Ahab was a perfect

The Word in His Prophets

example of how a religious spirit can infect someone—and how it marries Jezebel. Ahab was called and appointed by God to be king, but he did not do what was in the heart of the Lord for him to do. Jezebel set herself up, through Ahab, as head over the priests—not a place kings or queens belonged. The high priest belonged over the priests. That's exactly what these spirits do: they put themselves in places or positions where they do not belong or where God has not called them. The religious may want someone in a position, but God has not called that person to that position. In Revelation 2:20, Jesus says she *calls* herself a prophetess, not that she was one. In other words, they will infect people in high places with a religious spirit. While there, they become one and fulfill their own plans and destinies, not God's desired fruit. To that extent, even Lucifer and the fallen angels were, at one time, God-created and appointed with a task, until they did what was in their own minds to do.

These spirits may call themselves prophets, but there is little long-term history of accurate words being fulfilled. The control and rebellion evidenced in people being affected by it is there because of hurts in the people's lives. When we spot this, we can exercise many scriptural tools of inner healing and deliverance to restore these people, if they will allow that to take place. (See Matthew 23:37.) But once they come in contact with a religious spirit or Babylon in a leadership position, they will attack prophetic ministry and attempt to control that ministry's reproducing ability. The devil's antics have not changed. No matter what we do he will always try to convince everyone that a true prophet is false in some way. Ahab and Jezebel did this consistently. (See Deuteronomy 18:20 and 1 Kings 18:4, 17.) So did their son. (See 2 Kings 6:31-33.) Before Babylon carries the Jews away, Jeremiah is singled out by God to warn them. (See Jeremiah 14:13-15; 23:9-40.) When we study his book we see that for more than 20 years they accused him of being a false prophet. (See Jeremiah 12:6.) Finally, they attempt to kill him. (See Jeremiah 26.)

Fortunately for us today, we no longer use knives and spears.

Today most church people use gossip and words. Since these folks with religious spirits are in a place of authority, everyone believes them. It is quite possible for them to look good until a prophet shows up. Then these latent issues that have never been fully dealt with will crop up again. And sometimes God will bring people to test your resolve in this area, to see if you've been delivered from the stronghold issues of control or manipulation and bitter unforgiveness which can produce offenses. All of these prove our souls are in charge, not God's Holy Spirit.

True Religion

James 1:27 shows us what the opposite of a demonic religious spirit is. He shows us the example of what perfect, undefiled religion is. When we seek to help others in their calamities and horrors of tormented attack, not to judge, but to quietly provide relief by sowing the Word of God, we function in perfect religion. When we put faith to that Word by sacrificially providing for those so wounded, people get built back up in Christ. When there is no Word sown and no faith exercised it will produce separation and not Christ-like results (we will speak more about separation in chapters 8 and 9). When we take all of these factors into account, we have a much better picture of what the spirit called Jezebel wants. We must realize that a religious spirit and a Jezebel spirit are married—and thus the two become one flesh. Furthermore, they need a body (the Lord's inheritance) to do their dirty work. Unless we understand these things, we will never see how our own subtly sinful motives work hand in hand with these spirits. That's why they want people who function in the testimony of Jesus Christ. Sowing God's Word reproduces Christ in others. These spirits desire to steal the reproducing ability of the bride of Christ. They want to steal the health and vitality of a church by controlling the revelatory nature of the bride of Christ. These spirits do this by attacking the testimony of the Lord Jesus Christ within the church and those with that testimony.

The Word in His Prophets

Kill the Prophets, Defile the Next Generation

Let's go back to Ahab and Jezebel. In 1 Kings 18, Elijah defeats the prophets and priests of Baal. He defeats principalities and powers by the Word in power—in repentant submission to God by way of a sacrifice. Then he runs and hides. The sin for the prophets and Elijah is not in running or hiding from Jezebel. (See 1 Kings 17:2; 18:1–15.) The sin is in not recognizing the timing. The sin is in not offering the sacrifice at the appointed time and then standing their ground when the confrontation comes. We are told to present ourselves as living sacrifices. (See Romans 12:1–3.) Any Christian or prophet who will sacrifice his way for God's plans is always dangerous to Jezebel. When Jezebel hears about this sacrifice, what does she do? By the way, her actions were under the protection and authority of Ahab. Does she send an army? No. Does she send her police enforcers to seize Elijah? No. Does she send a military assassin or spy? No. She threatens him with words. In Revelation 2:21, what does she use to control people? Words in the form of teaching.

Look at Revelation 17:6 and 18:24. What is the testimony of Jesus Christ? Revelation 19:10 says that it is the Spirit of prophecy. Who or what is Babylon symbolic of? It is symbolic of false religion and idolatrous practices. Who does symbolic Babylon kill in verses 17:6 and 18:24? It kills the prophets and those with the testimony of Jesus Christ. Now look at Revelation 12. In verse 4, the dragon tries to devour the child. What tool is used? His mouth. In verses 15–17, the dragon tries to kill whom? He tries to kill those with Christ's testimony. And what does he use? Again, his mouth, spewing (v. 15). If the devil cannot get prophets to come in agreement with him, he will seek to kill them. Unfortunately, many times we confuse our own understanding with the Word of the Lord. When we do we taint what should be passed on to the next generation, thereby destroying the holy seed. This is why God sent Elijah, Hazael, Jehu and Elisha to wipe out everything that came from Ahab and

Jezebel. These spirits must use those in authority so they can legitimize their spiritually seductive ways.

Reproducing, Substituting and Teaching

Jesus mentions this principle over and over, but it comes home so clearly in Matthew 23. Two portions stand out.

> **Woe to you, teachers of the law and Pharisees, you hypocrites! You travel over land and sea to win a single convert, and when he becomes one, you make him twice as much a *son* of hell as you are... Woe to you, teachers of the law and Pharisees, you hypocrites! You build tombs for the prophets and decorate the graves of the righteous. And you say, 'If we had lived in the days of our *forefathers*, we would not have taken part with them in shedding the blood of the prophets.' So you testify against yourselves that you are the *descendants* of those who murdered the prophets. Fill up, then, the measure of the sin of your *forefathers!***
>
> —Matthew 23:15, 29–32 , emphasis added

Ahab and Jezebel substituted Baal's priests for the Lord's Levites and then sought to silence all the prophets through this substitution. Elijah was her splinter or thorn. Through Elijah preaching the Word, Jezebel's tactics were minimized, but never totally removed. It was when he moved in godly power that the prophets and teachers of Baal (her priests) were killed. (See 1 Kings 18:17–19:1.) In the New Testament we see this spirit teaching God's people again. Here Jesus gives this teacher time to repent. So we see an attack from the enemy on two fronts. If he can't get rid of some portion of fivefold ministry or a prophet, he will substitute his own person or people (priests). They, in turn will teach some things that may seem okay to the natural mind, but the teachings are not what God wants taught when He wants them taught.

The Word in His Prophets

Teaching Prophets

There have been several practices that I have noticed in the body of Christ that have disturbed me. The first is allowing someone to teach prophets with no mantle for the job. In other words, Elijah had a mantle to give to Elisha. They not only had a call from God for the job, but they had gone through the attacks of the enemy that would help them sustain others through similar devilish attacks. Before we see Elisha take over the company of the prophets, they were a little "off." If you were a prophet and saw that the mantle of Elijah rested on Elisha, would you argue with Elisha and try to control him in order to search for Elijah? (See 2 Kings 2:7, 15–18.) After Elisha picks up the mantle he begins to lead them and they start becoming effective for God's purposes to the nation. (See 2 Kings 9:1–10.) The right prophet with the right mantle causes them to become more focused and targeted. They move in God's direction, not off following this one or that one.

I have noticed a pattern of putting people in places to teach prophets, and these folks have never had to shoulder the weight of intercession for others. They have never had to shoulder the glory during times of attack by these spirits. They have never been called to be a watchman on the wall for any church. They have never presented themselves willingly as sacrifices. (See Daniel 1, 3 and 6.) In fact, as I have spoken to some of them, they have no idea how these enemies attack the body of Christ. Some I have spoken to have rarely prophesied and have no idea of the tests a prophet must go through. Yet they are charged with the sensitive area of teaching people prophetic ministry. I have heard the argument that there are older, wiser saints helping them. Those with mantles should not release the younger ones until their testing time is over and God reveals they passed the test. Elisha had a mantle. Paul had a mantle. These are spiritual gifts given to a body of believers. They not only reproduce other Christians, they shoulder the glory. They are given this responsibility because they have stayed in the heat of battle for many others. There is no substitution for this. God said even if Moses, Samuel, Noah,

BEYOND STRONGHOLDS

Daniel and Job interceded for Israel during her Babylonian captivity, they alone would be saved. (See Jeremiah 15:1; Ezekiel 14:14, 20.) The people of Israel went into Babylonian captivity because they refused to obey the Word of the Lord from the mouths of the prophets. If the mantles of those five could not save Israel from her attack by Babylon, how much more should we obey God's Word and rightly place the spiritual gifts of the people that He has called to do their jobs?

I would not want anyone reading this to go on a hunting expedition to search out people who don't seem to have a mantle or who are not mature in their ministry call. I would not want anyone to use any of this material as an excuse to further hurt already hurting people that are being affected by these demons. I believe the responsibility rests with leadership. I believe some in leadership will allow this situation because they are insecure, have low self-esteem issues and would rather not have a powerful mantle in certain positions. This leads me to the second reason why I believe we do not place people with mantles appropriately.

Society at large has a problem, and that problem has crept into the church. It seems we have raised a generation of adults who are still children. Whether as leaders or sheep, we want what we want and we want it NOW! I've made one observation while teaching God's people. I truly love the body of Christ, but many have the propensity for itching ears. I know many don't realize this. Children never want to eat their string beans or other greens. I have spoken with a number Christians who want to be taught prophetic ministry, but they cannot explain the doctrine of salvation. I don't mean a theological dissertation. I just mean their own basic justification and sanctification experiences as those experiences related to the Word of God. Many know what people write in books or preach, but they don't know the Word of God for themselves. One year a pastor friend of mine experienced a revolt because a married couple in the church wanted to be taught what they wanted to learn, not foundational teachings. They had great spiritual gifts, but absolutely no Biblical foundation or humility and character of Christ to sustain their

The Word in His Prophets

gifts. So they went and got a book by a wonderful prophet. There was nothing wrong with this book. Unfortunately, because they had no foundation or deeply seated Christ-like character, this book was too intense for them. Neither would admit that. They proceeded to tell the pastor how wrong everything was, based upon what they read in this book and then proceeded to split the church. I have seen many more mature Christians that want to preach, teach and lead, but many do not know God's Word. They have not gone through God's tests and received a mantle. If you confront them, even sweetly, they will make war or go behind the scenes to get their own way.

Mothers and fathers in the Lord have mantles to pass on. They should not let their "babies" get away with nonsense. My experience has been that there are many people with spiritual gifts that use their gifts to get what they want. Those with mantles who are called to disciple them should be able to see their shenanigans and put a stop to it. Of course, this rarely happens, because many leaders have their own issues to deal with. They do not want to confront people, and finding a scapegoat becomes easier. Even if correct discipline does occur, it can elicit responses of "Jezebel, control freak," and other such phrases. My goal and desire is restoration and the development of the character of Christ. So I tend to be a little more restrictive while I wait on the Holy Spirit to tell me what each person needs. I have heard some complain about this. I usually ask those who complain to put themselves in a pastor's shoes. If you were the pastor of a church and your people needed to be raised up in prophetic ministry, would you want them eating ice cream all day long and getting fat? If your church were going into battle how would you want your people trained? I'm not talking about being aggressive, unkind or rude. I am speaking about dealing with soul issues. Becoming a true prophet of God means dealing with deep-seated inner healing issues. Then prophecy becomes pure. It is taking on the nature and name of Jesus.

Contrary to popular opinion, true prophets do not need to be taught how to prophesy. In fact, God designs the training process of a prophet to be tough for a reason. They not only have to face devils, they have to speak God's Word so God's people confront their sin. I have heard the statement that what's being done is allowing people to learn how to hear God more accurately and be more comfortable when they prophesy. I disagree. When they learn how to overcome the fear of man they will learn how to overcome their pride. Then they will learn how to prophesy more accurately. This is part of the tough training that prophets must go through. What's really being done is we are teaching the flesh how to prophesy. Flesh gives birth to flesh and Spirit gives birth to Spirit. (See John 3:6.) God never taught my flesh to prophesy. He spoke His Word to my spirit man and commanded me to speak. Our elders warned us about the difference between the soul speaking and clouding the Word out, and the Spirit of God speaking clearly and plainly. (Please see chapter ten under "Open Doors to False Glory," where the practice of activations is discussed.) What we really need to do is teach people how to get rid of pride. Of course, this is a little hard to do if the leaders and teachers are immature in their call and full of pride themselves.

Make Disciples or Mentors?

Please do not think that I am speaking against discipling the body of Christ or discipling Christians in prophetic ministry. I wholeheartedly support discipleship and discipling Christians in prophetic ministry. Jesus commanded us to make disciples. But a subtle shift has taken place. I'm not sure exactly when it happened, either. Over the years I began to hear the word "mentor." When some people would say it in reference to discipleship I thought nothing of it. But after awhile others would use the word and a check developed in my spirit. After enough checks I turned to the Holy Spirit. He told me to look the word up. What I found grieved me. The word mentor originates in Greek mythology. Mentor was the elderly friend and counselor of the hero Odysseus. Mentor also tutored Odysseus' son, Telemachus. As the legend goes, the goddess Athena would

The Word in His Prophets

assume the form of Mentor when she appeared to either Odysseus or Telemachus. Over time the English word *mentor* became a synonym for a wise, trustworthy counselor or teacher. I need to ask a question. When did we decide that we were the wise counselors and teachers and not the Holy Spirit? The word disciple means one who is disciplined. As Christians we are to be disciples of Christ, not followers of some wise mentor.

It was Spurgeon, in 1869, who said that, "the Bible should be our Mentor." The root of the word mentor in Greek means "to remember, think, counsel." The Oxford Dictionary has the first English usage in 1750. Our English usage is less based on the Odyssey and more on Fenelon's romance *Telemaque*. Up until about the 1880's the word mentor was always used with an initial cap, referring to the actual legend of Odysseus. After this time we see small case mentor employed to signify it had developed its own meaning as opposed to being associated with the person of Mentor.[8]

While the world uses the term *mentor* to refer to one who counsels and teaches, many Christians use the term in reference to one who disciples. I understand how the usage of words changes over the centuries, and I believe the word *mentor* can be redeemed for Christ's work, as long as the focus is on Jesus rather than becoming someone's "wise counselor." The church desperately needs mothers and fathers in Christ to love, train, encourage and disciple God's people, but it must be for the purpose of establishing them in a relationship with Jesus and the fellowship of the Holy Spirit. True discipleship keeps the focus on the One for whom disciples are made. Nowhere is this more crucial than when discipling Jesus' people in an understanding of prophetic ministry.

Selling Kingdom Secrets

Another sad observation that I have made with many prophetically gifted groups is the banter surrounding the words that God gives them. I have no problem with sharing the things God allows me to share. But if we share them with pride in our hearts and publish or noise them abroad we may as well sell God's kingdom secrets. (See Jeremiah 23:17–40, KJV.) Isn't that what happened to Hezekiah when he showed the Babylonian emissaries what God had given him? (See Isaiah 39.) If pride is involved in our sharing, demons will certainly be able to comprehend what's being said, because sin is attached to the conversation. We may as well tell them everything God wants to do in our lives. I have had to shut my mouth in mid sentence when I wasn't paying attention to the Holy Spirit, as He told me to be quiet. I'd rather swallow my pride or just tell someone I can't discuss that subject and look foolish than be disobedient to the Holy Spirit. In this kind of environment these potential prophets are never taught the hard lesson that only the Word of God can be their strength and stronghold. If God does not come and rescue them or keep them, they return to their group dejected and hurt. They should not be coddled. They have substituted their feelings for God's Word. The Holy Spirit is teaching them a lesson. God alone is responsible for His Word. God alone will fulfill it. I can't base that upon my understanding. I can't make my soul feel better by sharing this word to see how everybody feels about it. I have noticed with these groups that they become very clique-ish. Evangelism and ministering to the broken and poor are not important. I've often wondered what the purpose of their prophetic gift really was.

Love Covers a Multitude of Sin

Never is this Scripture as crucial as when we talk about overcoming religious spirits, especially Jezebel. Discipline without love is legalism. Love without godly discipline fosters rebellion. Allowing an atmosphere of either legalism or rebellion encourage religious spirits to attack. If you have been involved in some of the practices above and the Holy Spirit is revealing you need to repent, then go deep! If you have been involved in self-promotion and pride and have refused discipline from a mother or father in Israel, then ask the Holy Spirit to reveal what attitude

The Word in His Prophets

or stronghold is rooted to your sin. If you're a mother or father in Israel and have encouraged an atmosphere of pride and rebellion, repent! When the Lord has graced me with people to disciple and I have seen areas where I know they will not overcome and they refuse discipline, I've learned that love covers a multitude of sins. (See 1 Pet. 4:8.) As I've prayed for them in godly love, the Lord set up circumstances that sometimes blessed them while challenging them to deal with their issues. (See 1 John 5:16.) Many times fasting and prayer preceded this breakthrough.

Word, Faith, Fasting and Prayer Exposes Motive

With this specific stronghold, the one human attitude that encourages a prophet to be attacked and also encourages people demanding their own way is pride. Not just any pride but the specific attitude that says, "You're not telling me what to do." The exact job description of a prophet is to relay the Word of the Lord that God wants His people to do. Many times they are called to just relay the word and then be quiet. (See Acts 21:10, 11.) At other times they are called to help in obeying that word. (See Ephesians 2:19–21.) This attitude of not wanting to be told what to do is so prevalent in our society that we have ignored how it has crept into the church. This is why we don't place fivefold ministry prophets where they belong. This is why many with prophetic gifts have become tainted. We don't want anybody telling us what to do. This attitude comes from wounding and offenses. If this is a stronghold, predictably one must silence or intimidate the prophets. Humans involved in this stronghold will cause dissension, division and strife. If demons are oppressing the people functioning in these strongholds, you will experience an atmosphere, both subtle and obvious, where women are minimized. After that, violence and abuse, especially extending to pornography and sexual or emotional abuse will manifest. With principalities involved, the church will take on some of their religious spirit characteristics. They will be very religious, hard working and bible "perfect." Where the spirit of Ahab and/or Jezebel is more of a problem, that church will be very "artistic." The region or church will have a history of homosexuality as having been a problem. They will act very sweet and demure. They may even use weakness as a sign of submission. But this is all a cover up for control and manipulation. (See 1 Kings 21:4–9; 2 Kings 9:30 KJV.)

Religious spirits will convince the church to be totally performance oriented. Factions and cliques can develop. "Sharing" can become gossip in an effort to strengthen the individuals' positions in the church. Church eventually becomes a rat race. People are never able to enjoy the church, the Word of God or the presence of God. They will never be able to admit to being wrong. The spiritual health of God's people is not as important as how hard they work. Remember that all of this can occur while people experience God coming in glory. Jesus, the Lord of Glory, was in the midst of Israel while all these issues were going on. Previous church fathers have seen these characteristics and implemented controls (no make-up, no artistic creativity, silencing the women, etc.) in an effort to rid the church of these spirits. Unfortunately, that played right into the devil's hand, because controls fix nothing. Addressing our own motives first always shows us our need for repentance. (See Isaiah 6:9, 10; Mark 4:11, 12 KJV.)

In Mark 9, we read of the transfiguration. Christ appears to James, Peter and John in glory. As they come down the mountain they learn of a mute (silencing spirit) boy being presented to the disciples. But what does Jesus find them doing when He gets there? They are arguing (dissension and strife) because they can't kick the spirit out. This should have told them that this spirit was already in charge. In verse 19, Jesus tells the disciples that the condition allowing this is unbelief. In other words, they don't believe God's Word on the subject (don't tell me what to do!). No Word allows no faith. This is what grieves our Lord the most. The disciples later ask Him why they couldn't cast the spirit out. Jesus answers that this kind doesn't go out except by fasting and prayer.

The Word in His Prophets

We fast because Jesus asked us to. We fast for what He desires. Fasting is done to be more Christ-like, not to get what we want. Repentance, fasting and prayer expose our own motives first. This makes sense because when we submit to God and resist all that is not of God in us, the devil must flee. A silencing or muting spirit does not go out except by our humbling ourselves (repentance prayers), denying ourselves and throwing any crown He may give us at His feet (fasting is an act of worship). With dissension, division and silencing intimidation manifested in the church, offenses take root. Gossip sets the church ablaze. When this takes place, our souls are in charge, not the Holy Spirit. When we lack faith and sow no Word, it is like bait in shark-infested waters for these spirits. They smell that bait and attack. It becomes very easy to divide and conquer a people when no one is in repentance, fasting or prayer. Pastors feel controlled or inept, so they can't care for the sheep as they should. Prophets feel attacked, so they go into hiding. While all this destruction is going on, these spirits sit back and eat up the Lord's inheritance. (See 1 Kings 21:3, 4, 16 KJV.)

Short-Circuiting Our Testimony

Why would satan put a wedge between genuine pastoral and prophetic ministry? Why would he sow stumbling blocks in the body of Christ? The answer should be obvious, and it reveals satan's motives. I believe any difficulties here would be an attempt to short-circuit the testimony of Jesus Christ. God's Word then never becomes sown to the full extent it should be. When that happens, it's easy for us to become sinful, prideful and unrepentant. That's why fasting and prayer exposes it. When we live in a spiritual morality and in a spiritual attitude of repentance, fasting and prayer, these usurpers never get a chance to get a foothold on the Lord's inheritance. When the devil uses these tools against us, he is just doing the same old thing he has done before. Who were the first prophetic witnesses? Adam and Eve. God created two—always the number for a faithful witness.

(See Deuteronomy 19:15; 2 Corinthians 13:1.) They were the first faithful witnesses on God's earth of His awesome Word. What are prophets? The first and foremost calling is to be faithful witnesses for God. Our enemy had to convince Adam and Eve to disagree with God's Word. When he gets Christians to doubt or refuse genuine prophetic ministry, or the person chosen by God to fulfill that task, he is just pulling the same old trick of getting a faithful witness to disagree with God's Word. Since satan can no longer stop Messiah from coming to earth, his motive is to stop those who can birth Messiah in others by the power of the Holy Spirit through God's awesome Word. Whether it is for initial salvation or for healing, deliverance or equipping the body of Christ, it matters little to the devil. For him, it's all the same, because we are attempting to further God's kingdom on earth.

Change Is Coming, and God Will Mess Up Our "Apple Carts"

Some today feel there are very few prophets around. I disagree. I see the need in the future for local and regional apostles, prophets and evangelists. True, there may not be as many national and international apostles, prophets and evangelists. But if our Lord should tarry even by twenty or more years the church is going to need a pastor, a teacher, a prophet and evangelist in every city or church. In fact, in some places, a pastoral staff, a teaching staff, a prophetic staff and an evangelistic staff will be mandatory. An all pastorally staffed church is not a balanced church, any more than an all prophetic or all evangelistically staffed church would be balanced. I am not talking about salaried or full-time workers, either. Remember Paul worked to feed himself and worked to spiritually feed others. I'm also not talking about usurping the pastoral staff in a church or trying to minimize its effectiveness. Prophets don't always make good pastors. Nobody can quite pastor like a true shepherd or shepherdess.

If striking the shepherd scatters the sheep, it stands to reason that when the rest of fivefold ministry lifts the shepherding gift up,

The Word in His Prophets

it will draw the sheep to the body. (See Zechariah 13:7.) It is then the shepherd or shepherdess' job to draw the sheep to Jesus, our Shepherd, High Priest, Prophet, Evangelist, Teacher and Apostle. If the shepherding gift will not do that, then God will deal with His shepherds. God knows how to deal with those in leadership.

When we substitute shouldering the glory, as God has required, with "apple carts," like David did, God will allow the oxen to stumble. When shepherds encourage their people to view the shaking process as wrong and allow them to put their hand to it like Uzzah did, somebody is going to get hurt. When there are no mothers and fathers with mantles teaching prophets that the shaking process must occur in their lives first, we raise up a stunted prophetic people. We, as the Bride of Christ, are in transition historically. We need to recognize that transition will bring changes, and change goes from the head down. If the heads prevent godly change as the Sadducees and Pharisees and ruling counsel did during the first century, God will judge these systems. He may not judge according to our timetables, wants or desires, but He alone is able to judge righteously.

Because God is the one that sets up different fivefold gifts in authority over different ministries, a pastor is not always the head of a particular ministry, as they are in most churches. I believe every ministry works better with a pastor, including a ministry of prophets; someone has to pastor them, even if it's a pastoral prophet. We should submit to whichever ministry gift God has placed as authority in a particular ministry (Eph. 5:21) with godly reverence, as servants of Christ, for our good. Am I proposing no clear head or leadership in our churches or ministries? No. We are supposed to be a body. Every body has a clear head. Within that head are body parts and organs. Then there is the rest of the body.

Is God totally done with one person running it all? Let's study the Word. We've already established that God is bringing the body of Christ into and through transition or change. This is why God has allowed us to experience more and more of His awesome presence in glory. When God sought Israel to change from a judge-priest hierarchy to a prophet-king-priesthood leadership,

BEYOND STRONGHOLDS

He established prophetic ministry for the nation through the leadership of Samuel. God then established David as king, along with Nathan and Gad as prophets. He gave them a revelation through worship-praise and appropriate leadership set in place as a key to maintaining the glorious presence of God over the nation of Israel. (See 2 Chronicles 29:25.) We call this key or revelation the Tabernacle of David. (See 1 Chronicles 15-16; 2 Chronicles 7:6; 8:14; 35:1-4; The Book of Psalms; Ezra 3:10; Isaiah 22:22; Jeremiah 23:1-6; Amos 9:11, 12; Acts 15:12-18; Revelation 5:5, 9, 10.)

While God used one individual leader to bring this truth to light, David's heart was that God was King or Lord. (See Psalm 110:1; Mark 12:36, 37.) This is why God established David and not Saul as king. Saul's heart was to control; David's heart was to further God in His people. (See Chapter 2.) Why else would David write the Psalms but to bless both God and God's people? This is an example of our Lord's death and resurrection and the meaning of the word *doulos*, or bondservant of the Lord, as they relate to the body of Christ.

But David did not take it upon himself to do all the work in God's house. He raised up strong-minded and anointed individuals who disagreed with him on many occasions and had the avenue to speak with him concerning David's problems—remember Joab, Gad and Nathan? Many times we start off in ministry with a right heart, but our own desires and motives occlude the will of God. This is one reason why God gave fivefold ministry to the body, along with all her other marvelous gifts. It is so we can help each other fulfill God's destiny call. I realize our hierarchy is different. We have elders and deacons. The gifts of fivefold ministries are spiritual. When they are put in place you'll notice how our adversary's devices and tools are pretty much made of no effect. (See Ephesians 4:12-16.) As a result, the purity of God's Word is made in full force and effect in our lives. How glorious! It would be just like the enemy to get us to try to thwart the powerful effect teams of fivefold ministers have on earth.

The Word in His Prophets

Jezebel's Effect

What was the effect of Jezebel and Ahab's rule in Israel? The effect was a setback of worship, temple ministry and God's plan for Israel. This is what satan's desired effect is for us today—a setback of worship before the throne of God and a hindering of the preaching of God's salvation plan for all mankind. The effect a Jezebel and a religious spirit have in the book of Revelation is death to prophets and those with Christ's testimony. What is a prophetic group of people's call when the glory has fallen? It is to restore an open heaven or to stand in the gap. In this way they take up the space occupied here on earth by usurping demon spirits. As they submit to God in fasting, prayer and repentance, they resist satan. He must flee! We see answered prayer and destiny fulfilled in our lives; people get saved and set free. Creativity, wealth and abundance are manifest. When God moves over an area, famine and drought disappear. I always found it interesting how Ahab believed the prophet was to blame for the drought—a clear indication of satan's smoke screen—when it was Ahab and Jezebel's own stronghold disobedience to God's Word that caused the drought.

Prophetic ministry is one of the arsenal weapons in God's military to help maintain an open line of communication to the throne. Of course, this is not limited to the fivefold ministry prophet gift alone. Sometimes God will use the people available to a church and then teach them how to overcome these spirits while in their respective positions. The whole of God's revelatory gifts given to the prophetic bride of Christ belong to all of God's people. Not everyone will function the same way, but gifts given by God are His Word. God's Word is living and active. If a donkey could speak it in the Old Testament to expose the madness of a prophet controlled by these stronghold attitudes, how much more can God use saints, blood-washed and Spirit-filled, to expose the tactics of the enemy as he tries to function within the church?

BEYOND STRONGHOLDS

God's Solution

Is there a solution to quenching these stronghold attitudes when God in glory shows up? Obey and submit to the Word of God. Unfortunately, we tend to be a slippery people, using Scripture to suit our own thought patterns as we deny God's gifts and people given as gifts. We compound our problems when God in glory shows up, by using the glory of God to act as if everything is peachy-keen. We resist the Word of the Lord, with which He can change our character, change our attitudes and change the way we do things. When God in glory moves upon most churches and individuals, we become like little children with a new experience. Thankfully we move on and try to search out why God showed up.

Most revivals settle for saving souls only. Only, you say? Isn't evangelism the crux of our purpose here on earth? Isn't evangelism the reason why we labor in God's fields of humanity? Yes, absolutely! And yet saving souls is only the beginning. Jesus preached the kingdom of God. You get into the kingdom by getting saved, but to maintain that kingdom it takes maturity. The final outcome is to see God in glory cover the earth as the waters cover the seas. Only God Almighty can do this. But He needs a repentant people, filled with His undiluted, pure Word, going forth in faith and discipling nations in an attitude of love. Thank God for the Great Commission. But we have been in the business of souls for thousands of years now and have, to some extent, neglected the end result of preaching the gospel. This is the totally manifested control of the planet by our Lord, and a totally changed human race, reflecting all of who Christ is.

I thank God for those saints that prayed me into God's kingdom. But I equally thank God for those saints that taught me who I was in Christ and how to receive fullness in living a godly life, thus taking back godly territory usurped by the devil. Birthing a child is a blessed thing, but it is quite another matter to train that child to become a warrior. Training God's people to receive the fullness of God's Word in glory on their lives breaks asunder stronghold resistances to that glory. Making disciples of all

The Word in His Prophets

nations, casting out demons, prophesying and healing the sick are part and parcel of receiving into our hands, from usurping demon forces, the results of what Christ has already received—ALL authority. (See Matthew 28:18; Luke 10:19; Matthew 10:7, 8; Ephesians 4:8–10.)

When the Word moves with all authority, beholding His glory is not so hard. (See John 1: 1–14.) It is a natural outcome of the Word becoming flesh and living among us. As we receive that Word in total fullness and do not resist, the Word dwells within us. The reason we do not see the glory breaking out on believers all around us is because we stop the fullness of that Word when it comes to dwell within us. Oh, it's fine to dwell among us and behold it from a safe distance. But to allow the Word to dwell within, and all the fullness of the Scriptures to be a controlling factor, is too much for some. Our pet doctrines have to go by the wayside. Our flesh and intelligence can become too embarrassed by the freedom and exposure that Word gives. What is at stake is spending another one thousand years letting a usurping enemy force eat our inheritance. We can go on disagreeing about healings, prophecy, women in leadership, fivefold ministry, signs and wonders. Better yet, we can let the Word have His full way and step back to watch as God heals, fulfills prophecy and returns in glory to abide and rest on Planet Earth, as His Spirit did in the beginning, over His people indwelt by His Word.

Certainly we are not bringing word of ourselves, but of Jesus Christ the Lord, we being only your slaves for Jesus' sake. Because the same God who said, "and now from the darkness, the light will shine," shone in our hearts to throw the light of the knowledge of the glory of God on the face of Jesus Christ.

—2 Corinthians 4:5–6, The Unvarnished New Testament

Chapter Five

HIS KNOWLEDGE

When God shows up, all of Him shows up. Therefore, experiencing the knowledge of God without experiencing His presence at the same time can leave you feeling spiritually dry. In fact, the Scripture says, "Knowledge puffs up, but love builds up" (1 Cor. 8:1). So without the Holy Ghost's presence, knowledge can do very little. Because of this fact, I had to resist my own desire to place the chapter on the presence of God before the one on knowledge. These two themes are so interwoven that even the resistant strongholds are the same. I don't think this is by accident. I believe God intended us to go forth in both His knowledge and His glory (Hab. 2:14). As a result, these next two chapters may read as one. I pray that you will be blessed with the uniqueness of both expressions of God as we study Him in glory.

I would like to set up a foundation concerning the kind of knowledge we will study that is connected to God coming in all glory. There are two areas of knowledge God in glory produces. As I've witnessed the glory of God come upon different locales, the Holy Spirit's internal moving and external manifestations were vastly different. Whether the manifested presence of the Father stayed or left had a lot to do with the teaching foundation that was put in place. The first kind of knowledge is Bible based foundational knowledge. I don't intend to get into specific different teachings. Literally, there are thousands of teachings we could look at that would get us to the same place. Many churches and individuals study the Bible over an extended length of time in order to grow and mature in Christ. We all grow at different rates and learn at different levels. We all have Christ's connection by His blood, as we're called to different works that employ different gifts. Thank God He has provided different teachings for us. Without the Word dwelling in us, we have no tools with which to minister. Compound that with the fact that different churches in different locations need to emphasize different teachings based upon their callings and purposes. All of this is accomplished as the Holy Spirit sees fit. It's easy for us, as Christians, to spot a resistance to learning about God and an apathy or lack of desire to study His Word. We can easily blame it on territorial demon forces. And, to be fair, some regions have a more difficult time with demonic activity in this area than others. But frankly, the real responsibility rests with us. The real attitude or stronghold is in us. It is best to admit that, repent for it, and make time to read the Word and attend weekly Bible teachings. It is much easier to spot this stronghold resistance to godly knowledge than it is to spot the second one.

Knowing

To explain the second kind of knowledge, one English word just won't suffice. We need to look at three very different Hebrew words that can relate the term "knowing." The first one is seen in Isaiah 5:13, "Therefore my people are gone into captivity, because they have no knowledge" (KJV). The primary word here means "cunning" or "knowing" (*da'ath*). It comes from a root word *yada*, which means "to perceive or understand as a seer does." The second word is seen in Proverbs 29:18, "Where there is no vision, the people perish" (KJV). The word "vision" here, *chazown*, means "to mentally see or have a prophetic understanding or revelation of." The last word is "prophet" (*nabiy, nabiyah*). This simply means "a person inspired by God to speak or sing, either in discourse, poetry or foretelling."

His Knowledge

Why these three words? The kind of knowing we are discussing here, besides the knowledge of good and evil in which we all function, is an intimate perception of being one with or seeing as God sees. I'm not talking about being God, but of allowing Him to infuse us totally in order to renew our minds. This is Holy Spirit led knowledge. Instead of speaking out of soul knowledge, it is seeing and speaking out of Spirit knowledge. When He shows up in glory He brings that knowing with Him. This is why it is difficult to separate God in glory into different aspects, because it is the washing by His Word, in conjunction with His awesome presence, that creates a knowing in us that is pure, as we present our whole bodies as living sacrifices. We then know His perfect will. (See Romans 12:1–2.) We are then made whole. Three words, *yada* (*da'ath*), *chazown* and *nabiy/nabiyah*, when taken as a whole, describe what we're talking about.

We spoke earlier of the three purposes of God for His creation: to save or redeem it, to bring forth Christ's bride, and to cover or fill the earth and all of creation with Himself in glory. But in two places in Scripture, Isaiah 11:9 and Habakkuk 2:14, knowledge and glory or the knowledge of His glory are interwoven with the covering of the earth with His glory. Furthermore, a common sense look at having God's vision and knowledge so one does not perish, combined with His ordained prophetic understanding so we are not taken captive, would reveal why satan must knock out any attempts made by God's people to develop this kind of God-knowing awareness. But how does the devil convince God's people, the very sheep of His pasture, to go awry in this area? It definitely starts with our lack of desire for, and laziness in reading and studying the Bible. I have seen several church leaders and individuals who read God's Word and loved when He came in glory, yet, they resist when the *chazown-yada-nabiy* awareness, or the God-knowing awareness, was prepared to be developed in them and their churches. Why? Is there any Biblical pattern to help all of us walk in a greater fullness with the Almighty in this area? The resounding answer is *yes*!

BEYOND STRONGHOLDS

Judgment

There is one main resistance to God-knowledge when He appears in glory: judgment—judgment as opposed to faith. Let's look at the examples of Noah and Abraham. Most theologians would balk at calling the flood a *theophany*. But the flood was an appearance of God in judgment. Whether He appears in judgment or blessing, His glory still accompanies Him. The human attitude or condition that existed, prompting this judgment, was man's desire to think, commit and learn evil continually. This generation of people couldn't think a good thought toward, about or concerning anything. God makes it clear His Spirit had been striving with that generation and its human judgment for quite some time until He finally had enough! (See Genesis 6:3-5) Thank God, Noah found favor in God's eyes. The Word tells us that Noah lived blamelessly among the people of his time, and he walked with God. (See Genesis 6:9.)

This word "walked" is the same word used when God walks in the cool of the Garden with Adam and Eve. So God found a witness—one from among the people who would be faithful to Him. I don't think it was an accident that Noah's name means "rest and quiet." His father, Lamech, prophesies concerning him in Genesis 5:29. Because the feminine article of the word for "quiet" can sound like the Hebrew word for "comfort," Lamech foretells that Noah will bring comfort to mankind despite the curse of the fall. While Noah may have brought a peaceful spirit to his surroundings as he lived side by side with his neighbors, I believe the comfort and quiet that Noah would give the Lord on the face of the earth was far greater. Hebrews 11:7 says that it was Noah's faith in who God was and his obedience to God's command that saved mankind from certain destruction. (See Genesis 6:22.)

When God shows up to walk with us on His terms, there is only one response—faith (belief, rest). Sin produces judgment on all involved. God came to rest and find comfort on the face of the earth, but found nothing except human judgment. What is human judgment, really? We're not talking about sizing up a

His Knowledge

situation or person and realizing there is danger there. We are not discussing common sense here. Human judgment involves an attempt to so control our surroundings and behavior that we crowd out God and His will, His Word, His knowledge, His presence and His name. Ultimately, this desire will crowd out any of His people that represent some aspect of God we don't like or understand. That kind of judgment is something all of us, as individual Christians and as corporate churches, do all the time.

You may wonder, what has this got do with knowing and God's glory? Look again at the statement made in Genesis 6:9 about Noah. It tells us that Noah walked with God. When the glory of the Lord abides in a place, God wants to walk there. He wants to know and be known. (See Genesis 22:12.) He wants us to know Him. Often that requires a time of preparation. Therefore, God sends us teachers, prophets and others to prepare us for different seasons of His visitation. All too often that sown word, and the people used by God to sow that word encounter resistant strongholds set up against them and the word they are carrying. These attitudes are really strongholds against God-knowledge. Where you find this kind of resistance, you will also find human judgment. To say it differently, you will find very judgmental people.

God sent Noah as a witness. If the people had believed Noah's testimony regarding what God was about to do and repented, things could have turned out differently. They might not have been judged. 1 Peter 3:20 tells us that God waited patiently while the ark was being built. For about a century God waited. How awesome it is to consider the Almighty walking with Noah during that time, observing mankind to see if any would believe and repent. Noah and the souls with him were willing to exchange their human judgment for knowledge concerning God Almighty. Rain had never fallen before. As a prophet, Noah stands up and says, "I'm building a boat to save us from the water coming from the sky." The people with Noah said, "we don't understand it, but we'll help you anyway." As a result, when the glory of God hit by way of a flood, they were spared.

BEYOND STRONGHOLDS

Why We Need Inner Healing and Deliverance

The opposite of human judgmental knowledge is found in the faith connection to the glory, as displayed in Abraham's life. Before we look at that, let's investigate another aspect of human judgment. What made me interested in this aspect of human judgment was really an observation from the Lord. After functioning in the Holy Spirit's gifts for a short period of time, it was exciting to see people being set free by the Lord. One thing kept getting my attention, though. The Spirit did not allow everyone to be ministered to. In fact, I sensed that I could pray with some individuals until I was blue in the face, but nothing was ever going to happen for them. I also realized that some Christians acted more like devils than saints. I wondered what was going on. I sought the Lord about these matters, but getting an answer took some time. Respected saints of God would share their experiences of helping believers get delivered from demonic oppression. Then, in the late 1980's, a pastor who was involved in inner healing came to speak at a church we were attending. It seemed the Holy Ghost was giving answers to the questions I had asked years before. The Lord then exposed me to teachings by the Sandford family. This family—a mother, father and children—have more than fifty combined years of ministry in deliverance and inner healing. Their books are a must-read for anyone called to inner healing and deliverance ministries.

John Sandford writes,

> **Inner healing is a misnomer. Healing suggests fixing something that is broken, whereas God has no intention of "fixing" our soul. That would be like putting a new patch on an old garment whereas God has but one answer for sin: death. "The soul who sins will die" (Ezek. 18:4).[1]**
>
> **Inner healing is actually the application of the crucified and resurrected life of Jesus Christ and His blood to those parts of my heart and yours that did not fully "get the**

His Knowledge

message" when we first received Jesus as Savior. Paul wrote, "Take care, brethren, lest there should be in any one of you an evil, unbelieving heart, in falling away from the living God" (Heb. 3:12). Because some areas deep in our hearts have not believed and accepted the good news of our death and rebirth in Him, the fullness of His work has not yet happened for us. We are new creatures in Christ, but some of our old nature continues to act in its ugly old ways, as though we had not yet received the Lord. Inner healing, then, is evangelism to the unbelieving hearts of believers. Paul refused to regard any Christian from merely a human point of view. To him, every born-again believer has been recreated: "Therefore if any man is in Christ, he is a new creature; the old things have passed away; behold, new things have come" (2 Cor. 5:17). But He also called us to work out that salvation "with fear and trembling" (Phil. 2:12). It is a "both-and" message. Positionally we have been made perfect, but we have to take hold of that salvation and make it effective in every area of our life.[2]

The aim of inner healing is to change individuals—and indeed, the entire Body of Christ—into "a mature man, to the measure of the stature which belongs to the fullness of Christ" (Eph. 4:13). Inner healing is effected by our listening to one another until God allows us to see whatever quirks in our old nature have not yet found their death on the cross.[3]

If and when demonic activity is found during this process, deliverance, in a Christ-like manner, can be effectuated. At the Sandford's counseling center, called Elijah House, they have four scriptural laws with which they make their diagnoses. But all these laws are centered on one Scripture, in my opinion. It is this Scripture upon which we will base our understanding of judging others. Jesus said in Matthew 7:1-2,

BEYOND STRONGHOLDS

> Do not judge, or you too will be judged. For in the same way you judge others, you will be judged, and with the measure you use, it will be measured to you.

John Sandford writes, "When we judge others with impure hearts—with blame, condemnation, anger, envy, jealousy or rancor—then God's immutable laws are set in motion to bring recompense."[4]

Sowing and Reaping Judgment

Judging goes from past to present and, in my opinion, affects our future. When we judge our parents for not being something they should have been, that same judgment falls back on us. We reap what we have sown—judgment! We eventually become what we judge in others.[5] The principle of sowing and reaping is seen throughout the Scriptures. When we sow finances, we expect to reap finances. When we sow time, God blesses us with God-ordained timing. When we sow blessings, we reap blessings. So we should not think it strange that when we sow judgment, we reap judgment.

Webster's dictionary gives us a first and second definition of *soteriology* as "the doctrine of the salvation of the Lord Jesus Christ as it relates to the health of the body."[6] When we get saved initially, that salvation works itself out in every area of our bodies and lives. Deliverance and specifically inner healing are valuable tools to help accomplish this. If we believe the enemy's lies—that we can get away with judging—we fall subject to judgment. There are countless lies that the enemy of our souls feeds us so that we miss Christ's total health for us. Inner healing and deliverance can uncover these lies so we can recognize them and stop the attitudes, habits or other practices that we follow, which support such belief systems. Many times these lies have been with us since childhood. Therefore, we need someone else to come alongside of us to help us recognize them and the effect they're having upon our lives.

His Knowledge

Judgments and Vows

Let me share two examples of how this became evident to me. For the sake of anonymity, I will say only that this person is a close friend.

I didn't realize it immediately, but the more I hung out with this individual, the more tired and sick I became, almost to the point of feeling like death. When I wasn't with this person, I was my old self.

Finally, one day while we were fellowshipping, this person let slip how difficult her parents had been to live with, constantly berating her while blessing and loving her siblings. Years before, while still a small child, she made a vow wishing that her parents would die! I learned firsthand Hebrews 12:15, "See to it that no one misses the grace of God and that no bitter root grows up to cause trouble and defile many." There were several principles at work here, but this individual was bound to the vow. A vow can involve the passing of a judgment upon someone before the time. (See 1 Corinthians 4:5.) My friend's bitter roots were defiling her and me when I was around her! Instantly we prayed. This person released her parents, repented of the judgment and the foolish childhood vow. We pled the blood over the vow and broke its effects in Jesus' name. You may say, "a silly thought like that in childhood can't possibly stick after Jesus has set someone free." The Bible is true or it is not true. Jesus talked about oath and vow making. (See Matthew 5:33-37; 12:36, 37; 15:3-6.)[7]

We've already talked about judging. If we have not opened our hearts up for the blood to wipe out these sinful areas that are still hidden, the law of God takes effect. This should not surprise us. This kind of judging affects churches in many difficult ways. I have spoken to several leaders who were wonderful people and loved their parents but ever so subtly judged them. As we would discuss the difficulties they were experiencing in the ministry, the Holy Spirit would reveal that their difficulties were directly related to their judgment against their parents. As was mentioned before, we can judge many people, not only our parents, and these situations can cause us to reap judgment if we do not repent of this sin.

Reaping a Harvest of Judgment in Ministry

Let me share another example of how this affected me personally and a church with which I worked. One year I had the unique opportunity of trying to get along with a minister who hated women in ministry. It didn't take long to find out that this man had been brutally beaten as a child by his father. But oddly enough, he didn't blame his father; he blamed his mother for not protecting him. It was quite obvious, though, that he judged his father also. The pastor of this particular church was a woman. She and I would watch as this man would share the gospel. It was the strangest sight. He would abusively berate people with the Scriptures. So much so that everyone in the church would run when they would see him coming. Some Christians would groan if they had to sit next to him during the services. There were certain "specialty" demons involved with this man, but it all started with his judgment against his parents—and for us as female ministers—specifically against his mother. While he never let us get close enough to get to the deepest roots of his problems, on the surface, it was obvious he blamed his mother. I thought it quite interesting that God would send him to a ministry with a female pastor. In vain she tried desperately and repeatedly to minister to him, even to the point of asking male leaders for help when it became obvious some of his problems were directed toward women. But he would have none of it. Eventually he was asked to leave that particular church.

A Weight of Judgment

Let's consider the magnitude of this judgmentalism. The church (or sinful and unhealed people in the church) has executed atrocities on people down through the centuries.[8]

Have we ever asked the world to forgive us? The world—or unsaved mankind—has judged all Christians on the basis of such atrocities. Yet, it is not their place to judge. So, in turn, the world reaps back on itself its own judgment. Some church people judge the world. Oh, isn't it sinful human flesh that commits murders, rapes, acts of violence and thievery? Yes! But isn't it our place, during the timeframe in which we now live, to preach the gospel and minister God's Word? And as God reveals the need, to cast devils off and bind demonic strongholds as they attack on earth, which will set the captive free? It is not time for us to pronounce judgment. If we judge humanity for its sins, we are bound by the law to have or see manifest some of those sins in our midst.

Entire churches can be involved in judging their own people. When new members come in we want to get to know them. After we get to know who they are, negative comments or thoughts can form concerning how they live. Or worse, we may have partial information about people and then make judgment calls about them or their situations based on that information. Someone may not like the decisions they make with their children, the way they dress, where they live, how they decide to run a business or you name it. It could be anything, but whatever it is, it is still judgmentalism. If a judgmental stronghold based on human knowledge is in place, we will swear that our ways of thinking or our judgments of that person are correct. We will believe that what they are doing or the decisions they make cannot be of God. We justify our judgments and build fortresses around them, as we gossip or "share" our opinions.

A Critical Eye

Many pastors and leaders have had churches burned by sheep in wolves' clothing. In an effort to protect the flock they judge everyone with a critical eye. I understand the need for caution. Many times, I have had to realize someone's motives toward me or a particular ministry were not pure. But I have also had to understand that I am not the Holy Spirit. Even if sin is involved with a person, it is not my job to change or judge that individual. It is the Holy Spirit's job. My job is to love him or her and share

God's Word. I may have to make a decision that an individual's sinful behavior is not something I want to be a part of. But I cannot judge that person. If a church is involved in this stronghold, results will be very important. What they do and accomplish will be more important than the spiritual health of their people. They will base how right they are upon how good their results are. When, in fact, fruit is the Holy Spirit's desire. He desires to build our character and our relationship with Him.

God's glory will wane and grow and wane again in a church where strongholds reside. This is to cause us to turn to Him and ask what's wrong. This is so we turn to His Word and find out where He wants to perfect us. When we discover that our stronghold, as a church or as an individual, is judgmentalism, we need to release those we've held captive by our judgments and repent of our judgmental ways. This will keep demonic spirits from using our judgments, as long as they are not already in place. If they are, deliverance is needed along with a persistent desire to root out the sin of judgmentalism in our lives.

Dedicating the Temple

The entire temple dedication prayer and response from God found in 2 Chronicles 6:12–7:22 is a promise. God's people are assured of freedom from territorial spirits and the resultant conditions of famine, death and destruction, if they will remain wholly dedicated to Almighty God. This applies to us as well. We must repent and ask forgiveness, not only to God for this particular kind of judgmentalism, but also to the world. If we will do so and remain faithful to Him, He will hear us when we pray, and He will deliver our land from famine, death and destruction.

Look at what a prayer of repentance according to this promise accomplishes in Daniel 9. Daniel did not commit the sinful acts Israel was being judged for at that time. In fact, he hadn't even been born yet. But his continued fasting and prayers of repentance broke through the territorial spirits' stronghold over that region. Within two years the pre-incarnate Christ appeared

His Knowledge

to him–the Lord of Glory Himself.[9] (See Daniel 10:1.)

From this, Daniel understands the time for the rebuilding of Jerusalem and the timing for Christ's appearance, death and resurrection here on earth! If this was so for an Old Testament saint, how much more for us who are partakers of that most holy blood!

Sitting on God's Throne

Practicing human judgmentalism is the same as setting ourselves up on God's throne to judge. What spirit does that come from? Isaiah 14:12–14 makes it clear that satan and his antichrist have a plan to set themselves up on God's throne in order to crash the gates of heaven. Our Lord took care of satan's ability to enter Father's presence in the heavenlies. So now he has desired to set up a throne here on earth. Why? It really goes back to Adam and Eve's God-given role in dominion on earth. (See Psalm 8:6.) In other words, they were supposed to provide a safe haven for what God had created, so the creation could mature and grow. They were supposed to use the tools that God had given them so God could walk on earth and rest with them, fellowship with them and be known by them.

Knowing what we're called to do is a tool that, when used in godly obedience, brings God's rule into the earth. Look at Ephesians 1:18. Paul wants us to know to what we are called. Several sermons could be preached on all the different things to which we are called, but one is to rule and reign with Christ. (See Ephesians 1:18–23; 2:6.) In that place, we are to execute godly judgments on the world and angels. (See 1 Corinthians 6:2, 3.) But we do not judge innocent people, only principalities, powers and worldly strongholds, exposing them as they attack on earth, while binding their ability to further corrupt God's creation.

If our first parents would have spoken forth God's Word on the subject of the forbidden fruit and stood in that knowledge, the serpent would have had no authority over them on the earth. (See Psalm 8:5, 6.) They forsook the glory of God and the knowledge of God it produced. Instead, God had to step in and judge all involved. Ichabod! It's just like the enemy to tempt us into judging against godly knowledge or godly perspective. He also tempts us, as we saw in previous chapters, to substitute our own knowledge for God's knowledge. The one tool Adam and Eve had was authority on the earth over the serpent, based upon their godly knowledge of God and His Word.

Disarming Principalities

Father has been attempting to teach His people for quite some time how to judge properly. I'm not trying to be critical, for all of us are still in a learning process. But, I don't believe we get it. To Israel, He gave the law, the prophets, the judges and the kings. The elders would sit at the gates of the city, which were symbols or places of political or earthly judgment. The priests were set in place to discern matters both legal and judicial, binding and loosing as it were, according to the law. They would look at a health problem, apply the remedy according to the law and wait for healing to take place. If it did not, they judged the situation and applied the law accordingly. (See Leviticus 13–15.) We are called priests under the New Covenant. (See Exodus 19:6; Revelation 5:10.) While we don't judge according to the law, we apply the blood to those areas of our hearts that still need healing faith, and bring to the cross any areas of sin the Holy Spirit reveals. This is why we need each other, as priests, to loose healing and deliverance in our "temples," casting out and binding anything that does not belong to Christ. Jesus said He would give us the keys to the kingdom of heaven. (See Matthew 16:19; 18:18.) Binding and loosing really had to do with the Levitical priesthood's role in adjudicating the law. But it is Jesus Himself who referenced it to demon forces in Matthew 16:19, Matthew 12:28–30 and Mark 3:27. We are told that Christ made an open show of demonic forces, disarming them. (See 2 Corinthians 2:14; Colossians 2:15.) Our Lord has won the victory and we are here to enforce it or administrate it on His behalf. (See Luke 11:20–22; John 12:31; 1 John 3:8; Isaiah 53:10–12.) However, as

His Knowledge

I've mentioned before, I am not encouraging the unscriptural practice of commanding or attacking angels in the heavens, fallen or otherwise. Our best tools of disarmament are repentance and obedience. I think we all agree that Christ gives us the authority to bind and cast off demon forces as they attack us here, in our arena on earth, and to loose God's desired purposes for the earth.

We will see His glorious purposes effectuated here in substance on the earth as we learn to move into what Christ has already accomplished. As was stated before, it is the testimony of Jesus Christ that makes hell's gates unable to prevail against us. (See Matthew 16:16–20.) Jesus not only restored our understanding of our priestly role in binding and loosing, and the authority it has in the spiritual realm as it affects earth, but He also gave us tools, or gifts, with which to conquer (Rom. 12:4–8; 1 Cor. 12:12, 13, 14; Eph. 4:11–16).

Releasing the Gifts of God's People

When the abiding glory of God falls in a place or upon an individual, you can expect to see various gifts flowing. If God's people are not permitted to function in their gifts, chances are that church or person is bound in judgmentalism. Noah used every tool available to implement the call of the Lord on his life. The people living during Noah's time refused His call and gifts. The reason for this manifestation of human judgment can stem from many different issues. As in the case of the man with the abusive father whose mother did not protect him, it could stem simply from unforgiveness. It may come from an inner childhood vow or a vow made later on in life based upon childhood experiences. These vows can sound like this: "I'll never let such and such situation happen to me again." It may come from some false teaching that claims that God only speaks to church leadership and it is only those called to that place who should be trained and allowed to function. It may just come from an inability to preach the Word on this subject, not sowing a balanced theology in order to raise God's people up in Christ's gifts. It may come from a stronghold attitude of judgment resident in a church because the leaders and members are constantly judging one another critically. Or, it may come from the oppression of regional or territorial satanic strongholds. It can even come from a combination of all of the above. But in each one of these cases, a judgment or decision has been made, whether consciously or unconsciously.

We should also clear up the misconception that all churches should look or function in the same manner. Each church is a blessed aroma of Christ to her neighborhood or region. Some churches have a calling to deliverance ministries; others are called to build worship teams. Still others have a specific call to see souls saved or to teach intercession. Of course, it's important to remember that the twenty-one gifts seen in Romans, 1 Corinthians and Ephesians should be used to bless every church's call. Each church has a different specialty call by God, and no one, in any way, should try to dictate that we all look the same or have the same gifts functioning in the same way, except within the confines of Scripture. I have seen very gifted shepherdesses whose only prophetic gift was receiving visions from God. I have seen evangelists with healing ministries and prophets who were very pastoral. I've spoken with people in some churches who were mighty intercessors, but they were not fivefold ministry prophets! When we house judgmentalism in our own temples we open the door for satanic footholds. (See 1 Corinthians 6:19, 20; 1 Peter 2:9, AMP.) Our gifts are hindered and our churches' potential in fulfilling God's destiny call is thwarted. God in glory comes on a place or person to kick stronghold usurpers out. If we refuse to kick them out because of our judgmental resistance to the total knowledge of God in glory, you will literally watch the flowing waters of that glory diminish and grow still—just at the point God was stirring them.

Is it possible then for us to judge or discern properly, as God would decree? The good news is *yes*! By faith we can believe God's Word, accept godly knowledge and change. Let's study Abraham, who is called the father of faith.

His Knowledge

Faith Overcomes Judgmental Unbelief

Hebrews 11 tells us of the saints of old. When you read it you almost forget how different in personality and calling each individual was. The writer inspires us with these saints' testimonies of righteousness through faith in God. But you couldn't get two more different men than Noah and Abraham. Noah is spoken of as a just man and perfect in his generation. When we first meet Abram he is a pagan, and not an especially candid one, at that. In fact, he settles in Egypt (a representation of the world) and Mamre, which comes from a word meaning "lusty," or "to lift up oneself or to rebel." The Amorites, (a representation of our old sin nature or of our enemies from within) gave the place its name. What transforms us from pagan idolaters to righteousness is belief in God. Abraham believed, and it was credited to him as righteousness.

The *theophany* appearance most of us remember when we think of Abraham is when the three "men" came to prophesy to him and Sarah. God had appeared to Abraham before that incident.

Sometimes the Bible calls the appearance of God a word, as we see in Genesis 15:1. On other occasions we aren't told how or in what form God appeared to Abraham; we can only surmise. (See Genesis 17:9–22.) On at least one occasion Melchizedek meets up with Abraham.

Building An Altar

With every encounter between Abraham and the God of glory, Abraham builds an altar or offers a sacrifice by faith. In chapter 17, it is the sacrifice of circumcision, and in chapter 18, he prepares his angelic visitors a meal. Whatever the circumstances, Abraham always responds in faith by making an offering. Chapter 15 is when we first read about a covenant. Before this time God had made promises. The custom of that time was to take animals and cut them in half, with the two parties to the covenant or contract walking between them. Call it a contractual agreement for land or other possessions. It is also that here. But the amazing truth behind this story is far greater. God Almighty Himself walks alone between these pieces. Abraham is knocked out by the glory of God. (See Genesis 15:12–13.) At this point, God prophesies to him and acts not only as the participant of the contract, but as the one who seals it with the holy vessels from the altar of heaven. Isn't it always fire and smoke that have accompanied His glory in the past? (See 2 Chronicles 5:13, 14; 7:1–3.) Wasn't it a cloud and fire that led the children of Israel out of Egypt? Why all this typology and fanfare? Not only did Christ come to represent the participants of the New Testament, He was the only faithful participant able to be The Holy Vessel and perfect sacrificial High Priest of the New Covenant with the glory of God totally manifested in Him. We are to be the exact same vessel for the earth. I don't mean that the shedding of our blood could redeem anything. Jesus did that once and for all. But when it is said of us—as it was said of Abraham in Genesis 15:6, "Abram believed the Lord, and he credited it to him as righteousness"— then truly all the nations of the earth will be blessed. Noah did not rely on his lack of understanding about rain when God spoke to him. Abraham did not rely on his neighbor's understanding of Jehovah when He told Abraham to move out of the neighborhood. When we by faith offer up our own knowledge and sacrifice our own judgment for what God knows, we provide a highway for God to enter in glory.

The knowledge of God and the ability to know as God knows allowed His glory to rest in Abraham. Over time, Abraham was graced to save Lot and receive strength and help for his final test of offering up Isaac. This knowledge enables him, while yet a pagan, to receive a name change. It helps him, who was called an alien to receive Canaan, the Promised Land. (See Genesis 17:8.) It helps him go through the pain of circumcision and gives him the resolution to put those born to him through the same ritual (See Genesis 18:19.) It helps him put out the bondwoman and her son, admitting the sins of his flesh and releasing control over them by trusting God.

His Knowledge

It has been rightly stated that we are the seed of Abraham by faith, for because of our faith in Christ, Abraham is our father (See Romans 4:11-17.) God used Abraham to bless the earth. When we, by faith, function properly in our priestly role, all the nations of the earth will also be blessed. (See Revelation 1:6; 5:10; 20:6.) When we release control of our judgments and move in faith, the blessings of Abraham are ours.

I specifically do not want to write about eschatology here, but, by way of example concerning God-knowledge and judgment, read Revelation 19 and 20. In Revelation 19:21, a sword comes out of the rider's mouth. I think most would agree that the sword represents the Word of God. Is Jesus here among us in the flesh right now executing the judgments of His Word? No! But who is? The Holy Spirit-indwelled church! What series of events in Revelation 20 does this Word create? Well, for one thing, the serpent, satan himself, is bound. As a result of being bound, the nations of the earth are no longer deceived, for 1,000 years, but are able to discern or "know." I'd say that was a real blessing! The next series of events we see in verse 4 are thrones that are set up for those that are given authority to judge. The antichrist spirit on the face of the earth today would do anything it could to usurp those thrones given by God to those who judge. Thus, there is a need to review these strongholds within us and pull them up or repent of them so that our enemy is not able to use them. As a result of doing so, the nations of the earth can be blessed to a greater extent by God's Word.

The Abundant Blessings of God's Presence

There is one last thought here that needs sharing. It was the blessing of financial prosperity Abraham received as a result of not resisting God in glory. When God shows up He gives abundantly. By the time Abraham is old, he still knows as God knows and sends his servant in faith believing for a wife for Isaac. (See Genesis 24:40.) What impresses Rebekah and her family are the gifts he sends. It's only after the servant tells them his story that they know it's from God. (See Genesis 24:50, 51.) In Genesis 24:53, Abraham's servant is able to give many gifts and presents to Rebekah and her family out of Abraham's wealth. It's a costly thing to start a nation. God knows this and blesses Abraham with His abundant glory. When we read the prophetic blessing Rebekah's family bestows on her, it is by no accident that they speak of her offspring inheriting the gates of their enemies—gates symbolizing places of elders judging in authority.

In each case of God appearing in glory, we see abundance reproduced. Even in our Lord Jesus' case, while he chose to forsake earthly comfort and riches, He produced abundance for those around Him. For instance, He fed the thousands and healed all that came to Him. In fact, the possibility for more abundance was so great that this must have been what the disciples were thinking when they tried to get rulers in to see Jesus. (See John 12:20–22; Matthew 15:12.)

Many preach a superior spiritual existence based upon poverty. But Scripture does not support this. Spiritual existence is based upon our relationship with Jesus. Whenever God in glory appears, abundance, on all levels, follows. It wasn't because there was no money in the bag that Judas Iscariot desired to be treasurer. Over the centuries, whenever God's glory has been poured out in a place or upon a person, an abundance of His presence can still be felt in the place even after He has departed with His glory. In fact, so much so that some churches still keep the artifacts. This is one of the reasons that God would not allow Israel (or us, for that matter) to keep these items. (See Exodus 20:4–6; Leviticus 26:1; 2 Kings 18:4.) They could become idols because His abundant glory would still have left behind an anointing.

Isn't it God's promise to us that, when we give the tithe of our wealth, He blesses the ninety percent left over so that it abundantly provides for us? Judgment always produces lack and a mentality of insufficiency. Defensiveness always leads to impoverishment. But when Christ shows up in glory, abundance

His Knowledge

is poured out. He asks us to willingly lay down our resistant attitudes so He can produce fullness in us—fullness of His glory, His Word, His knowledge, His presence and His name. When this takes place, we become His totally whole people with abundance overflowing to the nations. When Noah and Abraham moved in godly knowledge when His glory showed up, it reproduced an overflow to the nations. Praise God for the type of people Noah and Abraham were—true examples of people who functioned in faith and obedience when God's glory appeared to them. They left behind a legacy that still imparts in us God in glory and God-knowing faith.

If the service of death carved in letters of stone was born in such glory that the sons of Israel could not look straight at the face of Moses because his face shown with such glory, temporary though it was, how can the service of the Spirit fail to be one of even greater glory? If it was glory to serve what condemned you, how much more will it overflow with glory to serve what declares you innocent? In fact, there is no glory in the glories that were, in relation to this all-surpassing glory. If what is ephemeral passes through glory, how much more does what is permanent remain in glory? Having hopes of such nature, we can then act with great confidence, not like Moses, who put a veil upon his face so the children of Israel couldn't watch his glory fading to its end. Ah, but their senses must have become very dull, since right up to the present day their reading of the Old Testament is still veiled with the same veil, which has not been unveiled again, because it takes Christ to set it aside. Even today whenever the books of Moses are read amongst them, it is with a veil lying on their hearts. "Every time he returns toward the Lord, the veil is lifted." Now "the Lord" is the Spirit. And where the Spirit of the Lord is, that is freedom.

—2 Corinthians 3:7–17, The Unvarnished New Testament

Chapter Six

HIS PRESENCE

When the children of Israel followed the Lord beyond the Red Sea, He gave them a sign of His presence among them. That sign was a cloud by day and fire by night. What a sight! Over and over the Bible declares that God would come down to talk to them in the cloud. (See Numbers 9:15-23; 10:34-36; 11:17, 25; 12:5; 14:14; 16:19, 42.) There are many other instances of God in glory appearing to them, other than the few listed here. It is unfortunate, though, that some of these instances represent the many times Israel resisted the presence of God in glory. It's easy to be obedient when we feel or see God in glory among us. It is also easy to become too familiar with His glorious presence and start to try to control and manipulate His appearing. Even though God's manifested presence was among Israel they constantly manipulated and rebelled, always posturing for the benefits of more glory. The real test is when God removes the manifestation of His glory from us and we no longer feel or see His presence. It's during those times that faith and an obedient spirit are extremely valuable. We spoke about Abraham in the last chapter. His example suits us well here also. A substantial period of time elapses between God's appearance in glory to Abraham and the fulfillment of His promises. We don't know whether Abraham communed daily with God. The Bible is silent on this issue. It is likely Abraham offered regular sacrifices. Whether he did or did not, one thing is clear. When all hope of God's glorious appearing in order to fulfill the ten-year-old promise was long gone, Abraham still believed.

The book of Hebrews tells us that not all the promises given to the saints of old were realized by them in the flesh. (See Hebrews 11:13.) Nevertheless, they still believed and received by faith. By doing so, they have blessed many generations who followed in their footsteps. I wonder if we will be like them—able to learn from God's glorious appearances to bless many additional generations to come.

God's Abiding Presence

In the last chapter we talked about knowing as God knows. This kind of knowing is totally impossible without the presence of the Holy Spirit upon us in glory. Many times when we speak about God's presence people immediately think of worship. When I think of Him coming to me I think of meeting His needs—feeding Him. I think of continual communion in thought, prayer, praise or song—in total daily living. For me this is all worship. Children never think of meeting another's needs. It is only as they grow up that they start thinking selflessly. I believe that Father desires to mature the corporate body of Christ in His abiding glory. In other words, He stays and does not come and go. For this to take place we have to grow up some. As we grew up my mother dealt with our attitudes so we would become better adults. If earthly parents do as much, our Father in heaven will do far more. I believe this is why God will have us address these issues. However, I do not want to leave the false impression of some utopian society where, if we all believe "correctly" and act "correctly," perfection will be ours. We are human. We will make mistakes. All we can do is be obedient to Father and His Word. The rest is up to Him.

There are two parameters in which we experience or witness God's presence. He either abides continually or He comes and

His Presence

goes. In fact, in the Old Testament, God's Spirit rested upon some and left others, also. In the New Testament we are told that once Christ was offered up, the Holy Spirit came to abide continually. (See John 14:16, 17.) And yet, in both the Old and New Testament there is evidence of His manifested glory abiding for some time and also coming and going.

Why is there this need in us to feel, experience or witness the glorious presence of God? Besides rejuvenating and sustaining Christ-life in us, we feel as if we're right with God. God is pleased with us. The presence of God is a faithful witness to us. When His glorious presence comes upon us it is tangible evidence of His favor. Unfortunately, we can mistake this presence for the belief that everything within us is okay—that we have no need to change. We can also use it as a tool to show others we are superior in some way. This is the result when we mix our strongholds with the glorious presence of God. When we misconstrue the purpose for God manifesting Himself in glory, and we form opinions based on that misconception, we can miss the entire purpose as to why He is among us. Thus, our strongholds chase Him away (*tamei*) as we mix (*shaatnez*) our own ideas with His multifaceted purposes. Let's look at some positive results or witnesses left behind after God showed up in glory.

Glorious Witnesses Left Behind

Paul tells us this faithful witness of the Spirit has been given as a "deposit" guaranteeing our glorious redemption to come. (See Ephesians 1:13, 14; 2 Corinthians 1:21, 22; 5:5, KJV.) In every instance of a *theophany* appearance of God in glory, a witness or sign was left behind. For Adam and Eve it was the creation (See Romans 1:20.) For Noah it was the rainbow. (See Genesis 9:12, 13.) For Abraham it was a son and a promise. (See Genesis 15:5; 18:19.) For Jacob, his thighbone was never the same again. (See Genesis 32:31, 32.) For Israel, Moses and Joshua it was the fire and cloud and possession of the land. (See Genesis 24:7; Judg. 2:1-5; Deuteronomy 34:1-4.) Subsequently, for Israel it was the

BEYOND STRONGHOLDS

Shechinah glory over and in the tabernacle and later temples. (See Exodus 33:10, 11; 1 Samuel 3:3, 21; 2 Chronicles 5:2, 5, 7, 13, 14.) Samuel's role was to provide a change in leadership from judges to prophets and kings. He started what was known as the sons (school) of the prophets. We still have with us today some of the practices of teaching prophets that Samuel instituted. Even Gideon's experience with God in glory left behind a witness. His judgment or lack of faith moved him to ask the question, "If God is with us how come all this bad stuff is happening?" (See Judges 6:13.) His experience is a witness to us today concerning the answer to that question. Not only that, but he is an excellent example of how God overcomes our stronghold enemies (the Midianites) from within by faith. Many a baby Christian has put a "fleece" before the Lord to help find clarity regarding God's will in their lives. We can assume Melchizedek had glory experiences. He left behind a priesthood. (See Hebrews 5:6.) We don't normally view Job as having experiences with the glory of God, but he talked with God and the Lord spoke to him out of the storm cloud or whirlwind, like Moses and Elijah. What is Job's witness today? The early church understood Job's place as one who persevered in the face of demonic attack. (See James 5:11.) As long as our enemy is still on the face of the earth, entire groups of believers need the witness of Job.

New Testament Witnesses

In the New Testament, John the Baptist faithfully witnesses Christ. In other words, he witnesses about Christ's coming, and Christ Himself was left behind. Mary's experience with God in glory gave her Jesus. (See Matthew 1:18, 20; Luke 1:35.) For Christ's water baptism it was the Holy Ghost. (See Luke 3:21, 22; John 1:32-34; Matthew 3:16, 17; Mark 1:9, 10.) For Christ's transfiguration, the witness left behind was the glory. Except for Moses, no other human's face and appearance were so dramatically changed by God's presence. (See Matthew 17: 1-9; Mark 9:2-10; Luke 9:28,36.) If it were not for this earthly experience of our Lord, I

His Presence

doubt we today would be able to see, feel and experience God in glory as we do. For Jesus has already experienced everything we go through. (See 2 Corinthians 5:21; Isaiah 53; John 14:12, 13; 17:22.) In Luke's Gospel, we are told that Moses and Elijah came to speak with Jesus. It is interesting that Father sent Moses and Elijah. These two men both experienced the God of glory in very different and dramatic ways. It's as if Father wanted to show us Christ's glory from another place; so to testify of that glory He sent two witnesses from there. In Christ's death both blood and water flowed from His side, the cloud took Him up and the Holy Ghost descended with glory as a witness. (See John 19:34, 35; Acts 1:4, 5, 9; 2:1–4; Luke 24:51; John 20:22; Mark 16:19.) In all of these instances, what was left behind remained a witness of God's glorious presence for hundreds, if not thousands, of years.

In each individual that experienced God coming in glory, God made some portion of their lives a witness, testimony or custom for future generations. There are six individuals that are exceptions to this principle of God leaving a witness behind of His glory. These exceptions are Enoch, Balaam, Samson, Elijah, Isaiah and Ezekiel. While we have God's Word that they were witnesses, no other long-term, lasting witness has remained. Every time God showed up, either in *theophany* or outright glory, some example, custom or tradition was left behind because of the people that experienced God. But with these six individuals there has been no lasting witness, either by tradition or custom, that has remained that we can see or hear. All we have is God's Word as the witness that these people either lived in their communities or saw and experienced the glory and wrote about it. We have nothing else but the Holy Spirit and the Word to our hearts that this is so.[1] Let's look at the Scriptures and see what the Word may reveal about God's glorious presence as a witness concerning these individuals.

When God Paints by Numbers

In order to study these individuals further, we will be looking at them numerically. The numerical principle is a principle of Biblical hermeneutics. "Hermeneutics," as it relates to the Scriptures, is defined as "the science of interpreting the Bible." The "numerical principle," from a Biblical perspective is simply defined as "God's spiritual arithmetic." After all, the greatest mathematician is God. His creation—solar system, galaxy and universe—has boggled the minds of scientists. Music is nothing more than God applying seven letters to mathematics. Everything carries significance in the Scriptures, and numbers are no different. Some of the significance for this Biblical numbering system has to do with the fact that the Hebrew letters are also numbers. Each number, especially from one to twelve, carries significance. Numbers are usually (but not always) multiples of the numbers from one to twelve. For example, the number forty is always symbolic of God's judgment. Israel wandered forty years in the wilderness because of their unrighteousness. Yet forty is a multiple of 4x10 and 2x20. Our Lord fasted in the wilderness for forty days. Four is symbolic of what pertains to the earth, and ten is symbolic of earthly governments. Two is always the number for a faithful witness. Our Lord was and is the faithful witness to fulfill all godly authority to govern the earth. He would also become the perfect sacrifice to fulfill God's righteous demands for justice in judgment on the earth.

For some readers this exercise may be a little challenging if math was not your favorite subject in school. If that is the case, my suggestion is that you list these individuals as we separate them into numerical categories, along with the significant meanings of their numbers. After you read this section and look at your lists, your understanding for the awesome plan of God in this day and hour will be much clearer. For our purposes of studying these six individuals, let's look at their numerical significance and see if there is a pattern concerning God's presence when He comes in glory.

His Presence

Six Witnesses

First of all there are six of them. Six is the Biblical number for man or humankind. These six are witnesses to us (mankind). I believe, in our time, that these six individuals carry significance for companies of people like themselves from around the world that will have similar tasks from God to accomplish. These modern day companies of people may also have many of the same attitudes or strongholds, both good and bad, in them that these six Bible characters had. You may even see yourself represented by them. Because of their example, we can understand how to discern properly and not judge these companies of people improperly when God in glory moves upon us. We can also be prepared to repent of any of the ungodly strongholds that they may show us exist in our own lives. In that context, we can divide them into three sets of two's.

Three is the Biblical number for divinity or the divine, and two is always the number for a witness, as is three (Deut. 19:15; 2 Cor. 13:1). Their experiences divide them this way instead of two sets of three. Both Enoch and Elijah were translated. Both Balaam and Samson experienced the God of glory but also experienced failure because of their strongholds. Both Isaiah and Ezekiel saw God in glory in similar form and talked about the restoration of God's people, their worship and kingdom.

The last numerical category I would separate them into is two and four. Balaam and Samson are separated into one, and Enoch, Elijah, Isaiah and Ezekiel into the other. Balaam and Samson represent what can be both terribly corrupt and seemingly holy and godly, even while God in glory is among us. The other four represent the "see-through-me, God" kind of individual or, again, as we saw in chapter 5, those with obedient faith. This numerical division is interesting. In the case of Balaam and Samson the number two is a witness, but one (Balaam) quite worldly while the other (Samson) a part of God's people, both with glory experiences and both with the ability to repent.

The number four represents the other group. Four is the

Biblical number for the earth (four corners of the earth, four gospels, etc.). God will use these four modern day companies of people to bless the earth. Since all numbers are multiples of one, each individual is unique, especially these four (Enoch, Elijah, Isaiah and Ezekiel). Four is also a multiple of two. In these four individuals we have a double-portion witness for the face of the earth. Enoch and Elijah are witnesses to our glorious translation from earthly things to the heavenly realm. They have been with God in heaven and are relating their experiences to us as a witness. Isaiah and Ezekiel are witnesses that will speak about how to bring the heavenly realm into the earthly realm. These four individuals represent two companies of people today that will see God take them to the nations in order to manifest this double-portion witness that is upon their lives. As a result they become a witness and testimony to the people of the earth of who God is, and can be, in us.

Again, nothing but Biblical record is left of these individuals. True, many of their prophecies have come to pass, but nothing tangible is left: no custom, no tradition or company of people is left. We see the creation. We can see a rainbow. We know Israel forsook eating hip-joint meat. We know a nation was born, and we see the boundaries of the land they have encompassed. We know Christ historically lived and we know He heals and saves people today. There is medical evidence for this and the testimony of those of us He has redeemed and healed. Let's look at them as we have broken them down numerically.

Prophets Who Have Walked Before Us

Isaiah and Ezekiel were prophets who spoke symbolic truth about the God of glory and walked in it. To me, they exemplify a certain company of people in the body of Christ today who have a call to restore God's people to an understanding of heavenly worship around throne room glory. They are a transitional prophetic company of people.

His Presence

The next group, Samson and Balaam, were also prophetically gifted. However, they symbolize those who refuse and resist, but for a period of time they look good. It will be hard to tell the difference between these as wheat and tares. It was during a period of time of transition for God's people that God used Samson and Balaam. So they are also transitional prophetic types.

Enoch and Elijah were spoken of by Jewish people at Christ's first coming as witnesses who will return before Messiah's return. (See John 1:20, 21, 25; Matthew 16:14; 17:12; Luke 9:19.) Jewish history taught that Elijah and one of the other prophets (possibly Moses) would return before Messiah came. Jesus tells us this was fulfilled with John the Baptist. (See Matthew 17:12, 13; Mark 9:12, 13.)

But the Greek contains the element of the future. In both places the words "Elijah is coming" are used. Many people place different meanings to this portion of Scripture. But, regardless of what one believes, one thing is clear: in both Mark and Luke, Jesus used the transfiguration experience with the visitation of Elijah and Moses to back up what He said in the preceding chapters. He said that there are those who will not experience death but will be instantly transported to glory. While that is certainly in the future, the question can be asked, "can we experience the presence of God in glory as we live here on the face of the earth to such a dramatic extent that those that look on us see Father's glory? I believe Enoch and Elijah represent a company of believers that will walk so closely with God in power that a rapture of glory will surround them. Could this be possible, to some extent, before the Second Coming of our Lord? I believe the answer is a resounding *yes*! Let's study these individuals.

Resistances To His Glorious Presence: Samson and Balaam

In studying the knowledge of God in glory, we examined the strongholds first. We should also examine them here when we speak of His glorious presence. For no other word is used to embody resistance and great grief except the word *ichabod*. While *anathema* may convey some of it, *ichabod* stays in the conscience like no other. Even though Balaam appears in history first, let's review Samson's life first instead. Samson is born during forty years of judgment by God on Israel. He is also born during a transitional period of time. If we use Reese's Chronological Bible as a reference, Samson begins to judge (1096–1076 B.C.) in one area of Israel, as Samuel receives his call from God (1103 B.C.); Saul is born (1105 B.C.), and the Ark of the Covenant is captured and taken to Ashdod (1094 B.C.).[2]

Different scholars attach different timing to all these events.[3] Regardless of where one stands on the timing, Samson preceded, and to some degree lived during one of the more difficult transitions in Israel's history, the transition from judge to priest and from king to prophet. While Samuel is and should be credited with this particular transition from a prophetic point of view, we see no other judge so close to the transition period with the glory of God so uniquely abiding upon him as Samson. If one follows Reese's time lines, then the ark was taken during a period of time in which Samson, Eli and little Samuel were alive. If this is the case, it might explain why God would give Samson, one of the last few judges, an on-again, off-again glory experience (apart from his obvious strongholds) and then abide on little Samuel, the last judge and first priest/prophet.

Samuel then ordains and dedicates a new king, the king-shepherd/priest-prophet worshiper David. Transitions take time. When we look at the body of Christ today we see many people still functioning in worship in a very dry way, with no prophet functioning and certainly no pastoral understanding of the fivefold ministry for their congregation. Yet God is among them, bringing about His plan in their lives. In another region you may find a church with a pastor who has been raised to the apostolic office and has raised up other men and women as pastors, prophets, teachers and evangelists. Their church's worship is led by a team, functioning in prophetic release, and the glory of God is abiding on them and infusing them.

And then there is every level of church in between. Transitions take time. Inherent within those different levels of transition, one

His Presence

experiences or witnesses the presence of God differently. This was so during Israel's history. It is also true of us today. The danger and resistance that Samson represents are of taking the presence of God for granted, thus judging it. You say, "Oh, surely, a church in revival or renewal would never do that." Samson did just that, and to a greater extent, the same attitude that Samson exhibited prevailed in Israel up to the time that the Ark of the Covenant was captured. In fact, that is exactly what it took to get Israel's attention. While Samson was born during a forty-year judgment period by God on the nation, the truth is that the whole time of the judges was a testing period. (See Judges 13:1.) Judges 2:1–4 opens with the angel of the Lord proclaiming judgment on Israel for disobedience. Judges 2:16–23 tells us the first reason why the judges were raised up was because of God's divine grace and covenant responsibilities. The second reason was to test Israel's heart.

Why God Shows Up

Judges 3:1–2 provides a third reason: to teach those who are too young to remember how to successfully engage in warfare. I get the impression today, as we witness God in glory falling and the transition through which the body of Christ must travel, that God has shown up for exactly the same reasons. He has a covenant plan, filled with grace and mercy, and He also comes to test our hearts. He wants to give us an opportunity to see our own resistant stronghold attitudes. For those of us too immature or young in Christ, He comes to show us how these strongholds leave us open to enemy attack, thus teaching us warfare. Samson was the eleventh judge, if you don't count Abimelech.[4]

The number eleven in the Scriptures simply signifies disorder or incompleteness.[5] Interestingly, after the temptation of Judas we were left with eleven disciples. Deuteronomy 1:2 says that it was an eleven-day journey when the Israelites turned back in unbelief from entering the Promised Land. Had they traveled that extra day they may never have suffered forty years in the desert.

BEYOND STRONGHOLDS

Falling Short of God's Purpose

Jehoiakim and Zedekiah were the last two kings that reigned before Nebuchadnezzar took Israel away captive. Both rebelled against God. They reigned eleven years each. (See 2 Chronicles 36:5, 11, 12.) In fact, it was in the eleventh year of Jehoiakim that Nebuchadnezzar carried the Jews away, and in the eleventh year of Zedekiah he finished it.[6] How interesting that repentance or resisting temptation in each of these cases would have produced godly results instead of judgment, disorder and incompleteness, of which the number eleven is symbolic. As it was with Samson's life, we experience the same thing when God in glory falls upon our churches. The glory falls, but we don't complete or fulfill God's total desired plan at that location. We stop or get distracted by other things. We never press through to the other side. Our fleshly desires outweigh our spiritual need.

We all know the stories of Samson's less than godly desire for Philistine women. Frankly, this doesn't explain the real problem. In fact, Judges 14:4 tells us this desire was allowed by God who planned to use it as an occasion to confront the Philistines. Samson's real problem was in confusing God's manifest presence, in the midst of his less-than-godly choices, with that of God's covenant and plan for His people. How many people who experience the manifestation of God's presence on them for the purpose of blessing someone else think that everything that's done and said by them is all God? Or how many people feel that, because God showed up in glory, they did something right or prayed very hard?

God shows up in glory because He chooses to, not necessarily because of something we do or don't do. All we can do is set up His prescribed order on earth, present ourselves as living sacrifices and wait for Him to alight on those sacrifices.

Judges 16 tells us of the continual eroding and wearing down of Samson to the point where, in verse 19, the Scripture says, "his strength left him." Even then Samson thinks he can still operate under the same anointing of power. In Judges 16:20 we are told

His Presence

that Samson did not know that the Lord had left him. He had lost his discernment. He is no longer capable of discerning the purposes of God's glorious presence. But Israel is not affected by this sin. We are never told that the Philistines overcame Israel. In fact, Reese makes it clear that the Philistines weren't a real threat again until Samuel gathered Israel at Mizpeh.[7] The Philistines are defeated at that point. (See Judges 13:5; 1 Samuel 7:13, 14.)

Falling Short of God's Purpose: The Attitude of God's Leaders

Micah 2 and 3 describe the attitude of leaders that have fallen out of touch with God's purposes. They do what is right in their own eyes (Judg. 17:6), just as Israel did during Samson's term, lifting themselves up over God's people. Then when a true servant or prophet is raised up, they want to control what he or she says. (See Micah 2:7-11.) Micah 3:11 declares of Israel, "Her leaders judge for a bribe, her priests teach for a price, and her prophets tell fortunes for money. *Yet they lean upon the Lord and say, 'Is not the Lord among us? No disaster will come upon us'*" (emphasis added).

How could they say God was among them if some form of the presence God was not there? I believe that God's presence was there, and here are the reasons: First, as is so often the case, God always gives His people time to repent. Micah's prophecies were spoken long before Babylon carried Judah away. In fact, it took Nebuchadnezzar twenty-one years to complete the deportations.

There were seven deportations in all. These two numbers are significant because they suggest the divine completeness of what was done in judging the nation (3x7=21). Israel was judged for refusing God's will while His glorious presence was among them. During these times of graciousness, the presence of God did fall. (See Micah 2:7; 3:8.) But for whose sake? Simply for the sake of God to carry out His plan and for the sake of His people, the sheep of His pasture—to give all of us time to repent of our strongholds. (See Micah 4:6.)

In modern times, we have all seen how certain ministers have fallen into sin, and then they preach from pulpits and the anointing falls. This should not surprise us. Remember how both Miriam and Aaron grumbled against Moses? But only Miriam manifested God's immediate judgment. This wasn't because God hated her more. Aaron wore the mantle and anointing of the high priest. As a leader, God's people needed him. As long as he wore the anointing, Aaron was safe. God allowed Aaron to see His judgment on Miriam in order to give him the chance to repent. At Aaron's death, he was stripped of the priest's robe, then judgment came on him and he died.

We must be so very sensitive to the love and the requests of the Holy Spirit, or we will lose our discernment. It is a mistake for leadership to assume that God is there because of them. It is also a mistake to think that His presence continues to flow because every one is in good spiritual health. His presence falls to effectuate His plan and to provide relief and support for His people. It is notable, though, that Ezekiel 14:11 says God allows His presence to fall on a false prophet in order to draw His people back to Him so that nothing else is their God.[8]

Samson was not mindful of these things. Or perhaps he didn't stay close enough to the Lord, but chose to ignore them and his Nazarite vows. If we place the judges in the timeframe that Reese does, Samson's death is right before Samuel emerges as a judge. Since both kept a Nazarite vow, it would be important to review its implication relating to the glory of God during this time of transition.

The Nazarite Vow

Anyone could take a Nazarite vow—men, women, children and slaves. Only in the case of children or slaves could it be revoked by a parent or owner.[9]

There were three different lengths of time for making a Nazarite vow. They include:

- short-term, with thirty days as the minimum

His Presence

- perpetual, with seasons of reprieve
- perpetual, for life[10]

Scripture mentions three individuals who seem to have been Nazarites for life. They are Samson, Samuel and John the Baptist. All of them lived during glorious transitional times in Israel's history. Christian tradition mentions another one, and that is James the Just or the one the New Testament refers to as "The Brother of Our Lord."[11] He lived in a transitional time of change for Israel and the birthing of the church.

The vow itself had three restrictions:

- no defilement (especially from dead objects)
- no cutting of hair
- no imbibing or contact with anything that comes from the fruit of the vine

It was a vow of total separation unto the Lord. (See Numbers 6:1–21.) Regarding defilement, it was very similar to the law concerning priests. (See Leviticus 21:11.) In fact, most scholars agree that the word "Nazarite" conveys three meanings: "separation, holiness and the royal crown or the crown of the royal priesthood."[12]

This is the only place in the Old Testament where one could be separated out, almost as a priest, regardless of gender, age or ethnic background. I find all of this interesting in these respects. One, when God in glory falls on us, He totally infuses us, just like the Holy Spirit infuses us. Oil, water and wine are three Scriptural symbols for the Holy Spirit, in addition to the dove. Secondly, we are told by Paul to wear the helmet of salvation. (See Ephesians 6:17.) Our covering over our heads is to be Christ and His blood. Thank God our Lord wore a crown of thorns so we may "wear" our healing. Thirdly, sin is death, but the gift of our God is eternal life in Christ Jesus. (See Romans 6:23.) We never have to be defiled by death for all eternity. Lastly, Christ has made us a royal priesthood, separated to the Lord for all eternity. (See 1 Peter 2:5-9.)

When God in glory falls on us we are separated. It creates a separating process. Because of the Holy Spirit's involvement in all of this, salvation, or the process of salvation (soteriology), will always be evident. As the priest wore the mitre, or crown, upon his head (the Hebrew word is *nezer*), we wear the glory of God in salvation upon us. Remember how Moses' face was changed as a result of God's glorious presence? Scripture and Jewish custom give three time frames for this separating experience: short-term, daily life with times of reprisal, and never ending. I believe God wants to abide in a way that is never ending. I believe He wants to make a "vow" of salvation with unbelievers on earth today; to separate them out as He did with anyone in the Old Testament who wanted to keep a covenant vow with God. The Nazarite vow was an act in which believers could find a closeness with God. When Father comes to us in glory there is a closeness we experience that we never want to end. As God raises up an end-time people to prepare the way of the Lord, as He did with John the Baptist, the symbolism of the Nazarite vow will be important to them. They will prepare the earth for Father to baptize nations in glory. They will want to be separated and sold out to their King, wearing the glorious work of salvation on their heads with the stench of death to sin far from them.

Of course, there is a reality check here. God is so gracious. He knows we are but dust. So in graciousness He provided room within all three time frames of the vow for the Nazarite to make a mistake. Thank God! Offerings, sacrifices and other acts of cleansing were required. (See Numbers 6:9-12.) God uses Samson to teach us as Christians an important lesson. Even though His glory was heavily on Samson, it seems Samson never partook of these cleansing processes (Judges 14:8; 15:15).[13] Look at the symbolism in Judges 15:15-20. Samson gains a great victory by killing Israel's enemies with a jawbone. But a jawbone is death. It is from a dead animal. A Nazarite is not to touch these things. How often do we have successful church meetings and ministries

His Presence

and run great business or social endeavors, but we're doing it the same old way—the way that has worked for us in the past. We may even kill some enemies, but we're mixing this with God's glorious presence instead of doing what God wants us to do His new way. This, in effect, is touching something dead. The results look good, but it leaves us deficient, like Samson was for water. (See Judges 15:18.) We are left so deficient, in fact, that it looks like we shall perish. So we cry out to God in subtle accusation like Samson did, never realizing that we're in the place we are because we've been defiled. Samson calls the place of his "victory" *Ramath Lehi*. This word means, "hill or seat of idolatry of the soft flesh (the jawbone is the soft-cheek part of the animal). God is so faithful. He opens up a hole at jawbone hill and out comes water! We've seen God cleanse His people this way before. He did it for them with Moses and the rock. But Moses got in trouble when he tried to do it twice. (See Numbers 20:1-13.) God cleansed us once and for all time at Calvary when water and blood came out of our Lord's side. As a result a new name is given to the spring within *Ramath Lehi—En Hakkore*. (See Judges 15:19.) This means "the fountain of one calling." Hallelujah! After we've been cleansed from these areas of "soft flesh," or strongholds, God does not leave us. He still calls. Samson is given 20 more years to judge at this point. (See Judges 15:20.) God still used him, especially at the end of his life when his hair, the symbol of God's covenant, began to grow, and some form of desire for God grew with it. (See Judges 16:22, 28.) Even though revenge was in his heart, we must remember that this was Samson's calling from the Lord, to exact revenge on the enemies of God's people, thus providing peace and protection for them. (See Judges 2:16.)

The representation of Samson as a Christian, with God's glorious presence abiding all around him or her, should be both a lesson in gratitude and watchfulness. For while Father provided cleansing for Samson continually out of His grace, it is possible to go too far—even while the glory is still upon us. We must repent before it is too late. Our lamps must be full *before* the bridegroom comes. (See Matthew 25:1-13.) So while the job eventually got done, this eleventh judge no longer pressed in, and incompleteness was the result.

Pressing Into The God Of Glory

We forget that God has shown up in glory to fulfill a destiny purpose or plan of His own. How often has God's glorious presence fallen on our churches, only to find lack of effort in us when we stop pressing into our symbolic Nazarite vows. Therefore, we don't complete the painful process of renewal that must take place so that the enemies of the Lord are defeated and God's glorious presence finds perfect rest. The Nazarite vow has both negative and positive aspects. Not only do you abstain, but you also take action in obtaining a positive dedication to God.[14]

So it is in the case of pressing in, even though God's glorious presence seems to be abiding. There are times of abstinence from friends and family and other healthy entertainment. There are also times, no matter how good things look spiritually, of checking to see what more God has for us. Are we constantly seeking to "go up higher," as the apostle did on the Isle of Patmos, or are we satisfied where we are because our flesh says it's enough? (See 1 Peter 2:5-9.) Even though John was experiencing marvelous visions, seeing our Lord as the Alpha and Omega, it wasn't enough. (See Revelation 1:7-8.) He had to go up higher. Part of our problem is that we are unwilling to let others do some of the work. Change requires lots of people putting forth an effort. As with God's knowledge in glory, we don't raise up enough people to function in this new dimension. Or we want them all to look, believe and act a certain way. In reality this is greed. We become greedy for the glory. We don't want anyone else—a contemporary or someone "lesser"—to get a jump on us. This is more of a Balaam problem, and it takes time to manifest itself.

Greedy with the Glory: Balaam

We all want more of God. We are actually created spiritually to want more of God. Wanting more of God is one thing, but

His Presence

becoming so greedy as to say, "there's no more room at the table; you're not allowed in," are two very different issues. Jesus condemned the Pharisees for such practices. (See Matthew 23:13.) Yes, jealousy and selfishness are involved. But Balaam presents himself as a very interesting character, because, ultimately, fear itself is the effect of this judgmental resistance. We fear that someone else may get the credit. It may manifest itself in many ways like "glory snatching," self-promotion or church promotion. This kind of fear is best described by the term intimidation. We looked at faith versus unbelief concerning the knowledge of God in glory. To be sure, the opposite of faith is unbelief. But unbelief is fear (look at Jesus' parable in Luke 19:11–26), or a double-mindedness. (See James 1:6–7; 3:8.) John tells us this fear exists because we have not been made perfect in love. (See 1 John 4:18.) Whatever is not of faith is sin. (See Romans 14:23.) This kind of fear is an omission of faith we see in the resistance of God's knowledge in glory. Certainly we see parts of it Samson's life.

Yet another aspect of fear manifests itself in intimidation. For those who have not been perfected in Christ's love, those who are close to Father's bosom may seem intimidating. We need to distinguish this from real human intimidation or demon spirits trying to cause fear. Out of all the writers of the epistles and Gospels, the apostle John's writings speak about faith the least. Yet the theme of love (divine love or the character of God summed up in love) is mentioned the most. Eusebius mentions an instance in which the aged apostle went into the bandit-infested hills to retrieve a backslidden young man out of a recidivist life of crime.[15] He walked safely in and out of this environment, and no one dared touch him. Were demon spirits, which functioned with these bandits, intimidated, thus providing safety for the apostle?

When Elijah prayed and the fire of God came out of the sky to consume all, were the people somewhat intimidated? When Jesus healed the sick and exposed the Pharisees (and demon forces) for what they really were, was this intimidating for them personally? There is a place in which God flows through us so thoroughly that we can become intimidating to some people. We ourselves have no desire to intimidate. We're just functioning in Christ. But there is a subtle flip side to this. In a powerful anointing, we can begin to become polluted and desire others to walk in fear of us. We desire to control even though we profess otherwise.

In Balaam's case, Balak had to go to Balaam; no one else would do. Numbers 22:7 mentions the fee for this divination. Balaam could not hear from God unless he performed some kind of ritual first. (See Numbers 24:1.) Of course, the first problem with this is the desire for money. (See 2 Peter 2:15, Jude 11.)

Hearing God for Ourselves

The second problem, with even more dangerous implications for us today than the first, is the fact that it was generally understood by all that only Balaam could be in God's presence to hear. It is true that, Biblically, prophets have always been in a special place to hear God. But in the New Testament, Jesus makes it clear that the Holy Spirit has come for all who believe. (See John 14, 15.)

God is not shut up in one place or one person. Paul also makes this clear when he talks about the various gifts with which God graces His people. (See Romans 12, 1 Corinthians 12, Ephesians 4:11-17.)

This stronghold is based upon unbelief, and it produces fear. With it is the feeling or the attitude that only certain people are worthy to be in God's presence, or only certain people can bestow God's blessings when His presence falls. You must go to them or their location. This is extremely dangerous for obvious Biblical reasons. If God intended only a handful in one location to be blessed with the benefits of His manifested glory, why would Jesus have been sacrificed and the Holy Spirit poured out? (See John. 3:16.) To use the Holy Spirit's gifts in power to subtly control or intimidate is sin. To suggest that God only speaks to one person in a church or only a certain group is frightening. All of God's people can hear from Him. To be sure, some hear and experience His presence more powerfully than others. God sometimes separates out some individuals, groups or churches to

His Presence

stand out more than others in order to describe some aspect of His person or will. Down through the centuries, when God in glory has come to a location, one of the hallmarks of this visitation was the manifestation of His glory going back with those who visited. In this way His manifest presence and gifts were spread throughout the body of Christ.

Cursing Israel and Cursing Ourselves: Sabotage

God may have desired to start with one person, location or church, but His pattern of blessing us is to use that one person, location or church to bless others. When He separated Balaam out so Balaam could hear, it was as if to say, "I know you're a pagan idolater with problems. But if you remain obedient, I'll use you to bless my people and turn you from your idolatry and problems."

The purpose of God's presence is to change us all from glory to glory, to effect His plans and purposes and to go from one realm of glory and change to another.

To help in that change, God deposited five individual gifts, along with elders and deacons. Suppressing the healthy, free expression of God's presence when He has been made manifest in glory is the same as taking money to curse His people. Ultimately what's being done is suppression to propagate the desire of a few. These two outcomes, greed and intimidation, are from the same problem: a lack of faith, which produces judgment. Balaam, though, shows us a third and a fourth.

In his first conversation with God he is told not to go and curse Israel. (See Numbers 22:12.) Instead of relying on that word, his wicked desires cause him to go back to God again and see if these new, more influential princes of Balak will change God's mind. By doing this Balaam opened the door for his own motives to sabotage God's possible plan for his life.

Over the years I have seen similar situations take place. God shows up with His glorious presence and speaks a word. Possibly, it is a more difficult word than we expect. Or we may think that

He will fulfill it in a certain way, but He does not. Time goes by with very little evidence of this word being fulfilled. Circumstances or events take place to test the real desires and motives of our hearts, but we do not perceive that this testing is taking place. The word seems to not be bearing fruit, so we seek our own desires and a new word.

Sabotage Produces A Crossroad Word

I've come to call this next word a "crossroad" word. I've termed it this because it seems "so God." Actually, it is a test, and it is partially God. Let me explain. These words come at crossroads in history, crossroads in nations and crossroads in our lives individually. God wants to abide on us in glory, but going from glory to glory is an ongoing process. When we are going to the next level God will test us to expose what's in our hearts. These situations force us to go to the cross. Mary went to the cross before there was a literal cross. As a result, Christ was birthed on earth. When we go to the cross we pass the test. Not every crossroad word comes because we are sinning. Some crossroad words come to keep us on the right path because we don't recognize that we're deviating a little from God's order.

Some crossroad words test us before God takes us to the next level. Abraham had to be tested through offering up Isaac. In one instance God is saying to Abraham that his descendants would be as the sand on the seashore. In the next instance, He wants the hope for that promised seed dead on the altar! When Abraham became willing he birthed a nation. Ezekiel has to witness crossroad words when God pours out His Spirit on those He did not call as prophets run around like they're prophesying from crystal balls. He tells Ezekiel that He allows this "prophesying" so that His people will recognize their strongholds, repent and draw closer to Him.[16]

Passing God's Tests

When the school of the prophets followed Elisha around, telling

His Presence

him the Lord was going to take Elijah that day, were they right? Of course! But they did not see God's total plan for Elisha or for the nation. Only Elisha did. As a result, he was given the full understanding to follow Elijah and pass the test.

The leaders of the temple were tested by Jesus' words. They were in a crossroad situation as a nation, and spiritually as God's people. Either they were going to believe the Prophet and search out the Scriptures to confirm His Word—even though that Word challenges them to change—or they were going to reject the Prophet and see their seed affected by that rejection. Their disobedience is not evident immediately, for all continued to look the same. But in forty years' time, Rome destroyed the temple and killed and scattered Israel's seed.

When we fear God will not do as we expect, He will test us to see what we are going to do. When the rug is pulled out from under us and all we have left is God, we learn a valuable lesson of faith.

God may have a word for a church or person. When God has already appeared in glory and we fail to obey that first word, He may bring a second word. This one may actually be more palatable or easier to for us to obey. But if we go down the path of that crossroad or second word without fulfilling the first purpose or plan of God to change us, the second word may lead us to disaster. For we have refused to obey His first call to walk in the pathway of that first word.

These crossroad words literally can take one down two different paths. They show us what is in our own hearts. Balaam refused to look at what was in his. I include Balaam here because of his experience with the angel of the Lord, similar to the *theophany* experience that Joshua had. (See Numbers 22:22-35; Joshua 5:13-6:5.) Joshua's response is one of exposure. Balaam's is not. Joshua bows down, exposing the back of his neck to the angel's drawn sword. Balaam confesses, with an excuse, "I didn't realize you were standing in the road to oppose me."

When God's presence shows up in glory, the best thing we can do is be totally transparent or exposed before the Lord. No excuses! This is also one of only two places in Scripture where an animal has spoken in human language. The first one was when the serpent spoke with Eve. The serpent tempts unfaithfulness while the donkey exposes unfaithfulness.

Like Samson, Balaam does finally obey the will of the Lord. His prophecies in Numbers 23 and 24 are quite incredible. Not only does he have the concept of God as King, just as Samuel, but he prophesies concerning Christ. (See Numbers 23:21; Numbers 24:17.) In fact, some Messianic Jewish congregations today still sing Numbers 24:4-6 as a blessing over people. Unfortunately, Balaam's end is also very similar to Samson's. He is killed as a result of God enacting vengeance on the enemies of His people. (See Numbers 31:8; Joshua 13:22.)

Neglecting God's Presence

The final outcome of this stronghold of faithless fear that we see evidenced in Balaam is a lack of exposing oneself to the Lord's presence. We neglect becoming extremely sensitive to the Holy Spirit. We have seen how greed and intimidation with unbelief (lack of faith) in areas of our lives can produce disastrous results of judgment when God in glory shows up. But what happens when we don't feel God's presence? It is quite possible for God to be near and we never perceive it. As a result, we neglect fostering our relationship to Him because we don't feel anything. This is when reliance on the written Word of God must take place, since hearing it produces faith. (See Romans 10: 17.) This is because the written Word will expose our areas of sin (greed, lack of faith, etc.), as long as we will expose ourselves to Him. The written Word will bring a desire to foster God's presence.

Sometimes He delays His manifested presence as a test. (See John 11: 1-6, 11-15, 21-27 and 32-42.) If we keep our hearts and minds still before God and remain transparent to Him, faith and peace will come, furthered along by obedience. (See Psalm 46:10.) We may be expecting the spectacular when, in fact, Father desires to be a still, small voice. (See 1 Kings 19:11-13.) This danger here is evidenced in Balaam's life. When God doesn't

His Presence

appear the way we want, we're tempted to conjure up something. This is why the New Testament lambastes Balaam. (See Revelation 2:14,15.)

Please don't misunderstand what is being said here. When God in glory moves upon us it is exciting. It can be very noisy, as God's people shout and dance before Him. But we still must enter into the holy place and holy of holies. These places are far more intimidating for some in worship, because there is no one else present but you and God. You are totally exposed. It is in that place that prophetic release usually comes forth in the congregation. (See Psalm 29.) This is when transparency before Father and total obedience to the Holy Spirit are crucial. Some will shift uncomfortably in their seats. They are not willing to enter in. Others will keep shouting. They also are not willing to enter in.

Leadership will then do one of three things:

- Stop that aspect of worship.
- Keep up the hype of shouting.
- Teach and encourage God's people how to enter into new realms of God's glorious presence and how to properly discern God's voice.

Face the Wilderness of Dryness and Rebellion

Balaam knew only two ways of functioning—stop and deny. (See Numbers 22:13, 19.) This is evidenced by his "Can I go or not?" attitude. Instead, his attitude should have been, "What is your plan, God Almighty?" His denial was indicated by his desire to hype up things in places of worship. (See high places, Numbers 22:41–23:2.)

Balaam actually does come close to the third or more proper area of entering in. It is interesting that, as he comes close to that place, his last prophecy foretells the coming of Christ centuries before our Lord appears. What allows Balaam to enter into that place of worship is seen in Numbers 24:1–2. Balaam hears clearly when he no longer relies on his own terms of hearing God, but acts in obedience, sets his face towards the "wilderness" and lifts up his eyes. He no longer has to set up structures in order to hear God. He no longer has to fear what God will do.

It's not until we look at our own areas of dryness and rebellion (the wilderness) that we realize they will not work. When we finally lift up our eyes to see Father in all of His glory, we become willing to be exposed and see Him no matter how awesome the sight. Here we can become totally controlled by and sensitive to the love and leading of the Holy Spirit. It's at that point that we realize we no longer need the hype, and we are finally willing to enter a place where Father can speak clearly and reside among us purely. (See Isaiah 58:11, 12.) There is no fear, control or intimidation—just faith! Balaam came so close. He entered in. (See Numbers 24:15, 16, 17.) But his greedy desires and lack of faith caused his death. He never did enter in to the living blessings of God's people.

Struggling In Our Own Strength

Samson represents those within the body of Christ with resistances in place, who struggle unduly with their own sin instead of turning it over to Christ. They think they can fix the problem in their own strength instead of realizing that only the blood of Jesus can redeem or clean anything.

Balaam represents those on the fringe of the church. They believe they are saved or have made some kind of confession, but they never walk close enough to be changed by God on a daily basis. They may even be in leadership positions or have had experiences with God. That God in glory appears to them should not surprise us. That they can preach or prophesy truth should not confuse us. (See John 11:47–50.) But we should never mistake the manifestation of God's presence as a sign that all is perfect, holy or even becoming perfect and holy. It would seem that these individuals have become inoculated to the exposing

His Presence

power of God's presence. This is what I call transparency or the desire to be humbled—not just before God; to me that would be easy. But we must be willing to be humbled before all of our peers and colleagues so that God's plan may be fulfilled, instead of our own plans.

As we read the whole of the Scriptures and view history, it would seem as if God was preparing us to abide with Him for all eternity, so we no longer make the mistakes of those who have gone before us. We can be thankful that He has provided positive characters to teach us. When we speak about the presence of God in glory, these next four individuals, Enoch, Elijah, Isaiah and Ezekiel provide us with hope and joy for the future. Joy because our final end is translation with God, and hope for the remainder of our lives here on earth.

Beyond Strongholds: Enoch, Elijah, Isaiah and Ezekiel

Unlike Balaam, whose need for hype and show was evident, the Word simply states that Enoch walked with God and was no more. Unlike Samson's display of God-induced superhuman strength, Elijah was, well frankly, just Elijah. Elijah was very human, but with simple displays of all godly strength and power. While Balaam had to conjure or hype up the presence of God in order to hear, Isaiah walked in godly hearing and speaking.

While Samson had to be hoodwinked by his own desires into doing God's will, Ezekiel only had to be told. Both Samson and Balaam functioned within a transitional period of time for the nation of Israel. Both Isaiah and Ezekiel did the same thing. As we are in transition in our church age, so were they. But in the cases of Enoch and Elijah, no real transition was going on around them in the nation. Instead, these two became the transition. They embodied it through instant translation by the glory of God Himself! Each of the six experienced a *theophany* appearance of God, yet their attitudes were different. We already looked at the numerical and symbolic significance of these four. Let's take a look at them as people.

Not much is said scripturally about Enoch. Actually, I think that is the joy of him. He walked, one foot in front of the other, with God and then, simply by faith, he was translated. (See Genesis 5:24; Hebrews 11:5.) It is in our daily steps with Father that we learn faith. It is in our daily experiences that we learn not to judge God, but to believe Him by faith no matter what the circumstances. No one else knows those daily steps that you make with God but you and God. Sometimes the truth of the **purity** of your walk may only be evidenced after physical death, when the resurrection takes place, as it was in Enoch's case.

In contrast to the few scriptural passages about Enoch, many chapters are devoted to Elijah. Much is said of him. We see his **humanity** in the midst of difficult situations. But Elijah never hid his human frailty from God. Even when he was having a pity party, he did not hide it from God. He never put on about who he was or what he could or would do. (See 1 Kings 19:4, 5.) There was no denying his sin, but there was a **transparency** before God and in his dealings with others. The final display of this transparency is similar to Enoch's, from mortal life to immortal translation.

A Prophet's Unique Experience

Isaiah is born in Judah during Uzziah's positive kingly reign. Amos and Hosea are prophesying against the sin of Israel's kings in Samaria at the same time. Isaiah grows up under the influence of Uzziah and is probably anywhere from ten to twenty years old when Uzziah transgresses the priesthood and is stricken with leprosy. This is what facilitated his son Jotham's dual reign. (See 2 Chronicles 26:16–21.) Uzziah dies when Isaiah is a young man, and the young prophet receives a *theophany* vision of the Lord lifted up. (See Isaiah 6:1.) Is it just coincidence, in order to date this experience with Uzziah's death, or is there more involved in mentioning it in Isaiah 6:1?

To be sure, a kingship like Uzziah's would have had an impact

His Presence

on a young prophet, especially one who is connected to the royal family and is called to prophesy to the king and the nation. His vision and allegiance could only be **dedicated** and fixed on God. He could not be encumbered by feelings for the king or his family. This is probably why Isaiah didn't experience God in awesome glory until Uzziah was removed and the prophet's vision was totally centered on God.

Isaiah prophesied before and during Israel's transition from an independent monarchy to subordinate nation as a result of her own sins. (See Isaiah 6:8–13.) He saw the duplicity and the filthiness of the human heart, while, at the same time, he experienced some of the goodness of the kings' courts to which he had to prophesy. He experienced a natural love for his people, and yet he knew the pain in God's heart for His people. He knew much about the judgment their sins would elicit from that Heart.

In very unique ways, a prophet will experience what God is about to do. Sometimes this unique vision makes it difficult for pastors to understand the prophetically gifted people with which they are called to minister. While nothing but God can consume the vision of a prophet, all of fivefold ministry must submit willingly to one another and the body in general. (See Ephesians 5:21.) In fact, one aspect of maturing into the prophetic ministry is being able to understand experiences and know when God wants them spoken or wishes to keep them secret. We get a glimpse into that from Isaiah 6:6, 10. This is done in submission and obedience. It is never easy for a prophet to constantly speak good from the mouth of God when he or she knows God's judgment is not far off. One might accuse God of lying. This is nonsense. The Scriptures are plain and clear for all to read and hear. When we do wrong to each other and violate moral laws of honesty and integrity, should we expect anything less than judgment? It is God's goodness that leads us to repentance. (See Romans 2:4.) And so it is Isaiah's difficult task of being a part of God's goodness by prophesying restoration, while knowing that judgment and pain will attend to the lives to which he may prophesy. (See Isaiah 6:1–4.)

Nothing could blur Isaiah's vision in this respect, or else he would become useless as Father's mouthpiece—not fear of reprisal from rulers, not love for those rulers and not even love for his family. He had to be wholly dedicated and separated unto God while having free accessibility to the ear of the nation.

It has been traditionally believed that Isaiah was martyred by being sawed in half. (See Hebrews 11:37.) If this is true, it's a poignant reality. It was the dividing of the nation that led to Israel's weakness as a nation, along with her penchant for foreign gods. As her political monarchies would die divided, in the same manner, would they kill the prophet called to preach to those monarchies. Yet Isaiah remained **dedicated** and devoted unto God in both life and death.

Sold Out to God

If Isaiah was called to political Israel before and during its judgment, Ezekiel was called to spiritual Israel during and after its transition. I believe this is why their *theophany* experiences are so similar. Is there really much difference between the attitude and the integrity with which you go to church or function in God's house and the attitude and integrity with which you run a business or function in your job? There shouldn't be. The presence of God is the same. His purpose or work for you on the job or in church might be different, but His presence is the same.

God remained faithful to Israel both politically and spiritually. Ezekiel is born while Israel is paying tribute to other nations. So he never knows what it is to live in true freedom from hostile forces. Micah and Isaiah are long dead. Jeremiah and Zephaniah are prophesying during his birth. He is born during some of King Josiah's reforms in the temple. This must have produced hope for his family since they were priests.

As Ezekiel is growing up, Habakkuk and Daniel are on the scene. The first deportation has already taken place and Jerusalem is under siege. By the time Ezekiel is a young man, Nebuchadnezzar carries him away in captivity. He is believed to have been taken captive

His Presence

during the third deportation, when King Jehoiachin and his household are taken along with the precious things of the temple. (See 2 Kings 24:10-16; 2 Chronicles 36:10; Esther 2:6.)

God purges the dual Messianic lines of king and priest with one act of judgment. Yet God still leaves some witnesses behind. While Jeremiah is prophesying, "Woe be unto the pastors that destroy and scatter the sheep of my pasture" (Jer. 23:1, KJV), King Zedekiah and those with him are doing just that—scattering the sheep. As a result, Ezekiel becomes a part of those scattered.[17]

It's interesting that God never wants for a faithful prophet to speak to His people, but a faithful king is a lot more difficult to find. Could it be that absolute human power corrupts humans absolutely?

Ezekiel winds up prophesying to a spiritual people without much governmental structure. The authority over them is foreign and hostile. If there is the thought of some Jewish rule, it is a captive king (there will be other captive kings joining them). They are still thinking of a monarchy, or one-man rule. But God gives Ezekiel a vision of true plurality in leadership for the future, and Ezekiel prophesies Jerusalem's final capture in his present time. (See Ezekiel 1:4-28; Ezekiel 40-48; see Ezekiel 4:4-7.)

Ezekiel must tell of immediate judgment, while pointing them to the reality of a future government and a future temple filled with God's glorious presence. Ezekiel must see only the vision of the future God shows him. He cannot be encumbered by his feelings for those around him, as appropriate as the feelings may be, even for his own wife. (See Ezekiel 24:15-27.) He must feel the pain God feels for His wife, Israel. Ezekiel must be totally **dedicated** and sold out to Jehovah in order to be the mouthpiece God desires.

Purity, Humanity, Transparency and Dedication

As we've looked at a truncated review of these four characters, I have italicized four words: *purity*, *humanity*, *transparency* and *dedication*. These four words symbolize these four individuals. They exemplify four attitudes that must exist for God to remain and abide on us while we are in His glorious presence.

There must be a total dependence on the Holy Spirit, for it is only God that makes us pure. When we don't hide our humanity from Him, being willing to be totally transparent, a simple but profound dedication to Him becomes apparent. There also seem to be two different vessels or trains of thought flowing, similar to veins and arteries. We see Elijah and Enoch functioning with great acts of power and displays of virtue. They have gone on to be with our Lord. They know what translated glory is. These are like veins, carrying the old blood to be recycled through the heart so the body remains healthy.

Isaiah and Ezekiel remind one of the conditions of our New Testament heroes. Those were people living in hostile situations while putting their lives on the line to promote God's causes. They received powerful experiences with God in glory in order to help them make it through and to share with those around them. These are like arteries, pumping life-giving blood to every cell in need. This creates an interesting inversion or cycle, just as the veins and arteries meet through the hearts in our bodies. I know much has been made in modern times of an Elijah company of people. But I feel each one of these characters is a company of people.

Isaiah and Ezekiel remind us of those living throughout history after the close of the New Testament writings, up to and including our own day. They are obedient to God even to martyrdom, either in the actual spilling of blood or in sacrificial intercession and work. This sacrifice produces judgment from the hand of God toward those that resist their God-ordained message. And so another word is spoken—repent and look toward a new order of worship and government in Christ. Isn't this what Christ's death on the cross produced?

While this is going on, God is also preparing a people to walk so closely with Him in profound power that the natural next step is walking into translated glorification! This is so characteristic of

His Presence

God's glorious presence. He infuses history, flows through history, and yet, He is totally outside historical time so as to have no beginning or end!

Wow! What a God we serve! His presence has a glorious purpose. If we walk by faith in that purpose and do not resist through judgment, we will experience that purpose and His presence in our lives, both in glorious translation and glorious living.

I am coming soon. Hold on to what you have, so that no one will take your crown. Him who overcomes I will make a pillar in the temple of my God. Never again will he leave it. I will write on him the name of my God and the name of the city of my God, the New Jerusalem, which is coming down out of heaven from my God; and I will also write on him my new name. He who has an ear, let him hear what the Spirit says to the churches.

—Revelation 3:11–13

Chapter Seven

THE NAME

One of the final acts that God will accomplish with His people is to change our names. In the Bible, who you are in terms of your character and gifts is represented in your name. The name change in glory is one of the last steps God takes His people through before He fulfills most of His promises. God alone decides when and how that change will take place. Some people are ready for the name change first, while others—myself included—go through a more involved process! Understanding this process of change may be far easier than experiencing it.

Jesus Christ was called by many names in the Bible. His name, "Jesus of Nazareth" provided an explanation about from where He came. To call Him "Jesus, Joseph's son" provided more information about Him and distinguished Him from the other boys in Nazareth with the same name. To call Him "Jesus, Joseph and Mary's son" did so even more. The name "Jesus" or *Yeshua* revealed something concerning His life's work. His name, "Jesus the Christ, the Son of the Living God," sets Him apart from false christs—not only on earth but also in the spiritual realm where angels and demons function, for the most part, beyond our recognition.

In modern times, our names usually don't carry the same weight that the ancients placed on them. While our parents or guardians may have given us our names with special meaning, times have somewhat changed. Furthermore, we are given numbers also, especially in the United States where Social Security numbers stay with us until we die. Because our government is not God, who knows and sees all in every generation, there needs to be a way for them to keep track of us.

New Names In Glory

When God changes our names in glory He will be doing more than simply calling us something else—far more. Actually, this renaming will include an entire change of perspective concerning yourself and the environment in which God places you. Which brings us to the next point. It is God's idea. When we study the different instances in the Bible in which God appeared in glory, we cannot help but see the dramatic change that took place in each individual who encountered Him.

In some cases, God actually changed an individual's surname. In other places, everything concerning the person changed except his or her name. We are not talking here about the change that takes place after salvation or after we have an experience with God. Change in these situations is usually attributed to salvation and the infilling of the Holy Spirit. The change I'm speaking about is a direct result of God manifesting Himself in glory on us over a period of time. This appearance of God in glory in our individual lives happens for a specific purpose.

Let's look at Samson as an example. Samson was changed into a man of great strength when God's glory fell upon him, but he wasn't a changed man. It wasn't until his imprisonment and the subsequent re-growth of his Nazarite hair, which was symbolic of his obedience to the reappearance of the glory of God, that he became willing to die to himself to fulfill the call of God.

I am not promoting suicide. I speak of Samson's obviously self-centered life committed to satisfying his flesh. Later, he became a totally changed man. He used his last ounce of strength in sacrificing his life to save the people of Israel by enacting judgment on Philistia.

While his first change into a man of great physical strength is

The Name

obvious—just as our change from a life without Christ to life in Christ is obvious—the second, more purposeful change costs far more. The first change is far more apparent to us and everyone around us. This second change is not always as obvious to the casual observer, or even to ourselves.

Changed By The God of Glory

The first example of this name change in a Biblical character is that of Jesus. We will study our Lord first because He had no resistances, and the subtleties of this process will take time to review.

The best example of change versus stronghold resistance when God came in glory was Jacob, and we will review him later. On a corporate basis for church bodies, we will review the glory of God as He rested upon the ark of the covenant, the nation of Israel and the Jewish temple, where the name of God was placed.

Recent archeological finds have changed quite a few of our ideas concerning the environment in which Jesus was raised.[1] The only historical sources of understanding that we have about Jesus are the accounts of Him from the four Gospels and Acts. Very few ancient texts mention Jesus as a person. He was born in obscurity in the Middle East. We know He was a Jewish preacher that died as a result of being publicly executed. If we place His execution somewhere between 26 and 33 A.D., we get an idea of what life must have been like back then. Until recently, it was assumed Jesus was raised as a peasant, and not very well acquainted with social and economic issues of the world. But a closer look at Israel from 10 B.C. to 30 A.D. changes that attitude. Jesus was born when Israel was in captivity to Rome (Luke 2:1). The idea of the "Peace of Rome" or *Pax Romana*, as it was called, was a stronghold that had a life all its own. It meant that Rome ruled as God on earth. As a result of that rule, the provinces were "graced with quietness or peace." Every coin bore an inscription of the image of Julius Caesar. Under this image were the words, "Son of God." The ancient writer Virgil calls him the "Son of a God."[2] So Jesus is born into an environment in which society at large believes that

BEYOND STRONGHOLDS

Rome is God's agent and Caesar is recognized as God's son.

In this environment Rome took the notion of peace to its provinces very seriously. Any speech or action that disturbed that peace was met with swift justice (it is interesting how satan similarly lies to his worshippers, so much so that many witches, warlocks and satanic cultists fear for their lives if they speak against him or try to stop serving him).

Life in Caesarea

Ancient Palestine was anything but peaceful, with Judea creating a continual state of upheaval. Judea was the furthermost eastern province in the Roman Empire. Herod the Great was Rome's instrument of rule. Herod's building program for Jerusalem was immense. He rebuilt the Jewish temple and an expansive water system in the city of Caesarea.

The city of Caesarea provides scholars with an understanding of the worldly environment in which Jesus was raised. Caesarea was the Roman capital of Judea. Dedicated to Caesar in 12 B.C., it became a busy seaport, a thriving commercial center and one of the most attractive cities of its day. Excavations have unearthed theaters, commercial harbors, Roman temples, a synagogue, political buildings, an amphitheater and the hippodrome, which was a track for horse and chariot races.

Life in Galilee: Keeping the Peace for Rome

Jesus was raised in Galilee, whose capital city was called Sepphoris. Sepphoris was fashioned after the model of Caesarea. Sepphoris had all of Caesarea's cultural trappings and many of the same buildings. It is in this environment that Jesus is born. Most scholars believe Jesus was born before Herod the Great's death in 4 B.C. and that He was raised in Galilee near Nazareth, which was near Sepphoris.

Galilee was a hotbed of radical Jewish political ideas and was also a boiling pot for insurrection. When you read comments in

The Name

the Gospels such as, "Can anything good come from Nazareth?", the Jewish elite were referring to this political atmosphere in Galilee or Nazareth, not that it was considered some backward country region. (See John 1:46.) The priests in Jerusalem worked in cooperation with Rome to keep the peace. To them, unruly Galilee could spoil their efforts at collaboration and collusion. In order to keep the *Pax Romana*, they had to acknowledge, if not in word then by their collaboration and collusion, that Caesar was God's son and Rome was God's divine instrument. I use the word collusion because the priests worked with Rome toward a secret goal. The priests paid lip service to Rome because they believed God was going to set them up as the earthly rulers when Messiah came. Of course, Rome did not believe this. The priests were collaborating with Rome to fulfill their own high priestly positions. But what they didn't realize was that, by doing so, they were misrepresenting God and Messiah's true purpose for coming to earth. God has always wanted a kingdom of priests (Exod. 19:6), but the priests in Jerusalem no longer agreed with God's total plan. They substituted some of their own plans and mixed that with what God was doing. Thus, by this collusion with Rome they defrauded both God and the people, who needed to know God's purpose for their lives. So Jesus comes into an environment of both religious and worldly strongholds. Psalm 18:25–26 says, "To the faithful you show yourself faithful, to the blameless you show yourself blameless, to the pure you show yourself pure, but to the crooked you show yourself shrewd." The priests were acting crooked and distorted.

What they didn't realize was that God was about to act very shrewdly by using Rome as a divine instrument of judgment toward satan, the world system (including Rome), Israel and her priests. This enlightens Caiaphas's prophetic statement in John 11:50, "It is better for you that one man die for the people than that the whole nation perish." Many in Galilee knew that the priests were selling out to the Roman authorities. This should be a warning to us today to avoid attachments to a world system that tries to promise us peace and safety, along with religious systems that cause us to misrepresent who God is.

The Daily Life of Jesus

The excavation of the city of Sepphoris proves that Jesus did not live like a country bumpkin.[3]

As the capital of Galilee, Sepphoris was located only four miles from Nazareth, between Cana of Galilee and Nazareth. Since Sepphoris was built and fashioned after Caesarea, it had all the trappings of Greek and Roman life, including Greek and Roman commercial, political and religious life. Excavations here have uncovered a magnificent villa. Housed in that villa was a mosaic depicting the daily Roman life in Sepphoris of an upscale community. As the capital, Sepphoris was far more than just a town. It had a thriving culture with satellite villages settled around it.

With Nazareth so close by, doubtless it was one of these satellite villages. Such findings as these have caused some theologians to rethink Jesus' life.[4]

Instead of living a sheltered life, Jesus lived near a thriving urban culture. Daily, He would have dealt with issues similar to someone living in the suburbs of New York or Atlanta. Let's take, for example, an individual living in Warwick, NY, or Conyers, GA, who must commute to work in New York City or Atlanta. There are skills that this person acquires to do these tasks. For Jesus, it would have been no different. As the oldest son, he would have learned his "father's" business. He would have worked in Sepphoris, or at least gotten supplies from there. He would have been acquainted with bargaining and trading in at least three different languages.[5] Jesus was not socially or culturally naïve, for He could not have functioned in business or his trade without being aware of both social and cultural issues.[6]

Receiving a Name from God

On every level, Jesus was willing for His heavenly Father to define and name Him. It is easy for us to believe He was changed from infinite glory to finite human baby. But it is much more difficult

The Name

to realize that He had the skills and upbringing to be a Moses and deliver the Jews from Roman rule, but chose instead to take on the name and form of a lowly peasant and servant. He had to be willing to lay down the name of urban social structure and be identified with lowly peasantry. Maybe you don't consider this difficult. So imagine that you've been born and raised in the lap of suburbia, with TV's, telephones, fax machines, computers, dishwashers, washers, dryers, microwaves and the best education your parents could afford. You know you have a call on your life from God—at least you believe so. Your church associates, parents and friends know it. Your walk with God gets closer and closer until you sense His call to travel to India and live among the poor in the streets of Calcutta. At this point you are willing and ready to go. But the God of glory still has a work to do in your life. In the future, He plans to change what and how you define yourself.

Part of the difficulty in defining God's name change in us is found in how we define God. After all, the change in our names instills a portion of God in us. If we look at God from a balanced viewpoint and we are willing to see Him as He sees Himself, this process will be easier. If we believe He can't be trusted or He is harsh, this process will take longer. (See Matthew 25:14-30.) The more willing we are to receive, the more of God is instilled in us.

Moses had the same difficulty. His name, "the son of Pharaoh's daughter," no longer defined God's purpose for his life. It wasn't until, on Mount Horeb, he met up with God in the form of a bush that burns but is not consumed, that some things started to make sense. I believe this is why the people only knew God's deeds, but Moses knew God's ways. (See Psalm 103:7.) Moses was willing to walk through the process of total identification with God as a deliverer. So he got to know His ways as well as see His deeds.

When God Redefines You

So often we are defined by where we live. Our theology is defined by those with whom we associate. We define who God is by these things also. We box God in with these ideas. So God comes in glory to redefine our ideas in the light of who He is. When we start to study God and the life of Jesus, we realize over time that there is so much more there than initially meets the eye. Nothing about Jesus or God is easy to place in a box.

For example, Jesus lived in an upscale Roman-Greek culture, but His Jewishness was never diminished.[7] Jesus grew up in a community that was rich in Jewish culture. Much like Israel today, the Jewish culture was quite diverse, with many different religious sects.[8]

One of these sects, the *Essenes*, tended to be very apocalyptic. These Jews thought Christ was coming to overthrow the Roman government through violence. The problem with such teachings is that they tell God exactly how He should close the end of the ages. At the other end of the scale of people among whom Christ lived were the more secular Jews. These were people with varying degrees of devotion to Jehovah, living out their faith, or lack of faith, in their day-to-day lives. This also is not so very different from Christianity today.

It is obvious from a cursory reading of the Gospels that Jesus' cousin, John the Baptist, leaned toward the stricter, apocalyptic teachings of Judaism. He was not an *Essene*, but his lifestyle closely resembled their way of life.[9] Jesus, like others in His community, goes to be baptized by John. For those living in Jesus' day, this says something about Jesus. It defines Him as someone who wants more of God in a radical, and possibly, apocalyptic way. And yet we see the manifest presence of God in glory redefining the peoples' ideas of Jesus' end-time teaching when He says in Matthew 5:17, "Do not think that I have come to abolish the Law or the Prophets; I have not come to abolish them but to fulfill them." While this statement may have confused those who thought Jesus to be an apocalyptic Jew, and those who thought He needed to overthrow the Roman government, we see no such struggle within Jesus. He knows exactly what, who and how His Father defines Him. As the gospel story unfolds, we see the progression in this name change from one being baptized, to miracle worker, to suffering Messiah, to

The Name

Savior to King in residence. There is never a resistant struggle from Jesus, only from the religious crowd. Only once we read that Jesus asked for the cup to pass or be removed. (See Matthew 26:39, Luke 22:42.) But even in that difficult test He says, "not as I will, but as thou wilt." (See Matthew 26:39, Mark 14:36, KJV.)

Redefining a Miracle Worker

Just like Jesus needed to change the religious crowd's idea of Messiah, God comes in glory today to change our ideas and attitudes concerning Christ. For example, let's look at the miracles. Today we view the performing of miracles as special or different. But in that day, it was believed that anybody of importance performed miracles.[10] They believed, incorrectly, that there were many other miracle workers.[11] This thought strikes us as odd. But in Christ's day it wasn't the fact that Jesus could perform miracles, but it was whom He blessed by those miracles. To the Greek, Roman and even upper-class Jewish society, important, wealthy or pious people would consider themselves the just recipients of miracles. Yet Christ targets the poor and destitute. It is unbelievable to the Roman mind that God Almighty—if they even believed in one God—would use a Jewish peasant to perform miracles for other peasants and healthy Roman citizens, alike (such as the Centurion)!

The disciples, coming from a similar background as Jesus, view Him correctly as Messiah, but consider Him come as their Messiah to conquer the Romans. Yet God gives them the opportunity to view Jesus with Moses and Elijah in glorious transforming light. (See Matthew 17:1–3.) God gives them the opportunity to consider that Jesus' name is also King of Kings and Lord of Lords.

Peter does not understand this experience immediately. But decades later, when history tells us he requests to be crucified upside-down because he is unworthy to die like the Master, I believe he has finally come to understand.

Aren't we today very much like both groups? We consider that we need to be special for miracles to take place, or we have the idea that God would only speak through the leaders in a church. After all, isn't that how the church should be seen or be named? Why would God ever use a female like Kathryn Kuhlman through which to perform miracles? Popular thinking suggests that God would not use a woman in an apostolic way to speak to future generations about a relationship with the Holy Spirit. Our attitude is that God will not manifest His glory to sinners but only the righteous. (See Isaiah 65:1.)

And we know how it's all going to end, right? After all, don't the experts get on Christian TV and tell us? I'm not trying to be sarcastic, but we need a little confronting while we sit in our perfect worlds, soaking up God's blessings and telling everybody else how to live. I'm not criticizing or singling out any particular eschatology, nor am I trying to support any particular viewpoint on the subject. Nevertheless, could it be possible for Jesus to come back in a way that will totally fulfill all Scripture, but still surprise us all? He did as much with our Jewish brethren two millennia ago. Such an event would change how we name or view ourselves, just as He forced our Jewish brethren to do some 2000 years ago.

I'm not saying He will do that. But is it possible for Him to challenge our thinking? Remember the prophet whom God sent to prepare the way for Christ's appearing? (See Luke 7:26, 27.) He was the prophet who could only prophesy one message to Israel: make straight the way of the Lord. (See Matthew 3:3; Luke 3:4.) He never performed any miracles. Even John the Baptist needed confronting about Jesus' identity. John was probably closer to God dwelling in glory than anyone else living at that time, except Jesus. Yet he still asked the question, "Are you the one who was to come, or should we expect someone else?" (Luke 7:20). Could it be that Jesus did not fit the popular idea or expectations concerning the Messiah, even of those with an inside track? Although I do believe John was also asking the question, "Am I still one called to cry from the wilderness, or am I going to receive a name change straight into glory?"

This is why God comes in glory, to confront us, to confront

The Name

our churches, to change us, and to change our ideas about what we are, what we call ourselves and who we need to be.

Redefining Messiah: Holy Sufferer to Glorious Savior, Thy Kingdom Come

The Roman Empire named itself as being the kingdom of God. In other words, it considered itself the kingdom of God. That was its self-proclaimed name and identity. It permitted a plurality of religion and a tolerance for the adherents of various different sects. However, when you spoke about government, God, country and the world as one institution, you were speaking about Rome. If you were not speaking about Rome, you were considered an insurrectionist and, as such, worthy of death.[12]

Today we view the kingdom of God as being separate from our government or governments. My question has always been *why?* Jesus came to restore all.

The Scripture tells us that Jesus set His face like a flint to go to the cross. (See Isaiah 50:5–7; Luke 9:51.) After reading the Gospels, we cannot see any other end for Christ. After all, He is born under Roman captivity, and, in fact, Rome ruled the temple in Jerusalem. Oh, maybe it didn't rule how things were to be sacrificed, but there were standing orders between Caiaphas, the high priest, and the prefect, Pilate, on how to handle local dissidents.[13]

Frankly speaking, Jesus is nothing more to them than an annoying local dissident. This challenges our thinking today, because we want the death of Jesus to be named as bigger than life itself, and by purchasing our redemption, it is. But Father God did not intend for it to look that way back then.

At the time of that Passover there were hundreds of thousands, possibly even millions, in and around Jerusalem. I doubt Christ's death immediately changed the lives of a great portion of them. It isn't until about forty years later, when the temple is destroyed, that things change for the Jews. The crucifixion site itself is high on a hill. At that time it did not allow for thousands or even hundreds to be present. While Jesus' fame and name spread abroad, the effect the Romans wanted to have was one of warning and example. It would be like our large prisons today. Most of them are located away from the general population, but you can see their barbed wire from the highway or some other street. Yet you would not stop to stare, except to cast a quick glance. It's something with which you really don't want to be identified.

What was Rome so paranoid about? What were the priests in Jerusalem so nervous about if Jesus was, in fact, a fraud? We honestly forget that, from the beginning with Adam and Eve, God wanted rulers that would represent Him on earth. He wanted them to bring His kingdom to earth. We see Him confirm this desire when He commands Moses in Exodus 19:6, "you will be for me a kingdom of priests and a holy nation." In Revelation 5:10 (AMP), it says, "And You have made them a kingdom [royal race] and priests to our God and they shall reign [as kings] over the earth!" (See also Revelation 1:6, 20:6, 1 Peter 2:5, Isaiah 61:6.) The priests in Jerusalem knew they were supposed to be rulers and priests. Rome knew what the priests wanted. Rome knew what Rome wanted. God knew what was going to happen. God was going to have the people that would be under His rulership and His name as King of Kings and Lord of Lords. They would be men and women that would be faithful rulers and priests, as their High Priest and King had been faithful. What satan needed to do was stop God's kingdom in glory from coming in substance to the earth. He had to get the people who were supposed to be God's faithful priests to come in agreement with another kingdom on earth. It had worked once with Adam and Eve; he figured it would work again.

Of course what the enemy didn't realize was that he was walking into God's plan from the foundation of the earth. So, from an ordinary method of dealing with a criminal who is named or labeled as traitor for the crime of claiming to be king, God changes Jesus' name to Christ, Son of the living God. He was murdered at the hands of the captivity into which He was born. He knew all their history and was, Himself, able to be a leader

The Name

among even the intellectual elite. He now allows Almighty God to identify Him with the poor, the sick and the destitute, even though His name in heaven is King of Kings and Lord of Lords. He died a death defined by His contemporaries as meaningless and ordinary (the cross was Rome's electric chair). As a result, the glory of God is now able to infuse us, surround us and change us.

I wonder that God hasn't looked over the centuries at how many times He gave His people–Israel and the Church–the chance to rule, and He had to know we were not ready.[14] When we allow our own names to be identified with the suffering humanity around us and we are willing to lay down our own fame, God will begin to be able to trust us to be rulers. If we can come into agreement with God's plans and not the world's, we will be ready to be faithful rulers and faithful priests. First we must be willing to allow our names to be changed.

Our Name-Changes

Since Jesus had no ungodly human strongholds to address, Jacob becomes an important example to us of how God dismantles our human strongholds. Every *theophany* appearance teaches us something about God in glory. Jacob's experience is amazing, because he literally wrestles with God–and lives! Jacob must learn that his strivings and self-protection cannot save him. Only God can.

Jacob's story is replete with the examples of his resistance to God's intention of changing his name. Unlike Jesus, we all resist. We resist the changes God wants to make in our "names" or in how we identify ourselves.

Jacob is probably the best single example of this resistance and God's direct response. As individuals, each one of us holds some resistance to God changing who we are. It usually starts long before salvation, sometimes while we are yet children. Jacob realized and relied upon his skills of persuasion. If that persuasion crossed the line into deception, well then, the ends justified the means. (See Genesis 27:12, 20, 24, 35.) In Jacob's case, I would definitely classify his heart-attitude as stubborn or idolatrous. It didn't change with age either. He may have mellowed some, but he was always trying to persuade people in order to make events go his way. Remember the spotted and speckled sheep and goats of Laban's herd? (See Genesis 30:25-43.) If there is a stronghold of stubbornness or manipulation, control and rebellion (i.e. witchcraft) always goes hand in hand. (See 1 Samuel 15:23.)

We looked at control and manipulation—which are witchcraft and idolatry—in chapter 2. Because we looked at Jesus first, the resistance or stronghold may not be as obvious. The resistance is to change, itself. The stronghold is a resistance to God's changing us from how we identify ourselves to how He identifies us and names us. You may accurately say this would show itself as control and manipulation, which is the same overall resistance we saw to God when He is manifested in glory. But when we speak specifically about the name of God in glory, we are speaking about identity or the identity of God.

When Christ came to earth, He came to seek and save that which was lost—and much was lost. In order to be found, it takes change. We must change from our lost state to a found state. We may resist this change in our identities. Because of this resistance, we seek to manipulate and control situations around us. The resistance is our desire not to change. We are all willing to mouth a particular change. But we have areas or places in our personalities and attitudes that do not want to become totally dead in Christ, and that do not want to become totally submitted to the identity or name of God. Hence, our example of Jacob's name change. He went from a stubborn God-wrestler to a prevailing prince with the Almighty.

When God Allows Our Means to Justify His End

In Jacob's particular case, "usurper" defines who he was before God changed his name. What's amazing about Jacob's example is that God played along for so long. And isn't that the case with us

The Name

also? God placed Jacob alongside a man with an even nastier control and manipulation problem—his uncle Laban. It may have been with the hope that Jacob would see a portion of himself in the situation and chose to change. But Jacob's response was to out manipulate the manipulator!

We all know that it is scientifically impossible to alter the genetic structure of an animal by allowing it to breed in front of certain tree branches. We all know the story. (See Genesis 30.) Jacob asked Laban for speckled and spotted sheep and goats. When Laban agreed, Jacob placed the animals before certain manipulated tree branches, and all the young came forth as either speckled or spotted, enlarging Jacob's herds. I've heard the argument that certain acids from these different trees may have leeched into the drinking water to produce this outcome. This has never been borne out scientifically. I believe the real reason that Jacob prospered with his breeding program was because God Almighty prospered him. The only other solid theological argument that can be made is that of faith—Jacob believed it would work. But the overriding reason that it worked was that it went right along with God's plan for Jacob's life.

God played along with Jacob's manipulative ways just to bring him to the end of his own rope! How often do we think that God prospers us because of something we do? It doesn't have to be compulsive, workaholic-type stuff either. It could just be an attitude of self-righteousness. You know, the kind that says, "I don't smoke or chew, and I don't go with those who do." These attitudes or works of the flesh extend to most ministries today. I've seen lots of ministers who have taught the flesh to sing, preach, teach and even prophesy! Very few of us can see the difference. What has caught my attention over the years is watching God prosper these people. This observation has brought me to a better understanding of the graciousness of our God. But this prosperity has nothing to do with the flesh. God is doing the prospering to accomplish His plan and His purpose. There are times, though, when He pulls the rug up, right from under these efforts. He will even allow the efforts themselves to be the snare, as in Jacob's case, to finally teach us that He will not give His glory to another. (See Isaiah 42:8.)

Stubbornness in Jacob's Heart

Everything Jacob goes through before Genesis 32 is just a learning experience. I feel it's as if God is getting Jacob to a place where there is nothing left but God and Jacob. There is much prophetic typology in Genesis 31–32 concerning Laban chasing Jacob. This includes the witness heaps, angels meeting Jacob and, finally, Jacob dividing his camps into two large companies. (See Genesis 31:45–53; 32:1–2.) You can read the Scriptures for yourself. What I would like to draw our attention to is Genesis 32:4–5. Jacob uses the products of his fleshly efforts to persuade Esau. Lest you misunderstand what I call fleshly efforts, let me explain.

In the hands of other individuals these goats and sheep would be nothing but barter. I have seen people in business function in the Spirit with earthly items in a far holier way than some Christians function with what should be spiritual items. Our motives and attitudes matter. The item, event or effort has nothing to do with the work of the flesh. For God, it is always a matter of the heart.

Remember what God says about money? It is not money itself that is evil, but the love of money that is the root of all evil. (See 1 Timothy 6:10.) So Jacob tries to persuade Esau with these gifts. He surmised if that fleshly plan failed, he would divide the camp into two as a back up. He never realized that God has been in the details all along.

Genesis 32:7 says, "In great fear and distress Jacob divided the people." I'm not knocking Jacob for his efforts. If I had done to Esau what Jacob did many years before, I might have also been tempted to do the same. What is interesting is Jacob's prayer (verses 9–12). On the one hand, he functions totally according to his name or his perception of himself when he asks God to bless his fleshly works. On the other hand, he repeats God's Spirit-led plan for his life, asking the Lord to fulfill it. In Jacob's case they

The Name

happened to be the same. That is not always the case for us today.

Today, as God manifests His presence in glory to abide in different places around the world, He falls on flesh—sometimes carnal, sometimes spiritual, sometimes a mixture of both. This unfortunate pollution of the glory of God can only turn out two ways. We either remain resistant to the changes we will thereafter experience or we will allow God to change us.

In Jacob's case, God allowed his earthly efforts to be of no consequence. Jacob still doesn't realize this yet. God must get him alone. (See Genesis 32:24.) The wrestling that we see taking place is just an indication of the flesh and Spirit struggle that God finds, even when He moves in glory upon blood washed saints. It is by no accident that Jacob is marked or made lame by God in the strongest and largest joint in the human body. This is the painful result of resistance, even in an eventual God-appointed name change. I wonder sometimes what it will take for God to get His people to the end of all our busy-ness in order to get us totally alone with Him. What mark will be left on us if we struggle? I can remember one pastor many years ago saying, "when God shows up, just say *yes*." That's good advice for all of us. The reason I believe this mark has to be evident for Jacob is twofold. Remember all the witness typology in Genesis 31 and the beginning of 32? There had to be a witness for a prophetic change of the name of this people. The witness is Jacob's lameness. It witnessed to everyone that, even in lameness, God can make princes that overcome through Him. This example doesn't stop with Israel concerning God's glory. It also extends to the body of Christ as she becomes infused with the very glory of God.

A New Name

The second reason for the mark is for Jacob individually. Remember at this point he still thinks his gifts and other efforts are going to save him, hence the struggle. Jacob would need a reminder in the flesh of how big God is. He could no longer run away. What word does God speak over him when He gives him a new name? Instead of Jacob, the usurper, supplanter and heel grabber—the name that speaks of fleshly struggle—he is now called a princely struggler with God that overcomes!

At this point, this word still awaits future fulfillment. Unfortunately for our limited understanding God usually speaks about the future as though it already exists now. We all struggle with what God says and does. After all, His ways are not our ways. Everything God has created has, in some way, disagreed with the way He created it, starting with satan as Lucifer in the heavenlies.

The difference between struggling and usurping is the willingness to die to our own desires and to come in line with God. To struggle is not necessarily to sin. But to rebel in the struggle and want to go our own way is sin. How many students of the Bible have we seen struggle with certain theological concepts of God? Some put the struggle off to the side, continue to obey and believe God, until one day, He answers their questions. Others, though, struggle to the point of despair or unbelief, though teachers and those around them try to intervene.

When the God of glory moves upon us and He brings us through the name-change, we each must go up to a new level in Him. None of us wants to change, especially when God blows change through us. We wrestle. We refuse to let go until He promises blessing, just like Jacob did. He definitely brings blessing. However, the wrestle, depending upon how great our resistances are, will leave a mark—especially when we refuse to let go of one glorious level as God desires to bring us to another. When we hold on, making demands as we go, a mark is left as a reminder. This is similar, but not for the same reasons, to the after-flow of God's presence that we see in Samson's life. This after-flow is similar to the anointing left in some churches or other places where God was manifest in glory, but has now gone. It is a witness. In some cases it is a witness that God will return. In other cases it is a witness of struggling. In Jacob's case it was both.

The mark is the witness or reminder of Jacob's continual resistance to God's name-change. And yet, Jacob's changed name is a witness that God in glory will return to Jacob's seed. This should

The Name

give hope to all those that name the name of Christ, who have experienced God in glory in the past. It should give hope for His future return in glory if they overcome their stronghold struggles. We really don't see Jacob starting to comprehend the dynamics of this until Genesis 34 when Shechem defiles Dinah. Now we see the deceit of Jacob rise up in his sons as they kill the Shechemites. (See Genesis 34:13-30.) Again, the deceit of Israel's flesh (Jacob's sons) is overridden by the future plan of God in keeping the nation pure, both spiritually and genetically. (See Genesis 34:3.) It would seem that Jacob is more concerned with being attacked as a result of the double-cross of his sons. In this case, the sins of the father have passed to the sons. But by Genesis 49:5-7, Jacob speaks his thoughts concerning the deceitfulness of his sons and his desire to have no part in it. By now he knows only God can protect him. (See Genesis 35:5, 48:15, 16.) None of his own efforts will do.

The Apostle Paul

Before we go on to the corporate change of name or identity as a result of God showing up in glory, it may benefit us to quickly mention the apostle Paul. Paul has a *theophany* experience of the Lord Jesus Christ while he is on his way to murder and plunder the church. While some may argue that this appearance was not a *theophany*, remember the definition is "an appearance or manifestation of God or Christ that the individual can understand." While Christ may not have appeared in the flesh, something appeared in this realm, judging by the reaction of the men around Saul. To say Saul was functioning in the flesh is an understatement. Like Jacob, he is also marked in the flesh—but for a much shorter period of time than Jacob—by being made blind. By the end of that week, he no longer resists Jesus and eventually receives a name change. For those who believe Paul's thorn in the flesh was related to this experience, the Bible does not say, so I will remain silent. (See 2 Corinthians 12:7.)

Jesus' appearance to Saul changes how he defines himself. Saul means "asked." The name Paul means "to cease or quit." Saul asked, "Who are you, Lord?" (See Acts 9:5.) And God answered by allowing Paul to cease working in the flesh. The great apostle lays down his revered place in the Jewish hierarchy and identifies himself with a band of maligned and misunderstood Jews. For the sake of Christ, he then lays aside all to preach to the Gentiles. The church is forever changed by Paul's pen as a result of his willingness to accept God's name-change in glory.

God's Name-Change Over Us Corporately

God in glory changes the name and, thereby, the identity of His people as a corporate body. Several examples of this exist in Scripture. They read like the ebb and flow of waves over the shores of history. From Adam and Eve to Jesus, the suffering servant to the Lord of Glory, God has used them to give new meaning to the God-kind of living we need. From the first couple of faith, Abram and Sarai (Abraham and Sarah), to the first apostle of faith (Saul to Paul), God used His manifest presence to change them.

Jacob seems to comprehend this when he changes Benjamin's name from son of distress or sorrow (Benoni) to son of the right hand. There is a saying, "As the leaders go, so goes the nation." As Jacob struggled to walk God's way, so the Hebrew slaves struggled to be named Israel, which means "a princely ruler with God that overcomes!" The Egyptians had always referred to them as the Hebrews. It is an ethnic nomenclature, but the word "slave" was usually attached to it. In fact, one didn't even have to use the word "slave." In Egypt, as the years went by, "Hebrew" and "slave" had become synonymous. Thousands of years of deliverance by God have changed that for us today. We no longer view Hebrew and slave as the same. But they did then. God provided the deliverance of this former identity through the glory cloud and fire to safely lead them. The intention of God was to do this quickly. Unfortunately, the resistance of the slave mentality produced forty years of needless struggle. Sometimes I wonder whether, in more than two thousand years of Christian historical struggles, we have not outdone Israel's resistances. The good news is that Israel did become a nation of God's people.

Renaming Our Personal History

It is during that history that we catch glimpses of God in glory anointing His people synonymously with His name. We've talked about God's name and character, or nature, as being one with His glory. He wants to give each one of us a new name associated with His holy name. It amazes me how God decides to put each one of us in a certain environment that, to some extent, defines who we become as people. When I say that God wants to redefine us, I do not mean He does so by totally negating the environment into which He births us.

We talk about historically catching a glimpse of God anointing His people—and that's the point. History is a certain environment for each one of us. What I have lived through is different than what you have lived through. God knew growing up with a slave mentality would not help Moses deliver a group of slaves. Moses had to be in an environment of his own personal history of freedom that would give him the self-esteem and confidence to do the job. Yet that environment of Egyptian luxury could not bring any of its own baggage with it. God would have to give Moses a redefining experience with His glory. This is also true of those saints that satan has attempted to destroy at an early age through abuse, sufferings and hardships. God wants to give each one of us, no matter how difficult or how good our past personal environments may have been, a redefining experience with Him in manifest glory. In this way we can become the mighty people of deliverance that God wants us to be. This personal history of change usually takes place before we see a corporate change. Moses had to be changed before Israel could experience change.

BEYOND STRONGHOLDS

Whirlwind Worship: God Coming In Glory

Even the tabernacles and temples changed their geographical places throughout history. Once Moses had built the tabernacle, the glory cloud or fire resided over it, and when the tabernacle moved, it also moved. (See Exodus 40:34–36.) We also see this when Solomon dedicated the temple in Jerusalem. (See 2 Chronicles 5:13–14, 7:1–2.) The ark, the glory cloud, the temple and the name are either mentioned interchangeably or as one. (See 1 Chronicles 13:6; 2 Chronicles 6:5–10, 20, 24, 26, 32–34, 38; 2 Chronicles 7:16, 20.)

While the tabernacle and temples never changed their names, they did experience a change of location and identity in how they functioned. The tabernacle or temples were places of worship in warfare. They had God's name or banner over them in battle during temple ministry. The biggest change of identity in worship inside the temples and tabernacle—along with the change of location and a change of outward structure—came when David prepared for the temple of Solomon to be built.

We all know the external change of location quite well. It is the internal change in the style and structure of worship that we don't see as obviously. Before this time, it was God's good pleasure to have Moses' understanding in worship, as God flew the banner of His name over the tabernacle.

But when David came on the scene this changed. We call this change the tabernacle of David. While the banner of God's name remained the same, God's people were changed into a worshiping army through a new understanding of worship-warfare because of the implementation of David's tabernacle.

There is an order or foundation in place for God's glorious name to reside. While Moses was given an order for the making of the tent of meeting with all its articles and people of service (Levites), there came a time when God wanted the entire nation to become involved in prophetic worship. We see Him giving His people the understanding of a special place where He can be

The Name

found, according to a certain order in sight, sound, people, voice and function. This is called temple order.

We later see the same spiritual imagery applied to worship in the heavenlies (See Ezekiel 10:4–5, 43:1–5; Isaiah 6:1–7; Revelation 4) and in the upper room. (See Acts 2:1–2.) While the beginning of it all started with Adam and Eve walking with God in the Garden, strongholds within our human nature (sin) allow us to see God's part in restoring fellowship. (See Genesis 1:27; 2:8; 3:8) There is a progressive order to it, and God in glory is always on the scene each time.

Bringing the Ark Home to Jerusalem: The Tabernacle of David

David fails miserably when he decides to bring the ark home for the first time. (See 1 Chronicles 13.) He thinks he is doing all the right things. As a matter of fact, it looks a little like we do things today. He counsels with all the right people. They all assemble and start to dance, shout, praise and sing. (See 1 Chronicles 13:4, 5, 8.) They had read just enough of the Torah to think that they have got it, and there they go—off to the finish line with God's presence as the prize and God's name as their banner.

It's not until God breaks out of the boxed-in order in which they've attempted to place Him that they realize that something is off. (See 1 Chronicles 13:11.) It's their failure that teaches them to turn, humble themselves, confess and decide to do it God's way. Thank God, when we repent He calls us His children and continues to abide with us. This incident produced what the Bible calls the tabernacle of David. It isn't so much a place as it is a Spirit-led order of functioning in the army of the Lord. In this way God literally changes how we identify with Him in worship as an army.

It isn't the purpose of this book to teach on the tabernacle of David. There are already good resource materials out there on this subject. Certain phrases or words used in Scripture let us know that we are looking at the Holy Spirit's order for worship. Whenever

BEYOND STRONGHOLDS

you read about the sounding of instruments, the priests being set in their divisions or following the order prescribed by David or David's tent, we are looking at what we term the tabernacle of David. God always uses the shepherds, or kings, and prophets to institute His order for temple worship. Once it's in place, everyone functions in his or her respective role. In fact, it is never instituted by any other people but the kings and the prophets (apostles and prophets) throughout the entire Bible. (See Deuteronomy 18:15; Exodus 7:1; Luke 16:29, 31–e.g., Moses and Aaron.)

David, along with his prophets Gad and Nathan, originally instituted the order for Solomon's temple, and Hezekiah followed that same order some three hundred years later in 2 Chronicles 29:25. Nehemiah and Ezra were joined by the prophets Haggai and Zechariah in Ezra 5:1-2; 6:14. And of course, the early church was led and set up by the apostles and prophets. (See Ephesians 2:20.)

There are three overriding concepts for God's prescribed order of worship. It is Spirit led in prophetic sound, with appropriate leadership in place for warfare. This is so that God in glory, as the Commander in Chief and our King, finds a place to rest. In other words, the Holy Spirit anoints a declaration through voice, music and sound for God's name to rest on us. The Psalms read as a songbook for this order of worshiping as the army of the Lord.

As I've researched this subject I've often wondered, when we look at the tabernacle of David, whether we aren't looking at a nitty-gritty human perspective of the cloud of glory that the other prophets saw from more of a heavenly perspective. In other words, God in glory shows up when His prescribed and ordained order is in place. Order in worship, prophetic ministry and Word, with His prescribed leadership, will form an army in power for Him. This is the base of the glory cloud. As we look up, we see the rest of the heavenly host also engaged in warfare and praise. On top of it all is the Lord God Almighty–Jehovah–dwelling and coming to kick out enemy usurpers and to reside as King of Kings and Lord of Lords. (See 1 Chronicles 16:37, 39; 17:1-3, 15; 2 Chronicles 5:12; Ezra 5:1-2; Ezekiel 1:3, 3:17, 42:13; Isaiah 6:1-7; Acts 2:15, 16; Revelation 21:22-23; 22:9.)

The Name

In this way we go forth in battle with Christ's name, and the Holy Spirit maintains our battalion ranks as Father God directs. When we function in line with God's prescribed ways, He has an orderly pathway to come in glory. He always comes in glory according to His order, as is seen throughout the entire Bible from Old to New Testament. In this way, we become a full-time worshiping army, just like God showed David, along with the prophets long ago.

Restoration of Whirlwind Worship: Restoring David's Fallen Tent

Nevertheless, in Amos 9:11 the prophet declares by the Spirit of the Lord, "In that day I will restore David's fallen tent." I believe this is the day for David's tent to be restored. God wishes to restore, and even do a new thing, in our worship systems. In order for something to be restored, it has to be gone, destroyed or broken. We have to be willing to admit that something is broken before it can be repaired.

Sometimes certain things can still function in a state of disrepair. My husband works on automobiles. He comes home with stories of how far people will abuse their vehicles, even though these cars are still functioning. Have you ever seen folks drive a car on three tires? I have. It isn't a pretty sight. If I remember correctly, I may have done it once or twice myself. The manufacturers did not intend for that vehicle to function that way when they gave it a name. We as human beings, in our fallen natures, tend to abuse things. Have you ever known a child to need lessons on how to bang up and break her toys? Children know how to bang things up without any help.

God did not intend for us to function in worship impaired when He named us. So He comes to us with a supernatural order for approaching Him through His Son. Some enter in, and others refuse. He then invites those who receive Christ into a marvelous and burden-lifting way of worshiping Him, as He teaches us how to be an army. He ordains an apostle or pastor as a head for order, direction and covering. He ordains a prophet for insight to direction. As the other fivefold gifts come alongside, the army is able to reproduce. Singers, musicians and intercessors are ordained for warfare. Other leadership, including elders and deacons, are put in place, also, so the work goes on and the army marches forward.

There are those who receive and enter into God's order and those who do not. The excuses for not entering in are as varied as the instruments used—human and musical. He comes by Himself in glory to change these attitudes and to rename us. When God is getting ready to take us to new levels in glory, He will always require us to restore areas where "David's tent" has fallen into disrepair in our midst.

Why We Don't Enter In

Sometimes we do not want to change because we have become familiar with His presence, like a child with a toy (remember Uzzah?). (See 1 Chronicles 13:9, 10.) We have a saying in America: "If it ain't broke, don't fix it." Because we still feel His presence during worship we think everything is okay. What we don't realize is that God's glory cloud is a whirlwind that literally sweeps you off your feet. If we settle for something less during our corporate worship time because we are afraid of the whirlwind or afraid of the hard work it takes to change, we will continue to be swept away as our enemies fight us on earth. God designed it to be the other way around. As we worship in His prescribed manner we become incense on His altar, housed in whirlwind worship. Because we're in the center of the glory cloud we are at rest and peace with Him. On the outside of that whirlwind it is our enemies that are blown away.

I am not implying that every church needs to have the same ten-piece orchestra with a certain number of singers and that special worship leader. It's fine if God has provided that. Worship isn't about music anyway. It's about the King being in residence. As God moves by His name He is one with His glory, with His throne (place of worship), with Christ and with the Holy Spirit.

The Name

His presence and knowledge accompany Him. He desires to be one with His people! That should be mind-boggling to all of us. It is when we are in that place of oneness with Him that our strongholds become the most obvious.

He comes in glory to give us a new name or identity while using the environment we are in to make us into specialized vessels for His glory. We may not have arrived yet, but like the apostle Paul said, we are pressing on toward the high calling in Christ. God Almighty shows up in glory to change how we run our churches or worship Him, changing what and how we think of ourselves. As He changed His temples over the centuries, He wishes to change us. Likewise, He changed the rabbis' teachings concerning who, what or how Messiah should come, which eventually changed their names to be identified with Christ as Christians. He never leaves the foundation of Scripture, but changes us to conform to the totality of that foundation.

Many times He finds resistance to this change. Sunday after Sunday we continue with the same songs and format until, ultimately, the vehicle may work, but it has fallen into disrepair and it needs restoration. It needs an identity change. Could God ever break into a church's worship service with a prophetic song of the Lord from the congregation, or would such a song from an individual be viewed as out of order? How about prophesying on an instrument? Would that person be seen as trying to go solo? Do you always have to have your songs lined up on Sunday mornings like ducks in a row? If one of those sweet little handmaidens came up to your worship leader with a song from God, would the pastor reprimand that worship leader for allowing her to sing it? How about when the person that everyone knows has a prophetic anointing comes up to the pastor during worship and says, "God would like us to take a prophetic offering." These are special offerings in which God prophetically teaches a congregation something new about its people as they place their gifts in the baskets. (See Mark 12:41–44.) I am not talking about abusing this gift or prophesying for money.

Does the pastor fear because this kind of thing could get out of control? Perhaps a discerning Davidic shepherd or shepherdess will say, "I'll cover you; go for it." These are just some of the minor changes He wants us to make. There are many other "strange" things God wants to do in our houses of worship—and all of them have Biblical applications when we see God in glory with His name written upon our hearts in whirlwind worship. I'm not saying these things can't suffer abuse. I'm not saying we shouldn't always support such actions with Scripture and the direction of the Holy Spirit, for we should. But this is precisely why God in glory shows up—to burn off the dross and place the fire of God in hearts. He wants us not only to fear His awesome power, but also to discern godly order, not man's order.

I think one reason we do not function with this kind of spontaneity is because fivefold ministry would have to be flowing in the heart of God's worship with such spiritual gifts. It is very difficult for some pastors to admit that they do not spiritually sense whether someone from the congregation may be used by God to change an aspect of the worship. Usually this discernment is given to the prophet. But very few churches allow a prophetic minister or someone God has designated with similar gifts to come and help shoulder the work of the Lord. Because those churches do not have a fivefold prophet in residence, Father God will use whomever is available to hear from Him.

I don't want to leave the impression that prophets always know what God wants all the time. God often either speaks, remains silent or sends just a "plain old saint" to bless, correct or put us back on track.

Titles and Treasures

We may also resist God coming in glory to change our names because we enjoy what we have called ourselves and what others call us. It is sad to admit, but many churches give titles, and, though I am not against titles, an individual's spiritual calling has nothing to do with the title given them.

God told Gideon he was a mighty warrior. (See Judges 6:12.)

The Name

Yet Israel told Gideon his clan was the weakest in Manasseh, and his title was the least in the whole family. (See Judges 6:15.)

In our modern day church experience I think we get it reversed. I think we give great titles to people whose spiritual gifts and submission, one to the other, is the least in the place! Sometimes I wonder if we don't give great titles to those who are not mature enough to handle them. Another unfortunate practice we have is placing people into the fivefold ministry who have not had the death, burial and resurrection experience of our Lord Jesus Christ evident in their lives. In other words, they have not developed a foundation on which His name may reside (as we discussed in chapter 4 concerning mantles). I don't mean that they die physically—although physical sickness may accompany such an experience. What I mean is a real expression of a life experience that shows those over them that, unless God raised that person up, it would have been totally impossible for them to overcome. And through it all they were willing to allow God to take them through the process.

It is, however, easier in smaller churches to use this as a criterion, because if true change has not taken place it will become evident a lot quicker. In larger churches many people come in with wonderful stories, but the church is so large no one ever gets to check on the true heart motives of these people. Sometimes what they need is counseling for continuous inner healing, because their motives are not really obvious to them. My experience has been that those called in spiritual leadership over them (not necessarily church political leadership) will be given information by the Holy Spirit on how to help these ministers. However, if this is not done and they are placed in a position of leadership, I have found that most pastors will not remove them or make them sit out for the personal time of ministry that the Holy Ghost is requiring.

Another reason that I think we resist God in this area is because deep down we realize that our names will be changed forever. No longer will people look at the church or the leadership as those nice, sweet people on such and such a street. Instead, we'll be considered that crazy bunch trying to turn the world upside-down! This happened to the early church, as well. (See Acts 2:9, 19:9, 23; 24:14.)

Additionally, we often feel there is always a possibility of financial ruin. And you'd better be equipped for spiritual warfare! The devil hates to see us enter into our destinies by letting God change our names and identities.

If you feel for some reason or another that you cannot be a candidate for God to move upon you in glory to change your name, just remember that God delights in doing the unusual and the extraordinary, and He delights in doing it with very usual and ordinary people. The only issue is obedience. Israel left Egypt, its fruit, foods and culture. They identified so much with the slave label Egypt had given them that they easily accepted a slave mentality, even when they were set free. The Israel of Christ's time also refused to let her name be identified with the Messiah Jesus. She was afraid of losing her position in the world, so she came into agreement with Rome and suffered for it.

I pray that we will not fear losing our revered places within our communities, so we can come in agreement with what Christ desires to do in His Church. The Lord came from glory to take Israel out of her comfortable position and change her attitude and identity. If He desired and still desires to do it for them, He desires to do it for us also. May we all say *Maranatha*–Come Lord Jesus!

And all of us, mirroring with unveiled faces the glory of the Lord, are being reshaped into that image, changed from glory to glory by the Lord's Spirit.
—2 Corinthians 3:18, The Unvarnished New Testament

Chapter Eight

HIS IMAGE IN HIS PEOPLE

This chapter will look at God coming in glory to mankind, His people, and the human strongholds that He will find when He gets there. We will look specifically at the stronghold of gender and racial bias. When gender bias and racial prejudice are present in the hearts of a church's leadership and members, there's a good possibility a religious spirit is affecting them. It is quite possible that at that point, when such a spirit has found a place in the hearts of God's people, it will invite a Jezebel spirit to come with it. A Jezebel spirit will then produce the devil's desires in God's people, sidetracking and splitting God's people in two.

Several conditions are present that allow this to happen. In Chapters 3 and 4 we looked at the stronghold conditions that encourage a Jezebel spirit. They are offenses and unbalanced spirit-soul and body issues that can encourage stronghold attitudes against God's Word and the people that represent that Word.

What encourages a religious spirit is similar but slightly different. This spirit absolutely needs a Jezebel spirit to reproduce the devil's plans. We see this evidenced in Ahab and Jezebel in the Old Testament and the appearance of both Babylon and Jezebel in the New Testament. A religious spirit affects people who are ordained by God to perform a task. Instead, they decide to do whatever is in their own minds to do, not what God desires to be done. Ahab and Jezebel both functioned under the covering of a religious spirit. Babylon and Jezebel are both religious spirits named in the New Testament. Ahab and Jezebel had slightly different needs than what we see in the New Testament, but the effect of their ministry was the same. The effect of these spirits is death to the prophets and a setback of God's plans for His people. A religious spirit, which would also include Jezebel spirits, needs our judgmental minds in order to steal the authority that was given to us by God over the face of the earth. Our sinful judgmental attitudes will provide legal access for it to attack us.

Since the devil was never given any authority over the earth by God, he has no tools for the earth. He needs tools adaptable for earth to complete his job. The tools he seeks to use are the gifts given to us by God to fulfill our destinies on earth. Once he uses us to provide him with an excuse to be on earth through his lies, he can then steal our authority. Armed with what he's stolen from us, he can go about reproducing, as it were, his own desires, in opposition to God's plan. In light of the previous definition of a religious spirit, we can see that the whole human race can fall subject to these spirits if the impure motives of our hearts are not constantly being exposed by the Holy Spirit.

These religious demons would prefer to work in and through those in leadership in order to enact real change in a church. The two specific conditions that support their activity are our judgmental gender biases and our failure to have the mind of Christ. Throughout history, up to the present, we have functioned with these spirits because of our mind-sets, and we haven't recognized it. A religious spirit needs God's people to substitute their own minds and desires instead of living by the mind of Christ. Christ is our only substitution. Because of our failure to implement the mind of Christ, we can function with judgmental gender biases that will always open the spiritual doors for judgmental racial biases. Both of these conditions can operate together at one time, because they support and encourage one another.

His Image in His People

Radioactive Pollution: Targeting the Body of Christ and Her Leaders

All of us live in a state of imperfection as we learn to be more Christ-like. We all experience seasons of self-examination when we realize that our minds are not renewed in Christ in one area or another. When the Holy Spirit reveals to us that we are being too judgmental towards women, we can repent. But if the God of glory has already moved upon us and we are unwilling to change, an environment of spiritual pollution can result, called tamei, as we discussed in chapters one and four.

In the Old Testament, when we see the words "tainted" or "polluted" used concerning the temple, its vessels or people, many times we are looking at the Hebrew word *tamei*. Modern scholars have found that the only word that adequately describes this for us today is radioactive pollution. Literally, it means "a radioactively charged environment that is so toxic that it sets up conditions that chase the God of glory away."[1]

We don't realize how far we have fallen because of sin and how different our ideas are of God in heaven from what heaven is really like. We don't realize how toxic we have become as humans. This is why Christ's blood was shed.

What turns an already sin-filled environment into a polluted *tamei* environment is substitution. In the spirit realm pollution has many devastating ramifications. The first is separation from God, because our pollution chases Him away. The second is the separation or divisions that arise between each other because of our sin. Christ's blood paid the price for this contamination. But what happens when the devil has deceived us into believing that we're actually following God's Word in our judgmental bigotry? We never ask for forgiveness, and a polluted *tamei* environment remains. The devil can then seduce us into substituting some portion of his own desire for God's total and best plan.

Substitution starts out small and it looks very good. Remember how good that fruit looked to Eve? Adam had to talk himself out of following God's Word. He exchanged God's desires for his own.

BEYOND STRONGHOLDS

After they crucified Christ, the priests must have continued to look good with politics as usual in the temple. Priest-craft is simply politics as usual. Priest-craft is nothing more than leaders functioning under a religious spirit. We begin substituting our own understanding, or minds, and desires somewhere along the way.

Over time this environment brings disaster, and we never even perceive it. When Christians substitute their own plans and ideas for God's, they subtly abandon their relationships with Jesus and fail to live with their first love. Judgmentalism between the members of Christ's body becomes much easier when we've lost sight of our first love. This judgment separates the ranks of an army, making it ineffective against the devil. The devil knows that if things start looking too desperate, we will cry out to God and He will hear us. So he still allows things to seem okay—until it's too late.

Substitution's Effects

It starts by substituting our own plans, or our mind's desires, for God's and then calling it God's will. We then use our spiritual armor and the gifts given by God. Because they are our God-ordained gifts, the anointing of the Holy Spirit seems to fall, which we then mistake for God's approval. All the while, though, what we have really done is come into agreement with controlling, religious spirits (Babylon). This, in turn, mixes the anointing of the Holy Spirit with our soulish minds.

Now that our soulish minds, or our flesh, are involved, the devil can gain access into what was originally intended by God to be holy. In this way, we set up ideas, systems and programs within the church to protect our man-made ideas. Stronghold fortresses can now be set up within entire churches, allowing the devil to set up camp. If we would repent and change we would be set free. Because we don't, a *tamei* environment has been created. This environment eventually produces both spiritual and physical drought, famine, divisions and strife. It will not take long for sexual sins, especially ones committed against women, to start manifesting. Now a climate is ripe for bondage and imprisonment of half of the army of the Lord (the women) and for ethnic division.

It's not difficult to understand how opinions, attitudes, resistances and the demonic hindrances housed in those resistances can establish themselves in the very people who house the glory of God. Satan deeply hates God's people and will stop at nothing in his cunningly malevolent zeal to destroy them. His ability to kill, steal and destroy is directly linked to his lies (John 10:10). We humans don't always discern the lies. Many times these lies are presented as attitudes, character habits or opinions—especially opinions concerning the Bible. By hiding behind these things, the devil is able to snatch us unawares.

Sheltered by the Almighty

As Christians we are protected and provided for by the Word of God, as we dwell under the shadow of His wings. (See Luke 4:4; Psalms 91; 119:105.) Unfortunately, many of us as Christians never come to understand the place of refuge and weaponry that Father God Almighty provides for us by His Word in prayer, intercession and worship. (See Job 33:14, 23-26; Proverbs 27:12, 27:12, 17-20; Genesis 4:26; Psalm 65:2; Isaiah 56:7; Romans 8:26-27; Matthew 7:7; John 16:24; Ephesians 6:18; James 5:13; Acts 4:31; Matthew 6:9; John 17:1.) As a new Christian, I can remember God baptizing me with the Holy Ghost so my prayers could reach the throne without being intercepted by enemy "radar." I began to learn that was only one of the benefits of this marvelous gift. (See John 14:15-17, 25-26; 15:26-27; 16:7-15; Acts 1:4-8.) As I got a little older in Christ, I sensed that I had to be careful concerning what I said around certain people, because the enemy had interfering spirits that might attempt to thwart the destiny of God on my life. I didn't read this in books. The Lord revealed it to me, and I awaited His confirmation. (See Deuteronomy 19:15; Matthew 18:16.) On the occasions when I ignored these cautions, I often ended up feeling as if the enemy had eaten my lunch. It is sad to admit, but I learned some things the hard way.

Strongholds Cause Forty Years in the Desert

Satan is not playing church. He and those aligned with him know they are spending eternity in hell, locked up forever and ever. So they frantically desire to spot blood-bought saints and stop the church. But many of us in the body of Christ are playing church. We are not as committed to the entire body as God is to us or as the devil is against us. Those who should be a covering of health and wholeness build their own kingdoms, instead. However, they are the ones who should be giving themselves as gifts to others to see the body of Christ made better. They store up riches and power for themselves. Some younger believers see this warped example and decide they want the same thing. We must not continue to ignore the leading of the Holy Spirit when He lets us know that our attitudes and habits are not totally from God. Otherwise, it can become nearly impossible to separate the human strongholds from the demonic ones that can take cover in them.

This is what *tamei* causes, which is why God leaves and lets a whole congregation of His people die in a forty-year long desert trip. It becomes easier for God to go to the prostitutes, the lame, the homeless and the downtrodden, because they will believe and follow immediately and lay their strongholds on the altar.

The Foothold For Religious Spirits: Our Judgment Against Eve

Religious spirits convince us that we have no sin, so we remain in our sin. (See 1 John 1:18.) Any time we set ourselves up to judge, we sin. When we judge women as being ineffective or unable to lead, we reap back ineffectiveness and an inability to lead God's way. I say God's way because our way looks extremely good. I know for a fact that we would not get into half the messes we get into if we would follow God as a newborn doe follows its mother. I also don't want to leave some impression of political correctness here. Just because someone is female or has a different ethnic heritage than our own, doesn't make that person a better leader than someone else. What I mean as effective leader is the leader God has chosen. This is not based upon what I think. It's based upon what God says. Sometimes I know He has chosen someone to lead that I never would choose. Eventually they do just fine, with proper leadership and guidance. On many other occasions I have watched as leadership put someone in a position, and I knew for a fact God was telling me that He did not choose that person. In one particular case that I can remember, the anointing of God left immediately. But on many other occasions it took months and even years for those particular churches to reap the sour harvest of placing man's choice in a position, instead of God's choice. I often wondered why I saw it done so frequently. I knew I couldn't have been the only one that saw this. I began to realize God was teaching me something, not just for my own benefit, but also for the benefit of the body of Christ.

God Is First

The principle of first mention is seen throughout the Scriptures. Whatever is first belongs to God. God says whatever comes forth from the womb first is His. (See Numbers 3:11–13.) There was a festival of first fruits, because even the first of the harvest belonged Him. (See Leviticus 23:9–10.) It foreshadowed Christ, who was the first fruit of many brethren. (See 1 Corinthians 15:23.) Our tithe is our first fruit, and it belongs to Him. (See Malachi 3:10, 1 Corinthians 16:2.) Eve is the first woman mentioned in Scripture. She is mentioned as the mother of all the living. (See Genesis 3:20.) Housed within her was all of our ethnic diversity that we see presently. It has been scientifically stated that all humans can be traced back through computer-generated DNA models to one maternal source. That source was dubbed by scientists as "Eve." Every ethnic group can trace its origins back to this one female source. Adam thus spoke a prophetic truth for all generations.

When we judge Eve as inferior and incapable to lead because

the serpent could deceive her, we judge all women this way. What we do not realize is that we are also subtly judging our diverse ethnic brothers and sisters as also inferior, because we are judging our first mother. We then reap the judgment of division among the races. (See Matthew 7:1–2.) Adam was the first human created. If we judge Adam as unable to lead because he sinned, we will view all authority suspiciously and as incompetent to lead—male authority in particular. While the Scriptures are clear that Adam sinned and Eve was deceived, we cannot pass judgment on them and then carry that judgment to modern day man. (See 1 Timothy 2:14.) We then view our present day experiences with men and women through clouded glasses. These become broken glasses if we have had any difficulty in our personal experiences with men or women, such as an abusive father or mother. We will then interpret and cloud all Scriptures concerning male/female relationships through those clouded or broken glasses.

In effect, we are substituting what we think about mankind instead of what God says. Our human thoughts are in control, not the mind of Christ. At that point strongholds of protection are set up to keep our minds set in place.

Because both Adam and Eve substituted their own understanding for God's Word (Christ's mind) when they partook of that fruit, they experienced separation from God and from one another. Now God in glory stepped in to avert physical death by providing an animal to cover them, as a substitute. (See Genesis 3:21.) The next point along the human time line that we see God in glory providing a permanent redemption for human sin is when He moves upon Mary to deposit the Christ. In our first two parents the sacrifice covered human flesh. In Mary, human flesh now covers the sacrifice.

This follows another divine principle seen in Scripture: the last shall be first, and the first shall be last. (See Matthew 19:30.)

His Image in His People

The First Shall Be Last: Eve and Mary

Many things were first implanted by God that were lost, and these will be the last to be restored.

The apostle was the first ministry to function in the church. Yet, from our perspective, it seems that apostles are the last ones in our modern church day to be restored. While I don't mean to imply Christ was ever lost, when we look at His first and last recorded words spoken in human flesh before His resurrection, we can get a glimpse of this principle from a different perspective. As a twelve-year old in Luke 2:49, we read Him saying, "Why were you searching for me?…Didn't you know I had to be in my Father's house?" The King James quotes it as, "Wist ye not that I must be about my Father's business?" His last recorded words before His resurrection were, "It is finished." It is His first words that mean the most to us lastly. We have been searching for Christ's return for centuries and yet He says, "Why are you searching? You know I've had to stay in my Father's house, doing His business." My thought is that God's business is preparing a place for us, His children.

Faith operates upon the principle of a first and last exchange. Faith is exercised for salvation first, but the last demonstration of our faith will come first when we walk into heaven and our faith becomes sight! In the physical realm, dust is what our earthly bodies were first formed of, and it is to dust that they return. Woman was the first human to be judged in the garden and woman will be the last human to be restored to full function.

Another first and last exchange is connected to Eve and Mary. Because Eve is the mother of all the living, she was blessed. (See Genesis 3:20.) Mary spoke something similar when she said in Luke 1:48 that, as a result of mothering Jesus, all generations from that time forward would call her blessed. All the nations of the earth have been blessed as a result of Eve reproducing children, and all the nations have been blessed as a result of Mary's child, Jesus. The last being far greater than the first (John 1:1).

BEYOND STRONGHOLDS

The Holy Spirit Manifested In Glory

Let's look at some similarities between the first recorded expression of God in glory on the earth and the last expression we see with Mary. When we study God Almighty in Genesis creating, He is the Word in glory—an appearance of God in a form we can understand. Now, no one knows exactly what that looked like. No human knows what appearance the Spirit took when He hovered over the earth. We do know that the outcome was the literal creation, and Paul tells us that the creation reveals enough of God's glory for us to believe in a God whom we can understand. (See Romans 1:19–20.) But in other places, the *theophany* was in the form of a dove. (See John 1:32.) The word used in Genesis is *rachaph*. We talked about this in chapter 3. It means to hover or brood, to flutter (like a bird's wings) and, by implication, to rest or relax.

The King James translates this as "move" because of what a mother bird—and in some bird species the male also—does with its breast or undercarriage. It literally moves to create heat, shade and protection, thus bringing forth the embryos into chicks that can peck their way out of the eggs. If at any time during the development process this brooding-resting-heat motion is cut off, the embryos will not develop. So it is that the Holy Spirit, manifested in glory, brooded and "incubated" the earth, like a mother hen, to bring forth.

Likewise, in Luke 1:35, the angel tells Mary, "The Holy Spirit will come upon you, and the power of the Most High will overshadow you." A literal and amplified translation may help: the *pneuma*, or "sacred, holy, audible puff of air/breath or wind," will *epi*, or "rest, go towards, have charge above you," and the *dunamis*, or "dynamite, miraculous deed-ability of the supreme God," will *episkiazo*, or "shade or envelop you in a (warm) haze of brilliancy." Wow! All the components of brooding seen in Genesis are told to Mary in Luke.

This manifestation of God in glory in both places, but especially and more so over Mary, is a desire to bring to completion or unity. In other words, there is a desire for no separation. The earth was void or not complete, and the Holy Spirit had to complete it. It was out of order. The only begotten Son of God the Father emptied Himself and became an embryo in Mary to birth and finally complete the redemption and unity of mankind to God. He came to stop the separation and to bring God's order back to fallen man.

John 1:1–3 fills us in just a little more. I'll quote it from the Unvarnished New Testament because it expounds the first few sentences in a decidedly different light.

> **In the beginning was the Word, and the Word was toward God, and God was what the Word was. It was with God in the beginning. All things that have happened have happened through it and not one thing that has happened has happened without it. Within it there was life, and the life was the light of the world. And in the darkness the light is shining and the darkness never got hold of it.**

Our original translators and every committee since have translated this eloquently enough:

> **In the beginning was the Word, and the Word was with God, and the Word was God. He was with God in the beginning. Through him all things were made; without him nothing was made that has been made. In him was life, and that life was the light of men. The light shines in the darkness, but the darkness has not understood it (NIV).**

In the King James and most other Bibles, the Greek words *pros ton theon* are translated, "With God." But the phrase *pros ton theon* means, "Towards God" and implies a movement towards, thus, by inference, a separation from. In many instances it denotes time and place, thus the translation "with God." The early church always had to war against heresy. In this case, it had to do so even more since the Gnostics had a cultic doctrine about creation. Most of these myths dealt with creation as a cataclysmic event that took place as a result of a division or separation within the Godhead. To me this sounds a little like the "Big Bang" theory revisited. The second, and far more damaging heresy involves the deity of Jesus Christ, since this heresy would try to separate Christ from His divine nature. This sounds like Jehovah's Witness doctrine.

All of these theories substitute human thinking, or the mind, for the Word of God, or Christ's mind. Ultimately all of these theories would produce separation or division within the church. Fortunately for us today, we recognize these as doctrines of demons, and we can review John 1:1-3 in the light in which the darkness never understood it. The reason why we can understand this passage is because the early translators translated it with the best clarity they could. In fact, when one is teaching young converts in Christ, some of the most important doctrines of Christianity are much easier to explain when reading our authorized versions.

So, God spoke in movement through time. Remember, God is outside of time, but can, at the same time, move within time because of His omnipresence. That movement or Word created light (He is light). He, the Spirit, incubated or brooded over the creation. He was and is, the dynamite, miraculous deed-ability power that gloriously overshadowed Mary!

I am not trying to change or add to doctrine. Centuries of great scholars have not been able to understand all of the workings of God connected to John's prologue. I'm not trying to understand or explain it all either. God is too huge to explain. And yet, He describes Himself simply and plainly so we can understand Him. I'm just trying to expound on the simple, yet profound way in which God came in glory as Himself, the Spirit and the Word, to create or make complete.

He is first and He is last. The only way we can, as humans, understand God's desire to overcome our separation from Him and from ourselves is to have the mind of Christ. We must also view God's holy Word in the light of renewing our minds by the washing of His Word (See Romans 12:2; Ephesians 5:26.)

In this respect, God used two separate women, Eve and Mary, to describe two separate approaches to unity. This is not so strange. Paul speaks of a similar symbolism of two women in Galatians 4. He talks about Hagar and Sarah and how they represent law and grace. How strange that women, the very people most religions try to control and manipulate with the rules and regulations of a religious spirit, are the very people God used to implement freedom through Jesus Christ. He is truly our first, last and best hope for completion and unity.

Breaking Down Walls of Separation: Unity in God

God came in glory over creation to complete fellowship—to overcome a separation and to restore order. He moved over Mary when He deposited Christ to restore fellowship and overcome separation. Christ would restore God's order.

The resistance set up against God coming in glory in this last manifestation of the Holy Spirit is to separate God's people. When God shows up in glory and there is a manmade separation placed upon God's people according to gender and ethnicity, then a fundamental understanding of teaching the mind of Christ has not been in place. Where there is no resistance, the result of God's manifested glory is unity. At creation, Adam and Eve were in unity with God, formed after His image. That unity brought forth mankind. In Mary's case, the Spirit of God overshadowed her, impregnating her with the God-man, Jesus, to bring unity to a fallen creation.

God is extremely passionate about maintaining and keeping unity. He gave mankind the awesome gift of procreation. As humans who are separate and distinct, when we become united in marriage it results in procreation. This is why in Mary's case, not resisting God produced Christ on the face of the earth. In Adam and Eve's case, God had to step in because sin caused division. The outcome of resisting God's movement toward unity is a curse that causes a separation.

In Adam and Eve a separation existed in both of them, between one another and between God. God had to judge it, thus the curse passed on to creation. So when we refuse the mind of Christ, we substitute a religious spirit, which governs our judgment concerning women. Because Eve housed all the ethnos within her, this judgment produces racism (division) instead of unity. The outcome, or "offspring," of this religious stronghold is still separation between the genders, manmade rules separating the nations and, ultimately, separation from God for all eternity.

I am not talking about political correctness here. God loves our diversity. He created it. That's why there are so many different plants and so many different ways different cultures cook them. He has created a spectrum of color from the one light. There is nothing wrong with distinctiveness. There is something wrong with manmade rules to keep separation in place based on that distinctiveness.

You might think a church or individual functioning in godly glory can't have this resistance. Let's look at history and the Bible and see if there is a pattern.

Azusa Street

God sometimes comes in glory to use a person and a church to break strongholds. An example of this occurred in William Seymour and the Azusa Street revival. For those reading this who may not know of him, he was the man God used to ignite the Pentecostal revival as pastor of the Azusa Street Mission in 1906.[2]

No one can deny that God in glory fell upon that church at that time. I believe Father's purpose was not only to restore the baptism of the Holy Spirit, but also to place a spirit of healing in the body of Christ between men and women and those of different racial and ethnic backgrounds.

Far ahead of its time, the Azusa Street Mission enjoyed a racially mixed congregation where both men and women, African Americans and Caucasians functioned side by side in places of leadership. All were equal.

The Azusa Street revival birthed three different denominations: the Church of God in Christ, the Assemblies of

His Image in His People

God and, later, The International Church of the Foursquare Gospel. Why three different organizations and not one?

Dividing Along Racial Lines

Because he was an African American man, William Seymour's church was heavily populated by African Americans. The Caucasians separated from the early movement and started an all-white denomination, leaving the African Americans to start the Church of God in Christ denomination.

Some years later, Aimee Semple McPherson began the International Church of the Foursquare Gospel denomination at the Azusa site. As a woman who stood as apostolic head over the denomination, the International Church of the Foursquare Gospel churches remained open to women's leadership gifts.[3]

Many thousands of people from all over the world visited Azusa Street during the height of revival and took the glory back home to their churches. Quite a few of them also started churches.[4] I should also make it clear that the Pentecostal movement had started some time prior to the Azusa Street Revival.[5]

There is a religious argument for dividing this movement. In so doing, God diversified the church so it could be sent out to all different types of people over the globe. As a result, so many have been blessed because of these organizations. While it is true that God's plans are as multifaceted as He is in glory, this particular division was made strictly on racial lines.

Each time we see religious spirits function in our midst we see strife. Strife can gain a stronghold because the mind of Christ has not been implanted in us. But how is the door opened? I believe judgment opens the door. Arguments between various theological teachings that are not crucial to salvation or sanctification in Christ can cause us to be critical and judgmental. Satan will always use our differences to break up unity. The results will always be separation and division along the lines of those differences. Satan's desire is to remove or steal the effectiveness that each individual or church has within her own sphere of influence.

I believe the strife evident in the Azusa Street Mission set the move of God back in terms of delivering the church and the world from gender and ethnic-based strongholds.[6] I'm not suggesting that our all-knowing Heavenly Father didn't see this separation coming. Some may question why I mention this incident at all since many good works and great churches came out of this break-up. While this is true, and I believe that God always intended the movement to have a global reach, Azusa Street Mission had a definite anointing for racial diversity and gender equity. I believe that anointing would have reached beyond the Azusa Street Mission to the entire globe had strife and division not occurred.

Because of this break-up, the movement went global anyway—as God intended it to do—just without the anointing to remove many of the strongholds of bias within us. In other words, a slight substitution took place. We must realize, when God speaks in the heavenly realm, the earth hears. (See Psalm 19:1–4.) The church is supposed to be the mouthpiece for this revelation. But when she refuses to do it God's way completely, the unsaved of the earth hear God's Word and sift it through their unregenerate souls. In this way substitution takes place again, and now, instead of God healing our gender and racial biases, we seek for the world's remedy, which is never Christ-like. At that point a strange thing occurs. The church steps back and criticizes the way the world does the church's job. Because we're in judgment, we reap what we sow. We wonder why Sunday mornings are the most segregated day of the week, with 50 percent of the army of the Lord, the women, never getting out of boot camp.

A Spirit of Divide and Conquer: Gender and Racial

I am not suggesting that the entire body of Christ or the Pentecostal movement has religious spirits. Neither am I

His Image in His People

suggesting that the wonderful organizations and churches that have been birthed from this movement all have religious spirits. The church has many wonderful godly attributes that it sheds abroad through God's love. (See Romans 5:5.) Many marvelous saints have worked hard. Many of them have died for Christ's cause and for us who follow in their footsteps. The blood and toil of the saints of one generation provides fertilizer and nutrients into the soil of the lives of those whom Christ seeds into the next generation. I just believe now is the time God wants to expose religious spirits and their actions.

This spirit of division is not something new. Many Christians hated the Holocaust. Many Christians today speak out against neo-nazism and such movements. But do we realize that Martin Luther promoted hatred against the Jews by statements such as this: "What then shall we Christians do with this damned, rejected race of Jews?"[7] How about St. John Chrysostom's words: "I hate the Jews...It is the duty of all Christians to hate the Jews."[8]

Sadly, these weren't the first Christians to speak against the Jews. Let me recite a who's who in Christianity: Justin Martyr, Origen, Eusebius, St. Hilary of Poitier, St. Ephraim, St. Cyril, St. Jerome, St. Augustine.[9] Unfortunately, we could add more names to this list. We will speak later in chapter nine about God's love for Israel.

But it shouldn't surprise us when satan uses people–even God's people–to separate, divide and butcher each other. Such hatred produces many odd ideologies. One of them is that "inferior" people have smaller brains. We see this theory, which is a lie of the devil, promoted even today against many African-Americans. In past generations, this unenlightened theory was used by the United States government to collect bones from Native American burial grounds and have them shipped to experimental stations to prove that the skull size of these people was smaller; hence, their brains must have been smaller, also.[10]

Over the years, I've often wondered why it is that we in the church don't allow women to function in places of high calling, and we shun people with different features. As I prayed about this, Father explained it to me one day like this: suppose you were up against an army much larger in number, better equipped and with individuals of great integrity and honor. You cannot beat them in the conventional way; they outnumber you. First, you would have to hit their lines of communication between central command and the field. But that still wouldn't reduce the number of individual commanders and soldiers rising up to battle. You'd have to send some kind of interference among the soldiers in the field before central command had an opportunity to reestablish communication lines.

And that's when it dawned on me. The army of the Lord has two distinct groups—male and female. These are broken up into many different ethnic groups. Those are the obvious physical characteristics. Within that army are people with different spiritual gifts and job descriptions based upon whom God chooses, regardless of gender or ethnic culture.

Satan knows he can't beat an army led by our Lord Jesus Christ. Therefore, he had to sabotage communication lines between God and humans. We outnumber him from the time of Adam and Eve to the time of our Lord's Second Coming. In each generation, if we can grasp God's desire for us to function in repentance and unity, the cumulative defeat of the powers of darkness is astounding. So our enemy has to get us squabbling with one another over our differences, especially gender and ethnic differences. If he can get us looking at the natural realm all the time, we will never spot his tactics.

Whatever the enemy's plans are, the more exciting news is that God knows the end from the beginning. He prepared Christ before the foundation of the world. (See Revelation 13:8.) Nothing ever takes God by surprise.

God Knows All

This brings me to the following point: God knew that Adam and Eve would fall, and He knew what spirits would affect us as His body and what our reactions would be. We all know God allows

His Image in His People

His will to be birthed out of impossible, near-death human situations. These include Israel's flight from Pharaoh, Abraham's offering of Isaac, Joseph's imprisonment, Daniel and Esther delivering Israel and Christ's death, burial and resurrection. It seems to me that the redemption of mankind will be far more dramatic and complete than we could have ever imagined. (See 1 Corinthians 2:9.)

It had to happen this way. I'm not condoning sin, the fall or disobedience of any kind against God. But I firmly believe that as redeemed daughters and redeemed sons, we will understand what it means to be one with the Father as Christ prayed we would be in John 17. In this way we will learn the importance of unity.

A divided army cannot conquer. Satan knows this. He uses our differences with God and with each other to conquer us. I am not saying that God does not enjoy our differences. He ordains them. Nor am I saying that having different denominations within Christendom is wrong. In fact, each individual denomination, church and person has a unique call, message and gift that reveal some aspect of God that must be expressed. Without our unique individualism this may never be accomplished. God does use our differences. These very differences make us strong, and if we will function in repentant obedience to the Holy Spirit, God in glory will come to unify us with Him and each other. (See John 17:21, 22.)

Functioning In Unity

It is by taking the impossible human ideal of functioning in unity that God will break the backs of usurping demon strongholds that hold us, our churches, various geographic regions and even the earth captive. When God wanted Israel's freedom from Egypt He sent His Word through Moses proclaiming, "Let My People Go!" Each one of those ten plagues pronounced judgment on ten different deities that Egypt worshiped. These demons held the region captive. Once God judged these forces, it was up to God's people to obey the command of the Lord—to take the gold and go!

BEYOND STRONGHOLDS

Moses had to resist his desire to remain separate from his people and obey God. This principle is seen over and over in Scripture. Abraham, Elijah, Esther, Daniel and Joseph are a few people who experienced impossible situations. (See Philemon 1:17; 1 Peter 3:8; Ephesians 4:3; 2 Corinthians 13:11; 1 Corinthians 1:10; Romans 12:5; 1 Corinthians 10:17; Galatians 3:28; Ephesians 4:13.) I reference these Scriptures here to emphasize what the Bible makes plain. We say we move in unity because no one disagrees with us or we don't allow people of another culture or gender to function as leaders. When we are all the same with the same ideas, it's very easy to be unified. But once we have to work with someone of a different gender or ethnic background as a leader, then issues of rebellion and idolatry crop up, because our own minds are in control, not the mind of Christ.

Let me explain what I mean by rebellion and idolatry. Sexual sins are nothing more than gratifying ourselves in our own way, not God's intended way. This is one manifestation of rebellion, which is evidenced by our own way of thinking, not Christ's way of thinking. It's idolatry to be stubborn by doing things only one way and refusing to see that the multifaceted outcome of doing something another's way is possibly God's way. Our ways and systems become greater to us than God. This is arrogance. (See 1 Samuel 15:23.)

Those of another gender or ethnic background force us to confront our own personal ways of thinking in areas we may be unaccustomed to considering. I am not speaking about trying to work in a church with atheists. As I've made clear before, I am speaking about Spirit-filled believers working together in an environment. We all have strongholds through which we must work individually. In like fashion, when I speak about gender issues, I am speaking about God-ordained holiness, as Father God created men and women. My heart grieves for people caught in homosexual relationships. But I am not referring to those issues when I speak about men and women functioning in the body of Christ.

We must be united in faith, with sound theological principles, in order to work together in the body of Christ. We must allow the

His Image in His People

Holy Spirit to expose the biases in our hearts to us so we can repent.

Moving the Gates of Hell

Every generation gives us a psalmist who sings about moving or removing the gates of hell. These are earthly places of demonic political or organized community power. In order for the gates of hell to be a problem, they have to be somewhere near you. Jesus told Peter that it was the testimony of who Christ was that would make the gates of hell unable to prevail. (See Matthew 16:13–19.) The Greek conveys the meaning as "not proving stronger, or eventually overcoming." God has given us marvelous tools to combat the forces of hell. But the best and most effective are repentance and obedience. When we function this way in every area of our lives, we will give the devil no place to enjoy himself on earth.

Acts 3:19–21 states,

> **Repent, then, and turn to God, so that your sins may be wiped out, that times of refreshing may come from the Lord, and that He may send the Christ, who has been appointed for you—even Jesus. He must remain in heaven until the time comes for God to restore everything, as He promised long ago through His holy prophets.**

Peter makes this astounding proclamation to a group of people after they had been united in prayer in the upper room. While in unity, the Holy Spirit fell on human flesh of both genders. This resulted in people of all different tongues hearing the gospel in their own ethnic languages. We don't have to agree with one another on every theological point in order for unity to take place. But we do need to be restored, renewed and implanted with one mind—namely, the mind of Christ.

Resisting Unity

Why are there separations and divisions in churches, even when an effort is made to keep unity? It is because religious spirits maintain a false sense of unity, and a true renewing of the mind does not take place. There are many instances in the Scriptures where false alliances were formed. (See 1 Kings 1:1-50; 2 Kings 3, 10:13-14; Nehemiah 13:26.) It must have felt fine for the people involved in these relationships. It's obvious that God did not intend for these to take place.

There is no other way for unity to take place except that Christ restores us. When people resist coming into unity, based on gender and racial differences, it indicates that they are not walking in the mind of Christ, but have received a religious spirit instead. Ephesians 4:15-16 tells us that one of the outcomes of allowing men, women and different socially and ethnically diverse people to function as ministers is that the body will grow up to the Head, which is Christ. (See Galatians 3:28)

Paul exhorts us in Romans 12:2 to be transformed by the renewing of our minds. This will allow us to know God's perfect will. It is no coincidence that in the very next few verses he talks about the interdependent body of Christ, with her various gifts. Without the renewed mind of Christ, no part of the body could function. One may be able to hear without seeing and speak without walking, but without a head nothing works.

Integrating the Church: the Apostle Peter and a Religious Spirit

The mind of Christ does not function within us because of our denomination or diversity, but because of our willingness to resist a compelling religious spirit. In 1954, Spring Hill College in Mobile, Alabama decided to integrate amid great controversy. The head of this Catholic college, Father Smith, decided the Christian message could not get out properly within the confines of a segregated educational system, hence his decision to integrate. This Catholic college stepped out in a region of predominantly white Baptist and Pentecostal churches, which were stalwart in their segregationist beliefs.

His Image in His People

God used the Catholic denomination to champion a message in a region of the country known for its racial problems. These resistances are not always evidenced by what we say (everyone tries to talk a good talk!) but by how we act or what we do. As with the other aspects of God showing up in glory that we looked at throughout the Scriptures, these resistances are easy to see in Scripture, but more difficult to expose in our lives and our churches.

The great apostle Peter compromised under the pressure of such a spirit. In an effort to appease the circumcised crowd, He withdrew from eating and fellowshipping with the Gentiles, even though he had been with them all along. (See Galatians 2:9.) What is it about the mind of Christ that can change us from those who obey such a seductive spirit—one that even deceived Peter—to people of grace and humility?

The Mind of Christ: Purging Ourselves of the Flesh

Let's review the mind of Christ as seen in 1 Corinthians 2. We know the Corinthian church as a group of believers living in a society where immorality was rampant. Not much has changed over the millennia. Paul is obviously exhorting them to purge themselves of attitudes of pride, partying and immorality. This is why he made his opening statements regarding divisions among them based upon their foolish titles. He exhorted them, instead, to seek God's wisdom. It is in God's wisdom that He uses the lowly and seemingly foolish things of this world.

The Jews looked at the Greeks as foolish heathens, and many were. The Greeks looked at the Jews as being narrow-minded slaves to their own spiritual superiority—and many were. (See 1 Corinthians 1:22.) Both groups viewed women and slaves as inconsequential and limited. (See 1 Corinthians 1:25.) But God uses the preaching of the gospel through the "foolish" mouths of Jews, Gentiles, women and slaves to confound the wisdom in this world. (See 1 Corinthians 1:23-24.)

The difference between 1 Corinthians and the book of Romans

is both obvious and subtle. The book of Romans deals more with the strife between the soulish human heart, or mind, and God's will, or mind. This is one reason why Paul makes the argument to leave the inferiority of the law and live by grace. In Corinthians, he appeals to believers—many of whom were probably Gentiles—to put off the way the world does things and line up spirit, soul and body with the way the Holy Spirit does things. It is in this context that he calls the divisions foolish and tells them they are arrogant. (See 1 Corinthians 2:18-21; 1 Corinthians 4:18.)

He tells them to imitate him. (See 1 Corinthians 4:16.) How should they imitate him? He teaches us throughout chapters 1, 2, 3 and 4, but he drives it home in chapter 2. Here we are exhorted to have a mind that speaks according to the Spirit, not the flesh. It seems to me that he is telling them that the reason why they have divisions among them is because they were in the flesh. Our natural fleshly minds refuse to understand the things of the Spirit. We have taught our natural minds many things, but not all of it is of the Spirit. We've taught ourselves how to sing, teach, preach and even prophesy, but not all of it has come from God's Holy Spirit. Some of our actions are framed in spiritual language and religious sounding platitudes to look super-spiritual, but they are not.

Do Not Go Beyond What Is Written

Look at what Paul writes to the Corinthians:

> Now, brothers, I have applied these things to myself and Apollos for your benefit, so that you may learn from us the meaning of the saying, "do not go beyond what is written." Then you will not take pride in one man over against another. For who makes you different from anyone else? What do you have that you did not receive? And if you did receive it, why do you boast as though you did not?
>
> Already you have all you want! Already you have become rich! You have become kings—and that without

His Image in His People

> us! How I wish that you really had become kings so that we might be kings with you! For it seems to me that God has put us apostles on display at the end of the procession, like men condemned to die in the arena.
>
> We have been made a spectacle to the whole universe, to angels as well as to men. We are fools for Christ, but you are so wise in Christ! We are weak, but you are strong! You are honored, we are dishonored!
>
> To this very hour we go hungry and thirsty, we are in rags, we are brutally treated, we are homeless. We work hard with our own hands. When we are cursed, we bless; when we are persecuted, we endure it; when we are slandered, we answer kindly. Up to this moment we have become the scum of the earth, the refuse of the world.
>
> —1 Corinthians 4:6–13

As I read this and think of all the trappings we place on ministry, church and our individual success, I wonder how much of our own minds are in these things, not the mind of Christ. Paul makes it clear that he is not writing this to shame them (verse 14), but to warn them as a parent warns a child. Without Christ's mind, we are just like proud little children. We set up our own playgrounds and invite the people we want to play with. We function according to our own wisdom and boast that it's God's. These are the opinions, attitudes or strongholds that exalt themselves as better than the knowledge of God. (See 2 Corinthians 10:4–5.) Correction is a humbling experience. In some cases it is necessary for implanting the mind of Christ, in order to produce repentance.

What else did Paul mean when he exhorted us to let Christ's mind be in us? I see two words that jump out at me. One is found in Philippians 2:5. It is the word to "let," or allow. In other words, it takes an act of our will. The second word is found in Romans 12:2. It is "transformed," or changed. Much like the Greek word for repentance, transformation involves a desire for a 180-degree turn around, to change.

BEYOND STRONGHOLDS
Christ's Mind Changes Us

Change is essential where salvation is concerned. It is initial, continual and then final, when faith becomes sight. Our natural minds grow as we grow from infancy to adulthood. So why wouldn't the mind of Christ grow stronger and stronger within us as we allow it to? You may ask, "shouldn't this be a part of our foundational teachings as young Christians?" Of course, it should.

But suppose God has already shown up in glory in a specific location, and a real effort has not been made by leadership to teach or preach on the mind of Christ? The glory seen in the creation and then seen hovering or brooding over Mary comes to change a people. Instead of finding submission and willing hearts, the Lord of Glory finds a religious spirit resisting the very symbol of unity housed within men and woman of different races. There is a saying: "All it takes for evil to thrive is for good people to do nothing." What is it about having Christ's mind that would thwart this natural tendency in us to divide?

I will quote Philippians 2:1–5,

> **If you have any encouragement from being united with Christ, if any comfort from his love, if any fellowship with the Spirit, if any tenderness and compassion, then make my joy complete by being like-minded, having the same love, being one in spirit and purpose. Do nothing out of selfish ambition or vain conceit, but in humility consider others better than yourselves. Each of you should look not only to your own interests, but also to the interests of others. Your attitude should be the same as that of Christ Jesus.**

The Unvarnished New Testament translates it: "Keep the same spirit amongst yourselves that is also in Christ Jesus." It is translated by the King James as, "Let this mind be in you, which was also in Christ Jesus."

His Image in His People

Mind, Spirit and Attitude: Learning to Repent

Mind, spirit and attitude are three words used to describe the Greek word *phroneo*. There is one added meaning that this word conveys besides attitude, mind or spirit. It is a thoughtful obedience to exercise a thought or opinion; hence, the King James translators used the word, *let*.

Paul expounds upon the same theme in Romans 12:2 when he exhorts us to renew our minds. We know that renewing the mind takes the Holy Spirit infusing us and washing us as we read God's Word (Eph 5:26). But we have to be willing to allow it to happen and actively put off the old mind. We must be repentant about these divisive attitudes as soon as the Holy Spirit shows them to us.

We cannot merely repent at salvation; we must continue to repent for our unholy attitudes on a daily basis. This inoculates us against strongholds and the demons that can sometimes find a comfort in them. Repentance is the Holy Ghost's vaccine for mankind's strongholds. We function in repentance when the Holy Ghost convicts us of these ideas and we bring them to the cross. (See 2 Corinthians 10:5.) When this happens we begin to see others as Christ sees them, through His eyes. We begin to hear with Christ's ears, and we begin to react emotionally as Christ would react. All these functions travel through nerve pathways in the brain. But it is the Holy Spirit working through us and helping us in our infirmities that implants the mind of Christ in us. (See Romans 8:26.)

Correct Responses

We also need to be taught correct responses. These responses become a part of who we are and an extension of who Christ is in us. I like to use the example of teaching someone to ride a horse. When a horse bolts or spooks at something and instantly changes direction, most people try to grip with their knees to balance themselves. Unfortunately, this only pushes the person's seat out of the saddle even more. The proper response is balance. Balance is a whole-body response. Balance doesn't come from your mind willing your body to do it, but through repeated practice and relaxed lessons that teach you how to move with the horse as an extension of the animal. The jerk-knee response only gets you in trouble. That response comes from a fear of falling.

It's much the same when we learn that Christ is able to take care of any and all that happens to us. We learn that He has not caused a sickness or a death, and we can trust Him to catch us if or when we fall. That's when we begin to grow in faith. Over time, our responses become filled with Christ-like faith instead of the jerk-knee response.

Learning Humility: Facing Our Pride

The next idea I see repeated over and over again in Philippians 4, Ephesians and Romans is humility. Humility is not something that we can work up in our minds. We can't fake humility. Humility is a heart condition. This is precisely why we have to be willing to be renewed.

Christ's humility is inherent in Him, and as a result of it He bore the shame of the cross. Humility does not come easily to us. Sometimes life's difficult circumstances produce a harvest of humility in us. On other occasions, it comes from reading the Word and taking to heart the seriousness of Paul's admonitions to esteem others as more important than ourselves. (See Philippians 2:4.)

When we do, God works out His intentions in our lives. (See Philippians 2:12–13; Romans 12:2.) Humility is a heart condition that grows over time. It takes an active desire to allow our Christ-minds to grow in that direction. We can tell how far we've grown when the Holy Spirit brings proud words back to our remembrance, and we ask Him to forgive us for our attitudes. I doubt that we are even aware of how proud we are and how much our flesh enters into everything we do. We need the Holy Spirit to reveal this to us.

His Image in His People

When God says He shall not give His glory to another, I had previously thought He wasn't going to pour Himself out in glory on humans in an abiding and manifested way. (See Isaiah 42:8.) But as Father started to speak to me, He made it obvious throughout the Scriptures that it was His desire to pour Himself out in glory upon us. The "other" He is talking about is our human, resistance-filled minds. These minds produce all sorts of sinful desires that open doors for satan. In Genesis, God made it clear that He would not strive with our sinfulness forever. Isn't that what is really taking place when He comes in glory, and His presence wanes or eventually goes? It is not that He does not desire to stay. We chase Him away.

We can also chase Him away by wanting His glory instead of wanting Him. Many people desire spiritual gifts. There is nothing wrong with that. (See 1 Corinthians 14:1.) But do we want the gifts or the Giver? Do we want the glory or do we want the Lord of Glory? If we want Father, Son and Holy Spirit we will have to deal with our strongholds.

Learning the Word of God

The last concept that I see here is the natural outcome of understanding the mind of Christ: God's thoughts are higher than our thoughts. (See Isaiah 55:7-9.) In other words, there is absolutely nothing we can do to earn or merit the mind of Christ. It is higher than anything we can comprehend.

So instead of trying to understand and strive for everything, which is what causes division, why not just read His Word, view others with higher esteem than ourselves and allow the Holy Spirit to change us? Everyone seems to try so hard to be right about Scriptural things. When someone comes along with a different, but equally correct view, we fight him or her.

James called Christians—not the unsaved—double-minded. (See James 4:8.) What was the remedy? He told them to repent—and not just some half-hearted repentance. He said to "grieve, mourn and wail!" If we would do just that when God shows us our sins of prejudice and pride, the church would be a much friendlier place in which to function.

The second step in James' remedy was to, "Humble yourselves before the Lord" (James 4:10). The third step was all God's doing: "And He will lift you up." Instead of us lifting ourselves up, God will promote us His way.

Just as salvation is initial and continuing with a final outcome, so is allowing Christ's mind to be implanted in us. We must initially allow the Holy Spirit to work it out in us and then daily take up our crosses and follow Him. Finally, and with each step along the way, He will implant Christ's mind in such a way that the double-minded patterns of a religious spirit will stick out like sore thumbs. If we do not "grieve, mourn and wail" to change our biases, we will lose another generation in which God in glory will not abide or remain, but come and go.

In the next chapter let's see if we can reveal where we have substituted some of our own thinking in this area. Let's see if we can expose where Christ's mind has been stunted from growing in us.

Set up road signs; put up guideposts. Take note of the highway, the road that you take. Return, O Virgin Israel, return to your towns. How long will you wander, O unfaithful daughter? The Lord will create a new thing on earth—a woman will surround a man.

"This is the covenant I will make with the house of Israel after that time," declares the Lord. "I will put my law in their minds and write it on their hearts. I will be their God and they will be my people."

—Jeremiah 31:21–22, 33

Chapter Nine

HIS PEOPLE IN HIS IMAGE

In the last chapter we spoke about God's purpose when He appeared in glory on Eve and Mary, and the separating resistances we humans set up against that glory. In this chapter we'll discuss the Scriptures concerning relationships between men and women. I will make a distinction between the conditions of women in ministry and the husband-wife relationship. It is only as we desire to loose Eve or cease to judge her that healing can take place concerning men, women and the rest of God's people.

We all judge our parents. In chapter 5, we talked about how there are consequences of this, especially when we are not willing to walk in repentance for our actions. When we refuse to stop judging, we receive judgment back on us. Mary was ordained by God to be an instrument to overcome a separation between mankind and God through birthing Jesus. Eve was similarly ordained to procreate the different ethnos (or ethnic groups) in unity. Consequently, our judgment of women will reproduce ethnic and gender division.

The outcome of this division will put a wedge between faithful witnesses of the Word that God has ordained for this planet. The two witnesses in the beginning were Adam and Eve. There are also two witnesses mentioned in the book of Revelation. By placing strife between men and women, especially husbands and wives, the devil is able to take us off our testimonies of Jesus Christ. We then disagree with God's Word. We no longer become faithful witnesses of His Word to the earth. Sin is able to enter in. When we get caught disobeying God's Word we play the blame game just as Adam did. We do this to protect our stronghold belief systems.

I firmly believe that we must stop blaming or judging everyone else in order to receive God's outpouring of Himself upon us more fully. The manmade rules and regulations set up against women are really nothing more than our own judgment against Eve. We fear falling into sin, either by deception or rebellion, and we fear Eve, or the woman, will bring us there again. Religious spirits make up some hideous and some seemingly benign conditions by which women must live.

As Christians we are aware how wrong it is to judge based on ethnicity. But we don't realize that, to judge ethnically is, in essence, to judge Eve or woman. I can handle the believer who says, "It's true, we should allow women the same opportunities to minister and rethink our stance on some husband and wife issues, but how can we reconcile this with Scripture?" That kind of an individual can be as pure as Mary when she asked the angel Gabriel, "But how can these things be?"

When we ask in faith, Father always answers our questions. It is the Pharisee that troubles me. Ultimately, he looks down his nose as soon as a woman or a person of different ethnic background approaches. This stronghold will taint every decision made concerning that person.

There were only three entities judged on earth as a result of sin: Adam, Eve and satan. Subsequently, the curse passed to the earth and all of creation. As long as we continue to judge Eve and her descendants, all the ethnos housed within her will continue to judge each other. Race relations will never become healed as long as we insist upon this judgment.

In Christ, women have been set free. But the effects of our sin remain. Our attitudes need to change. Because of this, it would

His People in His Image

make sense to review some New Testament Scriptures concerning male/female relationships. Some Scriptures you may wish to study are Galatians 3:23-28; Ephesians 5:21-6: 9; 1 Corinthians 7; 1 Timothy 2; 1 Timothy 5-6:1-2; 1 Peter 3 and Romans 10:4.

It's almost impossible to properly interpret Scripture in this area when we look at these Scriptures with our own minds and not the mind of Christ. What usually happens is a mixture of God's grace and law (Sarah and Hagar) which, in turn, pollutes the Spirit of the Word—turning it to law.

There can be no mixture of these two concepts. The apostle Paul goes to great lengths to make this clear throughout the epistles to the Romans, Galatians, Thessalonians and others. It is the goodness of God that leads us to repentance and obedience, not some mandate or rule.

Some in the church fear that a wishy-washy, gooey grace will take over and render us powerless. So they really preach the law. But if you have ever experienced the love and goodness of God, all else pales in comparison, including legalism.

Romans 10:1-4 talks about Israel's desire for righteousness. The apostle makes it clear that Christ is the end of the law for everyone who believes. In other words, women are free. Whenever groups or denominations make rules concerning women in their midst, they really seek to create their own manmade righteousness. It is this self-righteousness that Paul condemns. When we live by the Spirit in grace and faith, no manmade mandates are necessary. Whether the group is Jewish, Christian, Muslim or some cult, whenever we try to mandate in order to subjugate, we are erecting a building to our own righteousness and telling God His covering is not enough. While other religious organizations might get away with this, we as blood-bought saints should expose the lie.

Equals Before God

Galatians 3:26-29 makes it clear that in Christ we are equal—ethnically, socially and between the two genders. So much so,

BEYOND STRONGHOLDS

that in chapter 4, Paul goes on to talk about receiving all the authority pertaining to inheritance, as would a first-born son. Wow! So it is clear that no structure, rule or regulation for leadership, gifts or calling should be erected based on ethnic, social or gender differences.

It is well known historically that the early church was originally led by not only the twelve disciples, but other men and women of great calling, as well. In fact, many Roman and Greek men would not receive the Lord because they could lose their status as Roman or Greek citizens.[1]

So when the Judaizers show up and demand circumcision they find a frightening sight—women in leadership! How are you going to make a case for circumcision when God has outmaneuvered you and placed people in leadership who can't physically function in circumcision?

The only way to subjugate the women is to make their gifts seem unclean or of a lesser value so they act in doubt and fear instead of love and faith. Once you've got them questioning, then you can continue to divide and conquer.

Paul went to great lengths to purge the early church of this spirit. Unfortunately, it is still alive and well today. Additionally, an understanding of the mind of Christ is not properly taught. Then Scriptures concerning head coverings and other Jewish customs are inserted to substantiate their rules. This plan of attack works. How do I know that? Not just by modern day observation. It was so powerfully persuasive that Paul addressed it in Galatians 2.

Remember, we are talking about what is freely ours in Christ—calling, grace, mercy, love, faith, walking by the Spirit, gifts—both leadership and spiritual—and our unique exhortation as believers to grow up to the head, which is Christ. We may also take on His mind—among many other wonderful aspects of our inheritance. These things can be accomplished by prayer, reading the Word, worship, teaching, preaching, leading churches, serving and sacrificing for one another selflessly, among many other diverse ways God uses us. The Judaizers wished to separate people based solely upon ethnic background, which would also have divided

His People in His Image

along gender lines and, ultimately, down social lines. You see, once you start separating, it's like an avalanche. It starts small, but just keeps on building.

Galatians 2:9 says that when James, Peter and John realized the grace and anointing given by God to Paul to preach to other ethnos, they agreed with it and sent Paul out. This is how he got his description as the apostle to the Gentiles. Now, other admonitions concerning idols, morality and the like would come later. But none of these guidelines divided people. In fact, they are things all Christians should live by.

So Paul and Barnabas get on their way. While in Antioch, Paul watches the duplicity of Peter and reproves him. The Word states that Peter agreed with Paul earlier and continued that attitude on the mission field until some people from Jerusalem, along with the Judaizers, show up. At that point, he withdraws and separates. (See Galatians 2:12.) The Bible states the withdrawal and separation was a result of fear—fear of brethren from the circumcision group. This stronghold reproduced itself in other people (verse 13). So much so that even Barnabas, who was sent as a fivefold minister—a prophet—to cover not just the Gentiles but also Paul's back, was drawn away and seduced by this attitude!

When even apostles and prophets can be seduced by these kinds of strongholds, we as the body of Christ must take heed. God's truth rested upon Paul, the "freshman" apostle, to bring clarity and light to the murky teachings of supposed submission to supposed truth.

Ethnicity

Read Galatians 2:14. For purposes of expounding on this issue, let's remove the ethnic descriptions and just call us humans. For the purposes of this grammatical exercise, I will place the actual Biblical words in parentheses. In Galatians 2:14, it is Paul speaking:

"When I saw that they were not acting in line with the truth of the gospel, I said to Peter in front of them all, 'You are a [human being] (Jew), [living like one] (Gentile) and not like [anything else]

(Jew). How is it, then, that you force [other human beings] (Gentiles) to follow (Jewish) customs?'"

We can see from this grammatical exercise that when we try to cause others to submit to certain standards based upon gender, ethnic background and social status, we have resisted the Lord of Glory—the very Lord of Glory who spoke the universe, the earth, Adam, Eve, Mary, you and me into existence! God places no difference for leadership or other callings between yellow people, white people, red people, brown people, black people, male people, female people, old, young, rich, poor, educated or uneducated. He uses us all.

Controlling Half the Army of the Lord

There is another Scripture concerning men and women outside the marriage relationship I would like to look at. In 1 Timothy 2, Paul seems to say women shouldn't do anything in the church but have babies. This attitude is quite prevalent today and is subtly taught in many seminaries.

A look at history or society as a whole and a look at to whom Paul was speaking might help. Paul was talking to Timothy. Not only did he know Timothy, but he also knew Timothy's mother and grandmother. (See 2 Timothy 1:5.) It is common knowledge that Timothy was raised in Lystra. There was no synagogue or place where Jewish children could go to learn. Timothy's father was a Greek. So it would have been mandatory for Timothy's mother and grandmother to be his "rabbis" in learning the Scriptures, receiving an appropriate Jewish education and trained in living a holy Jewish lifestyle. In order to do that, they would have to be more than just caregivers in Timothy's life.[2]

Also, we know for a fact that women functioned in the highest levels as apostles, and they were in leadership in other places.[3] (See Romans 16:7.)

So what is Paul addressing here? First let's view the Scripture in context. In Chapter 1 he is dealing with heretics—and probably violent and adulterous ones, at that. In keeping with demanding

His People in His Image

purity in light of the seduction of these heretics, he instructs Timothy how to conduct a worship-teaching meeting.

Secondly, they worshiped in a separated way, like Jewish custom demanded, with men in one area and women in another—very much like the meetings we see in 1 Corinthians 14:33–35. We are also dealing with an environment in which women were property, just like slaves. It was illegal, during that timeframe, for women or slaves to be over or above anything. These women get saved and now the only authority over them is Christ—great liberty, but not much maturity within them. Remember that most of them were not allowed a formal education. You also have harlots and other people coming out of lifestyles of idolatry. Add Jewish customary mandates, and Paul needed a huge dose of wisdom to deal with an immediate problem—not to mention a dose of Holy Ghost aspirin! What does he do? He does the best thing custom and propriety can dictate. He turns the heretics over to satan, so they can't continue to pollute these impressionable people. He demands holiness in dress and action. He must continue the demands of Jewish custom in maintaining a separate male-female worship system, but these ladies are still boisterous. Just learning their freedom, they may have been a little out of order as the whole church was in 1 Corinthians 14:35.

Remember that legally, by the standards of the world at that time, these women were property. It was also illegal, during that timeframe, for a woman to rule over a man in anything, just as it was illegal for a slave to rule over a freed man or to run away. Paul must keep them silent in public meetings and not allow something as illegal as a woman over a man. Likewise, he exhorted Onesimus to go back to being Philemon's slave. (See Philemon 12.) Of course, slavery is now illegal, and so is discriminating against a woman in job status or owning another human being as property. But, as Paul told Philemon to accept Onesimus as a brother, he gives the absolutely astounding command for the women to learn.

Astounding, you say? Yes. Women were not taught so much as how to add, except that they had to go to market. They really were viewed as chattel.[4] Now Paul exhorts them to learn, but quietly, and under the legal purview of their husbands. Remember, they are still their husbands' legal property. Again, the safest pastime during that time period in history for a woman was to have children. Some of these new converts from prostitution would be quite safe in that respect. Paul then seems to exhort the women who do have any understanding to help those that don't.

When these Scriptures are used to control the powerful effect that teams of holy men and women can have on earth to save and deliver, something is wrong. Scripture that is interpreted properly should, in the long term, have the effect of delivering people from human and devilish strongholds. God's Word always results in a closer walk with Jesus and more fruit of the Holy Spirit in our lives. People get set free, not placed in bondage.

Childbearing

There is one other point to be made for Paul's exhortation to childbearing; it is the concept of sacrifice. When we talk about having the mind of Christ, we talk about His love and His ultimate sacrifice for us. Men are exhorted as husbands and fathers to embody this in their families.

While women are never specifically mentioned to embody Christ in this way, it is the very self-sacrificing act of bearing and raising children that the bride of Christ does to reproduce Christ's disciples on the earth. At that time, many women died in childbirth. These deaths were quite common. The love of God-ordained self-sacrifice always makes its way as intercession before God's throne.

There is a saving grace for some women in children and childbearing that they otherwise may never have had. So I don't think Paul was exhorting women to be mindless children, never learning to function as thinking adults. And I don't think he was saying that being mothering baby-machines was their highest call in Christ.

Since we have loosed the attitudes of slavery from ourselves, isn't it about time we got rid of the subtleties of women as property? The world has in a much faster way than the church.

His People in His Image

Unfortunately, this worldly freedom has caused licentiousness and sin. But do we in the church fix that by legalism and a jerk-knee response, or do we speak about grace and submission to Christ and the Holy Spirit? It's about time we stopped implementing the law and, instead, implemented the mind of Christ.

The Marriage Vow

While most individuals and churches can recognize a demonic attitude that tries to separate, they seldom recognize how it pollutes us with its murky doctrines where the marriage relationship exists. Some take their resistances—strongholds of the mind—and seem to find an outlet or place for them to rest when it comes to the male-female relationship in marriage.

While women or men can be equal leaders regardless of gender or ethnicity in the church, there is one distinction in the marriage relationship—and only one. Again, studying this one distinction must be done in the light of God's glory, with the whole of Scripture. We must see it with the eyes of God's Spirit, through the mind of Christ. In other words, it must be all of Him and none of us. This is very seldom done. We all love to add our own pet teachings, or stronghold ideas, and they in turn are used to subordinate other human beings.

First, let's celebrate the fact that men and women are different. God ordained this difference to be as striking as that between the rich and the poor, the educated and the uneducated and one ethnic group and another. Truthfully, I have learned equally great lessons from those who have no money as I have from those who do. I have learned just as many lessons from those with polished and trained minds as from those who never made it out of grade school. The Italians have a wisdom that the French do not possess, and the French have a wisdom that the British have not discovered. But when we learn from one another and enjoy these God-ordained differences, we grow in ways we could never have grown alone.

So why is it that, within the marriage relationship, the church makes it seem like one God-ordained difference is inferior to the other? Why do we take Scriptures and twist them to puff up a supposed superiority? This is sad. If we continue to do this in our marriage relationships, we are in danger, like Peter and Barnabas, to miss the glorious will of God for a whole generation.

Female Subordination

Having already established an understanding of the mind of Christ, let's look at Scriptures that resistant ideologies use to support subordination as submission: Ephesians 5:21–6:9 and 1 Peter 3. Looking at 1 Peter 3, Peter is primarily dealing with those married to unbelievers. Nevertheless, he makes several good points about living a godly lifestyle. So many make an issue of the words "master" or "lord" used here. Again, this is done without understanding the times or the language. The word *Baal* (Hebrew) means "husband, lord and master." There is no other word. They were all synonymous. This stemmed from the property-ownership system in which wives were owned. Hence, their husbands were, indeed, their masters. They had no choice but to obey, as a slave would. This word is still the same in the Hebrew language today.

Being a devout Jew, even though this is written in Greek, this is precisely what Peter is referring to. We should take heed, though, for this misunderstanding of the language is a similar trip-up when Israel goes "a-whoring" in idolatry to the Baals. We miss the magnitude of what calling these gods "Baal" meant. The word meant exactly the same then as it does now. Israel exchanged marriage to God Almighty for worshiping, or marrying, the foreign gods, termed as Baals (we will look at God's marriage to Israel shortly).

The second inaccurate doctrine that is sometimes developed from reading 1 Peter is that women are somehow inferior because they are the "weaker" vessel. Peter is speaking physical weakness here. He cannot be speaking of anything else since he calls them the weaker partners—KJV says *vessel*—and in the next phrase says they are "heirs (joint) in the gracious gift of life."

His People in His Image

Now, to be sure, some men marry women that are inferior to them in many respects, and some women do likewise. But this is not always the Lord's doing. When people find themselves in this type of a marriage, Ephesians 5:21, which precedes all else in our discussion of submission in Ephesians, will be the overriding factor: "Submit yourselves therefore one to another."

Husbands and wives must cover each other, submitting to one another and recognizing each other's differences, strengths and weaknesses. They must make the marriage team stronger by helping each other where one partner's skills are weaker or where the other's are stronger.

One other incorrect doctrine that stems from an inaccurate reading of this passage is that husbands should make all the decisions in the household. Well, then, why is Peter telling them to live in harmony so that nothing hinders their prayers? Why are they praying together for godly guidance if the husband is making all the decisions? Some then use Ephesians 5:22-23 to substantiate this error. It is here that Paul describes a superseding headship that the husband does have; he likens it to Christ's headship over the church.[5]

Because of this headship, many infer that all the decision-making belongs solely to the husband. After all, doesn't the head do that? Well, sometimes and sometimes not. The brain provides all the connections for all bodily functions; remember, though, our minds are to be the mind of Christ, which is not limited to male/female, Jew/Gentile, bond/free boundaries. It is Christ, through the Holy Spirit, who helps us all make some tough or easy decisions.

The ancients did not consider the seat of thinking to come from the brain but from the heart (called a *leb*). They considered the head as a concept of order because the head is what is birthed first. When we talk about the head, we talk about order and direction—and not just any direction. In this case, we refer to the direction of some specific areas that come up in a marriage relationship only. This would be when a decision cannot be based upon mutual agreement, either in prayer or by natural understanding. (See 1 Peter 3:7.) When this situation arises and we follow the head, order will always be maintained because of proper direction.

Getting Direction

Direction is not always decision making. If your head loses its sense of direction and vertigo, dizziness or double vision sets in, your body is not going anywhere. You are out of order. Christ gave His bride direction: preach the gospel, make disciples, heal the sick, prophesy and cast out demons; occupy until I come. Within the parameters of those directions many different decisions can be made. Jesus gave direction when a ragtag group of confused believers could have gone off in half a dozen different directions. They were excited, elated and full of hope that He was alive. But once He had left, if He had not given those directions and sent the indwelling Holy Spirit, one disciple would have said, "We need to do this," and another, just as powerful and gifted disciple, could have gone off and said, "no, we need to do that." But God gave direction, and they came with one accord, submitting to one another in the upper room on the day of Pentecost. In that way, order would be maintained. After the church was birthed they came together as men and women of God in order to make decisions on certain issues.

Likewise, there are some severe life situations where a husband and wife need direction—not necessarily a decision; the direction may produce a decision. Such was the case with Joseph and Mary. We have talked about the great anointing upon Mary, an anointing that really is only superseded by Christ Himself. For none of us saints can imagine what it took to risk our lives to bear and birth the Lord of glory. And yet, the direction of where to go, where to travel and where to live was given to Joseph, not Mary. It was Mary's decision or choice whether to accept the responsibility to birth and raise Christ under Joseph's direction.

Sometimes, tough life circumstances come up, and you have two powerfully anointed people moving in submission, one to the other, but they cannot make a decision on a given subject. In such a case, the husband will most always have the right direction. In that place, while the wife might not agree with the decision that follows, she knows how hard it was for her husband to seek the answer from God on the subject; his attitudes were pure and his motives were holy. She should willingly obey God's command. Her husband is her head and she should submit.

Submission must be total. We say we submit, but we have attitudes that can stress the family unit beyond fixing. Our submission must be in accordance with the mind of Christ. We must have a godly attitude, exercise godly thoughts and habits and speak with godly speech. And I stress both husband and wife living in appropriate Christ-like submission, even though the husband is the head.

They cannot hold a false sense of authority by confusing it with a domineering personality or some supposed piousness that says, "Oh, well, I'm just the woman; my husband must make these decisions." This is cowardice and lack of faith, not healthy growth in a Christ-like environment. When God says Eve is a help meet for Adam (KJV), it is exactly the same Hebrew word used in the Psalms to describe God as our present help in times of trouble. (See Psalms 20:2, 33:20, 70:5, 115:9–11, 121:1–2.)

When Direction Follows Order

God's wisdom amazes me. While mothers are generally tenderer in nature, it is the very strength, necessary for raising their sons, that teach a woman how to deal with strong-minded young men. At the same time this teaches the boys a proper sense of submission in the household, as they watch appropriate submission of their mothers to their fathers. It also teaches them how to respond appropriately to women in authority, as well as in personal relationships in the future. Fathers tend to be stronger in their dealings with their children. Their daughters are prepared by God to make fathers softer in areas in which they need to be softer. Fathers usually treat their sons in more of a rough-and-tumble kind of way and treat their daughters more tenderly. As this interaction is going on in the family unit, this teaches their daughters how to respond to men appropriately in the future, both on the job and in their personal relationships. In the same way that an unhealthy family environment is created when a mother usurps her husband by lack of submission to his authority, an equally unhealthy family environment is created when a husband subjugates and subordinates his wife's God-ordained authority in the household.

Love and Marriage

One of the last issues concerning marriage I'd like to address is seen in Ephesians 5:24. I will quote from the King James Version: "Therefore as the church is subject unto Christ, so let the wives be to their own husbands in every thing." Let's also quote from Ephesians 5:33: "However, each one of you also must love his wife as he loves himself, and the wife must respect her husband" (NIV).

Why does Paul tell wives to respect, but husbands to love? Is it because wives don't have to love their husbands, only respect them? And is it because husbands only have to love their wives; respect is not an option? We err in not knowing the times in which the apostles lived. Try, if you will for a minute, to ignore over a thousand years of church dogma. We talked about this before concerning 1 Peter. Wives and children, like slaves, were owned. Wives, especially, were "special property." They did not marry for love. While Jewish law afforded women and wives far more rights than the Roman-Greek world of Paul's day, women and wives were still property. Marriages were arranged, and women were paid for with dowries provided by their fathers. Love for a woman in those days was not as women marry for love today. When these women got saved, they realized they were no longer owned by anyone. Christ had purchased them—redeemed them—and paid a dowry for them. Christ was their new provider, or husband, if you will. The Hebrew word for husband, *baal*, is the same word for master—the exact same word. Christ was their

His People in His Image

new Master or Lord. Some of these women were looking on their former masters, their husbands, with contempt, much the same way the slaves were. Paul had to arrest this dangerous attitude before satan could get a stronghold on it and, thus, pollute the church. That is one reason for the admonition in verse 24 to submit in everything and respect.

What about the admonition for husbands to love? Have you ever owned a dog, cat, horse, cow, fish, bird or other animal? You may have loved it, even respected it, but would you die for it? It's your property—you own it. It serves you. Even if you love and care for it, you would never die for it. But that's the kind of love that healthy marriage produces. Ancient marriages were not primarily relationships in which the husband would die for his wife—maybe a son who was the heir, but not the wife. He could always get a new one. After all, he was her owner, master or lord. Paul must admonish these husbands who were new believers to love. It must not be just any love, but the "I'll-die-for-you" kind of love that Christ has. We have some better understanding of this today because of what Paul had to write to these husbands in order to arrest a similarly dangerous attitude in the church. Satan already had a better stronghold here.

It is a real testament to the love of God shed forth in the body of Christ that arranged marriages are almost a thing of the past. Unfortunately, they still carry on extensively overseas, largely due to Muslim religious teachings. But it was Paul's profound revelation to newly converted Christian husbands that helped to destroy the attitude that says, "my wife is my property." I must make a sad observation, though. Many churches still teach marriage relationships based upon subordination to male superiority. Instead, they should stress mutual team marriage based upon the mind of Christ in love, unifying men and women in marriage—even in their God-ordained differences. It breaks my heart to hear these teachings that bring disunity. When holy Christ-like submission is taught, it never brings rebellion. It will deal with our control and manipulation issues. When we teach true Christ-like submission, the love of husbands grows stronger, and wives trust them and their leadership even more. As this interaction takes place, both partners realize the strength of team ministry under the husband's direction (head) to Christ's orders. May God help us to have the mind of Christ, who loved us enough to humbly bear the role of a servant to unify us to the Father.

If all husbands had Christ's mind in them when it would come to areas of disagreement concerning direction, wives would willingly acquiesce. They could be confident that God was using their husband's humility and submission toward God's greater good. It is the burden of both partners to intercede as priest for direction and decision-making. God places the greater responsibility upon the husband because of his symbolic analogy to Christ and His church. This greater responsibility should actually produce more humble attitudes, even during difficult times. Instead, we have abuse of all kinds, even within the body of Christ. These attitudes of domination are camouflaged as submission and can eventually lead to outright physical violence. Because this attitude is a substitution of true Christ-like submission, it will never lead to health and wholeness. It is the little foxes that spoil the vine. (See Song of Solomon 2:15.) It is this slight attitude shift that many people buy into wholeheartedly, especially within Christendom, that produces so much contention. James asked where fights and quarrels from within us came from. (See James 4:1.) The answer James gave for overcoming these sinful behaviors was submission to God; resistance to the devil; repentance in the form of grieving, mourning and wailing, and choosing to humble ourselves before God. I pray we will take action and commit to this kind of godly mind. Possibly—just possibly—the Lord of Glory will find rest among us at that point, so He may abide continually.

Overcoming All Slavery

Let's look at another issue concerning subordination. Some Greek scholars argue that Paul must condone slavery, since he never speaks against it but, instead, seems to support it.[6]

His People in His Image

We need to look at Paul's stance on these issues in the light of history, the legal systems of the world at that time and cultural mandates. As I said before, because he seems silent on the issues of women as property and slavery in general, some have concluded that he supports this subordination. But does he really?

God wrote Scripture to give countless generations guidelines to live by. God has Paul condemn the root causes of these evil practices. Attacking the practices of slavery and women as property would have done nothing for the church or the world at that time. God shows us today, by the example of the early church, how to eradicate these stronghold mentalities. Submission, repentance and love for one another, even in the face of persecution and certain death, will cause God in heaven to hear our cries, come down and quash these mentalities.

It is because of the early church's sacrifice in these areas that large portions of the earth no longer practice the ownership of one human being by another. So when Paul exhorts women to submit to their husbands in everything, it should not surprise us. He was just exhorting them legally, just as he exhorted slaves to be submissive. And yet we have seen the reality of to whom wives should be submissive. They are not instructed to submit to a domineering personality, someone full of the pride of who he thinks he is. Rather, submit to a humble servant of God, who has been given the greater responsibility of praying for and seeing his family lifted up. In this way, love for one another will give our Lord a highway on which to come to earth. Satan will have no open door by which to use his oppressive tactics.

Living on Earth

We must remember one reality that we see over and over in the Scriptures: faith has not yet become total sight. In other words, we are not physically in heaven yet, and the end of the ages has not passed into eternity. We still live in our mortal bodies. The ramifications of this fact hit everywhere you and I live.

When God passed judgment in time and space on Adam, Eve

and the serpent, certain things took place. Adam had to toil the ground, and Eve was then made subject to Adam. (See Genesis 3:16–19.) Before that time, Adam did not toil, and Eve was not subjugated. Many think it was because the earth just produced fruit, and weeds did not choke other plants. While this outcome is absolutely true, the cause or catalyst was God speaking His Word. (See Genesis 2:4–6; 1:11–12.) Over time, had Adam and Eve not sinned, they would have had the ability to watch God speak His Word to the earth, and the earth and all her creatures would have responded.

So Adam and Eve would have had the ability to watch Father God speak. Likewise, to the extent God gave them, they would have been able to speak His Word or will to the face of the earth, so the Holy Spirit would move on the earth, and the earth would have responded. Adam would not have had to toil in the flesh, and there would have been no serpent attackers. Hence, Eve would not have had to be subjugated.

She would truly be his equal partner. Because of sin, God now had to work backwards from sin to salvation. Sin is backwardness for God. It is totally alien to Him. He had to judge the serpent first and then all the way up the line to Adam. So, in similar fashion, because of Christ's death, Adam received freedom first, then Eve, then creation.

Of course, I don't ever mean to imply that satan, as a part of creation or otherwise, will ever be redeemed. This will never happen, as is made extremely plain throughout the Scriptures. I am speaking of the judgment of the creature, the serpent, as representing other serpents—just as all Adam and Eve's descendants were judged through them. To be sure, satan was judged both then and emphatically right after Christ said, "It is finished." I am separating the difference between the serpent as a creature of earth and satan as a created spiritual being. (See Genesis 3:14, 15; also Isaiah 14:3–20.)

This is not just a woman's issue. If we can get a grasp of this as the whole body of Christ, the ramifications are astounding. As holy men and women, especially within the bonds of marriage,

His People in His Image

God has given us the ability to speak forth to God's earth today. We can become the deliverers Moses, Elijah, Joseph, Ruth, Daniel and Esther were. We can become even more so, because we are going forth under the banner of Christ's holy Word, or name, and in His glory.

Attackers on Earth

Because of this, it is time for "Eve" to be restored to her fullness in Christ as an equal partner. Nevertheless, we are still on earth. So why does Paul exhort the wives to be subject to their husbands in everything? While we have discussed some reasons for this, one seems quite plain: there are still enemy attackers, or "serpents" on earth. So from a marriage point of view, the husbands must function in their priestly roles before Christ for their wives and their families. One might ask, "If this is the case, why is it different within the hierarchy of the corporate body of Christ?" (See Galatians 3:28.) I believe it is different because of the extensive leadership covering in a church or other ministry organizations. When these bodies move according to the Word of the Lord, fivefold ministry, elders, deacons, singing priests (worship teams) and sacrificing priests (intercessors), along with all the Holy Spirit's marvelous gifts, are functioning in place. There is almost too much covering for the devil. He can't openly attack such a defended army successfully. He has to separate and divide in order to conquer. In the smaller hierarchy of a family unit he can do that easily. There are only two in that context. In order to be successful, marriages must function according to the attitudes and hierarchy that the Word of the Lord has placed to govern them. It is the very attitude of sacrifice that Christ had that delivered His bride from certain death.

This attitude of repentance and sacrifice by husbands protects wives and families from demonic attacks. The same principle is seen in nature. Whatever seems to be in the best interest of preserving the species is what the practices are for the two genders within those species. In the lion and lioness structure, the lionesses do most of the work. The lion's main job is marking their territory to keep jackals and hyenas away from the pride.

Within the United States, there are two wild bands of horses left. One interesting thing that researchers noticed while studying these two bands was that, in one band, the broodmares ran the show, and in the other band, the stallions did. The main focus of this study was to preserve the wild horses and to see what it was in their daily lives that humans could do to help. After studying these herds, the researchers noticed this male/female oddity of leadership. Upon closer study, the main difference became clear. Within the one herd there were many more predators, mountain lions being the primary source of attack. Within the other herd, there were few or no predators. Within the band where the mountain lions attacked, the coloration was muted. The bright white and spotted colors that would draw the attention of the mountain lions were changed over the generations to blacks, browns and other "quiet" colors. Within the other herd the coloration was still loud.

Within the herd where the mountain lions were a problem, the broodmares ran the show. One might wonder about this. But when we study horses, we understand that stallions know only one purpose in their lives. That is to constantly breed. This constant desire to breed creates chaos within a herd. With the broodmares in charge, the herd would be much more cautious and much more attentive towards survival instincts over the long run. Breeding would still go on, but the main objective would be survival. For this, broodmares are a much better source for leadership. Within the other herd, the stallions ran the show. This herd's lifestyle was more chaotic. They didn't need to be constantly on watch for the mountain lions or other predators; therefore, the stallions could rise to the top in leadership, and breeding would be the main objective. Eating and other survival goals would still be accomplished anyway. This herd's main contribution towards the survival of the species would be multiplication. Therefore, the stallions would be more needed as leaders.[7]

This is not a Darwinian evolutionary theory, and of course

humans are not lions or horses. We also see this principle at work in the Bible, as well as ancient society. Depending upon whether a household had more sons or daughters, what their ages were and whether they owned goats or sheep, either girls or boys would be selected to be shepherdesses or shepherds. This is one reason why we see Jethro's daughters tending the herd and Jesse's son, David, tending his father's herd later on. (See Exodus 2:16-19; 1 Samuel 16:11; 17:15.) It was usually the youngest child or children who tended the herds. In other words, it was what the family needed to survive based upon the family's individual make-up.

While God may be outside our time and space, we are not. God uses our time and our environment for His better plan and purpose—or for our health and well-being. We are not animals. We have spirits, souls and bodies. In the spiritual realm, while we are on the face of the earth, the hierarchy role of a husband makes sense for the survival of a family because of our attackers in that realm. As it relates to the leadership gifts within the church, Christ has already dealt the blow to the devil's antics there. (See Ephesians 4:1-16.)[8]

Husbands and Wives in Leadership

We have already talked about transforming our minds with God's Word to gain the mind of Christ. We've also discussed how the headship role of the husband should manifest itself in love, holiness and dedication within the marriage bonds. The next question that arises is this: if women can be called into leadership roles within the greater body of Christ, what happens when God calls a woman who is married into a fivefold leadership position, but her husband is not so called? This should not confuse us. As long as the husband has no objections to his wife's calling by God, then he remains her elder anyway. His headship should not be circumvented. They will simply need to work out the family duties and the extra burdens placed upon the family that the wife's call may bring. In other words, don't male pastors, evangelists, and prophets have their wives as elders who speak godly wisdom into their lives? The husband would lose no authority in that place or over the family. He is still head of the household. This particular situation might actually place a greater burden on him to be in constant prayer for his wife. He must also learn the hard task of not usurping her call, yet he must understand his unique place as teammate and elder in that calling. This is very similar for women whose husbands have a fivefold call, but they do not. The wife may have no place in that fivefold call except to pray for her husband and speak wisdom into his life. So this may also be the case for a husband whose wife has a fivefold call. The only difference is that he is also her head and the head of the household. Not to state the obvious, but no one should be placed in an elder position if their household is in disarray. (See Titus 1:6.)

When Both Are Called

It becomes more challenging, and yet somewhat easier, when both have a fivefold call on their lives, as it is assumed that Priscilla and Aquila did in the New Testament. But we must remember that just because these issues become more challenging, it does not mean they are unscriptural. God's gifts are as multifaceted as His Word and as diverse as His people.

Aquila and Priscilla must have functioned appropriately, since there is no mention of any trouble with them. In fact, out of the six times they are mentioned in the Scriptures, her name precedes his three times. They are always mentioned as leaders together. And it is not because, as some would state, the writers were being chivalrous or polite by mentioning her name first. This just does not line up with the plain fact that, legally, Priscilla was Aquila's property. Considering the restrictive climate in which women lived, the only explanation is that they must have both been strong leaders together.

It is not the purpose of this book to delve into the subject of women in ministry. My purpose here is to expose attitudes or strongholds that separate and hinder the body of Christ from being one healthy bride, blessed with God's continuously abiding glory.

His People in His Image

A Father's Love: Go and Make Disciples

What is the devil so afraid of concerning women and ethnic diversity in ministry? We forget the declaration of the Lord in Genesis 3:15. While certainly there is dislike between women and serpents, or snakes, and their heads can be easily crushed in the natural, I believe we would all agree that this is a spiritual proclamation. When we study the judgment God places on the creature—satan—the creation and mankind, it is judged in three areas and three time frames: spirit, soul and body; past, present and future. So it should not surprise us that satan hates women or that there is special enmity there, as proclaimed by God. The enemy knew Christ would be born, and searched for Him constantly. With Christ's victory on the cross, satan is defeated. If he can prolong the final judgment, he feels he can still succeed, in some deluded way. So from satan's point of view, why not continue to attack women, constantly striking at her offspring. The other reality, though, is that satan knows his time is short. Once he sees women restored to functional freedom in Christ, creation is the next entity to be restored. His time is up; he will receive the final manifestation of his judgment and be locked up forever.

There is another question that needs asking. Why does satan try so hard to keep Christians captive to these divisive ideologies? In a spiritual sense, when we as believers learn to wholly submit to the will and ways of God, we will die to the resistant strongholds of our natural minds and become pure and holy. We will then become able to birth Christ in others and reproduce other disciples for Christ on the face of the earth. We will become better able when we release the other 50 percent of the army of the Lord into full service. The devil hates Christ being birthed in others. It represents God's love to us as Father, Husband and all in all. Satan wants to destroy all examples of this.

Remember, if unity can be restored and we are as faithful to one another as Christ is to us, this love will reproduce itself as Christ in others. (See John 13:34-35.) And this love will be a witness of Christ to others. I am not sure how much our domination and demands of legalistic justice for Eve's sin damages the evangelist's preaching of the gospel, but it can't help.

Jesus tells us in John's Gospel that the love shown one to another is one of the best ways to witness to people. He says, "*All men will know that you are my disciples, if you love one another.*" In other portions of Scripture where the gospel is preached, it is to limited numbers of people with the ability to receive or reject it. But Jesus says that *all* men will know… (See John 13:35.) By loving each other everyone will know we are Jesus' disciples. That's remarkable.

I am not recommending to love only, without preaching the gospel. By all means, preach, teach, prophesy, heal the sick and cast out demons. Do everything that is needed to reach the lost. But this goal can only be accomplished as men and women work together in holiness, love and humility towards each other and the people they need to reach. We know the hindrance that legalism has upon the church. Why would we think that a legalistic, male-dominated mentality wouldn't be even more devastating? Love covers a multitude of sins. (See 1 Peter 4:8.) This is especially true in matters of marriage. Where there is prophecy, it will cease. Where there is knowledge or other gifts, they will cease. But love remains because it is the greatest. (See 1 Corinthians 13.)

When husbands relinquish their rights under the law and realize that even the prophecies of judgment over Eve have ceased, then and only then will "Eve" be free. This is the purest example of Father God to mankind. Eve is stated to be the mother of the living. Adam is never stated "as the father of all living." It isn't because God didn't favor Adam in this way or that Eve was better suited for this task. God created Adam just as He wanted Adam to be created. It is because God, the eternal Father, is Father of all the living. I don't mean to imply that all of mankind is blood-washed and children of God. Many are not. But to those that are, the love of our heavenly Father is all sustaining. Because of Christ's blood, we have forever been restored to the love of Father God as no other human beings can be.

His People in His Image

Until this revelation is sealed in our hearts, we will all demand justice from the law, when Christ has already satisfied the law. By maintaining our stronghold judgments concerning women, we are maintaining some portion of the law over our lives. Father God could have demanded legalistic justice for our sin, but instead, He sent Christ, His own Son, as payment. Father God relinquished His rights under the Law—once Christ's sacrifice is accepted—so that judgment is averted. Judgment has been imputed to Christ, so Father God imputes righteousness to us. When we relinquish our strongholds, judgment is averted, and righteousness can now flow to every area of our lives in which the law has held us.

God's Wife: Israel

Since we're talking about love, husbands and wives, it would be out of order not to mention God's wife, Israel. (See Isaiah 54:5; Ezekiel 16:1-41; Hosea 2:2; Isaiah 50:1.) While both Israel and the church are His people, and the church has been termed the bride of Christ, God has made it clear that He has not forgotten His wife, Israel. (See Isaiah 54:6-10; Ezekiel 16:42, 59-63; Hosea 2:14-3:5.) This reality hit me hard when I studied this stronghold set up against God manifested in glory. While satan hates "Eve" for her ability to bring forth, and the church because of her ability in spiritual purity to bring forth Christ in others on earth, he hates Israel because she brought forth Christ the first time on earth. This is why this stronghold in us produces such jealousy, and this is why our enemy is able to use it so well.

Jesus makes it plain that He will come back to His people—both groups of them—when they (Israel, His brothers) seek Him or ask for Him. (See Malachi 3:1-4; Matthew 11:9-11; Isaiah 42:1-4; Matthew 12:15-21; John 19:37; Zechariah 12:10-14:21; Revelation 1:7.) There are many Jewish believers in Christ, but as a whole, the nation of Israel has rejected Jesus as its Messiah. (See Romans 10:1-4, 16.) When God restored David to his throne after Absalom's revolt, David's tribe Judah did not come to welcome him back. David said he would not return unless they did. (See 2 Samuel 19:11–42.)

Paul tells us that Israel's falling away from Christ is God's will so that we, the Gentiles, might be grafted in and brought to a fullness in God's kingdom. (See Romans 10:19–11:15; 11:25–29. See also Romans 12:2 in reference to passages on renewing the mind.) I believe when we restore "Eve," or woman, to her appropriate position in Christ, God will remember—with a longing you and I cannot comprehend—His wife, Israel. When He does, it will be right on His time schedule for Israel to receive and remember her Brother and ask for Him to come to His throne! (See Hosea 2:16–20.)

If the Lord God Almighty would not forget Israel, His wife, why would we think He would forget to restore woman in general to Christ-like fullness? He has seen all the bigotry over the years. He has heard the cries of millions of women over the centuries that have been ignored, or worse, brutalized. God has not forgotten, nor will He forget.

The Bible says,

> **But Zion said, "the Lord has forsaken me, the Lord has forgotten me." "Can a mother forget the baby at her breast and have no compassion on the child she has borne? Though she may forget, I will not forget you! See, I have engraved you on the palms of my hands; *your walls* are ever before me."**
>
> —Isaiah 49:14–16, emphasis added

With this in mind, I'd like to look at a portion of Scripture in Malachi 4:5–6 (kjv). The prophet says,

> **Behold, I will send you Elijah the prophet before the coming of the great and dreadful day of the Lord: And he shall turn the heart of the fathers to the children, and the heart of the children to their fathers, lest I come and smite the earth with a curse.**

His People in His Image

He never talks about the mothers. Why? While taking nothing away from a husband's headship role, we should begin to understand that, as men die to their rights under the law to judge Eve's descendants, and as they renew their minds by receiving the mind of Christ, they release freedom to all of Eve's children. The result is that male, female, Jew and Gentile—all those who are bound—are allowed to be free! This extends beyond the absentee father, for it has a spiritual application, too. This is a place of intercession before God. Christ interceded before the throne that we, as sinners, should not receive the penalty due us. Similarly, husbands, and by implication, fathers, can give up their legal rights to rule over their families. Instead they can view them with Christ's mind, and work with their wives as partners and mutual leaders. It will require an understanding of their responsibilities to pray and fast for direction, and to lift up their family members to be the leaders in Christ they were destined to be.

Restoring the hearts of the fathers means to restore their hearts to their daughters as well as their sons. God has truly changed attitudes over the centuries. I've talked to many fathers that grieve for the bondage in which they see their wives or other women when they are discriminated against because of their gender. I've noticed many men adamantly refuse to allow that same bondage over their daughters. Men are realizing that their daughters, as well as their sons, can be leaders equally and in the full sense of the word. Fifty years ago this thinking was not as prevalent as it is today. God is truly restoring this understanding to fathers and husbands so that each subsequent generation can be released even further in Christ to see limitless possibilities in the sciences, the arts, government and theology.

Christ, the Second Adam

While we are speaking about a husband's place of intercession before the throne, there is another place of sacrifice that husbands are required to make. When marriage takes place, a woman gives up an internal or hidden place of purity. For a man this is not so. And yet men are created with an internal sense of government. Adam was created as the federal head for the human race. But in Christ, we have a second Adam or new federal head.

Husbands must give up that sense of totally ruling or governing their own lives and decide to submit their own governmental decisions for the better overall health and well being of their wives and families. As a result, this internal submitting or giving up becomes a place of sacrificial intercession before God's throne. It is a witness. I take nothing away from a husband's place or proper headship in a household. The witness of which I speak, as a sacrifice, is that of the glory of God for the world. Marriages should, in each individual way, represent the faithful giving of the bride of Christ and the faithful giving of the Lord of Glory–the sacrifice of both to one another and the world. Instead satan has convinced even some in the church to represent witchcraft and idolatry. What I mean by witchcraft is a desire to so control families so that everything must go our own way. Idolatry is similar, because the "weaker" partners never control; instead, they subtly manipulate.

I am not at all attempting to be judgmental or to pass judgment of any kind. Neither am I saying that only men control. Men and women can enter into control and manipulation equally. Sin is an equal opportunity employer. Its wages are death. (See Romans 6:23.) What I am saying is that some marriages have become war zones in many homes. As the bride of Christ, we should expose the subtle ways in which our enemy exchanges the glory of God for a lie. When we don't recognize the lie, we have a hard time perceiving the Lord of Glory coming to bring abundant life to an area of our daily living. (See John 10:10.) When we base our marriages upon the lie, hell is invited to the wedding as well as the divorce. When we base our marriages upon Christ, abundant life is manifested. Pulling down these stronghold attitudes brings Christ to every part of our lives.

His People in His Image

Restoring True Unity To Christ's Body

When both genders lay their respective God-ordained creative gifts at the feet of the cross, God then restores them to each of us individually. We may still have children in the flesh. But when we allow God to restore us in Christ, men may be able to birth children spiritually, and women may be able to govern. The entire body can be restored to the head, which is Christ.

God's people truly perish without Christ's vision and they are taken captive by satan through ignorance (See Proverbs 29:18; Isaiah 5:13.) Of course, freeing woman is also the best example of freeing the bride of Christ. As those who were originally given federal headship release it to the Lord of Glory, He sets His order in place, freeing all who are bound.

The true body of Christ is the best hope the world has for unity. I pray that we do not abdicate this responsibility by exchanging the fullness of God's glory for a slavish adherence to religious, legalistic spirits. I have heard many say it is too difficult to allow men and women to work together in the body of Christ. My response is always this: if God has called and chosen a person, God will sustain the situation as long as we act responsibly. We must always strive for holy living. We must all exhort one another in holy dress and behavior. But James says, "Let no man say when he is tempted, I am tempted of God" (James 1:13, KJV). When we are tempted we must acknowledge that a portion of flesh remains. When we are as dead to sin as a dead body is to insults, no amount of provocation will work. Instead of covering up a desire to sin with a rule or regulation, we must realize the necessity for Christ to expose, crucify and purge it.

Redeeming the Earth: the Prodigal Son

Even the world recognizes the church's need for law as sin. This is why they shun our hypocrisy. Recently, God reminded me of the prodigal son. As I listen to people and read the news, I hear an underlying human spirit that honestly believes there is a God and that His Son is Jesus Christ.

The problem with many of the unchurched is they are like the prodigal son. They need to establish their own way while the "good" son acts obediently on the surface, staying home and taking care of father's house. It isn't until the one who was lost is found that the sin of the "good" son is revealed for what it is—jealousy, bitterness and rivalry. These are strongholds that are used to protect our positions.

The same demons that inhabit the world's strongholds of infirmity, disunity, rebellion, and idolatry inhabit the church. Infirmity is caused by a lack of affirmation. Disunity is caused by substituting a religious spirit to create a false sense of unity, instead of thinking through the mind of Christ. Corporate America functions this way frequently. Rebellion is control. This can ultimately foster adultery, rape and murder, because we want things our own way. Idolatry is just a stubborn arrogance to our own human systems and agendas. All these strongholds are in our churches. It is our destiny to cast them out and bind them from functioning on the face of the earth. (See Luke 19:13.) How will we be able to walk into places of political human strength and recognize the lie and the subsequent demonic attachment when we can't even recognize these things in our own churches? We don't even allow those who can recognize them to cast them out and bind their continual ability to deceive.

God can come in glory upon us, but sooner or later the prodigals will see that many of us are not genuine. When we decide to remove the hypocrisy from our midst by removing these strongholds, the prodigals will come home. Jesus did not redeem the world back to God to make Adam and Eve's descendants happy in a garden. He redeemed mankind to teach us how to complete the fullness of the whole earth's redemption.

The Scriptures make it clear that the earth is the Lord's and the fullness thereof. (See Psalms 24:1; 50:12; 1 Corinthians 10:26.) Satan is an intruder. He intruded in the garden before sin ever took place. It was up to both Adam and Eve, in unity, to recognize the intruder and kick him out. Adam could not have done that alone; otherwise, Eve would never have been created. Eve could not do it alone. They both had to eat the fruit in order for sin to take place. Conversely, they both had to stand their ground against the intruder. This takes unity. It takes an equal partnership and an understanding of the other's strengths and weaknesses. For those descendants of Adam and Eve who are not in a partnership of marriage, it takes an attitude of humility with an understanding of our brother's and sister's strengths and weaknesses.

An army must stand in unity and in line with a clear chain-of-leadership command, for divided it will fall. There is no unity when we try to make someone else subservient to our own desires and add to our hypocrisy by calling it scriptural. Dominion in the spirit realm, after the order of God Almighty, is nothing more than maintaining the health of God's environment. This is so that God's creation can grow and mature in order to fulfill its God-given destiny.

It is our job to establish or maintain a spiritual environment on earth so that God may abide and rest. The Great Commission is still the best and most complete way to do this: preach, prophesy, teach the gospel or sow into the heavenlies by speaking on the face of the earth the Word of God. (See Mark 16:15.) And the Word, combined with the Holy Spirit, will produce new converts (verse 16). At that point, cast out the usurping intruders (demons). And with the power of the Holy Spirit (verse 17), heal those who have been wounded by them, and take back and occupy the ground and all creation in those areas that have been tainted by the influence of those demons (verse 18).

Restoring Breaches: Reflecting God's Glory

All of this can only be done in submission to God's Word and authority. Submission must be total. There must be submission in attitude, in godly habits and godly speech. Whomever God wills and chooses within His body as leaders should be submitted

BEYOND STRONGHOLDS

to with godly reverence. But we remain in rebellion to Christ's federal headship when mankind demands its own headship back. This is why justice is not found within us, and deceit becomes the way we do things. (See Isaiah. 59:12–17.)

When we say, "Oh, Lord, all headship and honor belong to you," He places those whom He chooses in leadership. We are restored. (See Isaiah 59.) Women are called to bring peacefulness to a headship position outside the marriage relationship that sometimes a man cannot give.

As seen in Isaiah 58, when women are restored, a breach is repaired. But God is preparing us for eternity beyond the confines of earthly rule. (See Matthew 22:30; Mark 12:25; Luke 20:35.) God is preparing us for eternal purposes where we are not given in marriage, but are like the angels. He is bringing us to an understanding of the heavenly life. This is why we must forsake these strongholds. God is so good. I believe He is giving us a transitional period of time so we can examine these issues.

I believe this is why we are hearing more balanced and scriptural theology on this subject. And yet, I have seen many women in fivefold ministry go through horrible persecution from people who refuse the leadership gifts in which God has placed them. No one seems to understand the rebellion that is evidenced by these biases. I have no statistics to prove my experience, but when I get an opportunity to see or study certain churches or denominations that specifically persecute or shun women in leadership roles, I have noticed an unusual amount of emotional abuse, as well as spousal abuse. Sometimes this spousal abuse is subtle, and it is sad. It seems that what grieves father's heart no longer grieves us. What breaks God's heart should break our hearts. Isaiah 58:1–3, 6 speaks to God's people and says,

> Cry aloud, spare not. Lift up thy voice like a horn and declare unto my people their transgression...Yet they seek Me daily...As a nation that did righteousness... Wherefore have we fasted, and thou seest not?...Is not this the fast that I have chosen? To loose the fetters of

His People in His Image

wickedness, To undo the bands of the yoke, And to let the oppressed go free, And that ye break every yoke?

—Masoretic Text

I don't know how bad things need to get around us before we realize that it is our responsibility to change before the unsaved do. (See 1 Peter 4:17.) Isaiah tells us that we must attend to what breaks God's heart and grieves Him. When we fix those things, the result is the following:

> They that shall be of thee shall build the old waste places, Thou shalt raise up the foundations of many generations, And thou shalt be called the repairer of the breach, the restorer of paths to dwell in.
>
> —Isaiah 58:12, Masoretic Text

The first breach was between God and mankind. The second was between Adam and Eve. Christ came to restore all breaches. 2 Corinthians 3:18 makes it clear that all of us mirror Father's glory. Women have God's glory inherent within them that shines of Father. Men have God's glory inherent within them that shines of Father. They may each shine that glory in slightly different ways. But as each individual allows God's glory to shine, he or she will reflect Father's glory back to Him. He, in turn, reflects His glory to them.

Father's glory is then reflected throughout the face of the earth in Christ. That glory dispels all darkness. As we allow God's people to shine with Christ's glory, it is quite possible they will say, with one accord, the apostle's words in Revelation 22:17, 20:

> And the Spirit and the bride say, Come. And let him that heareth say, Come. And let him that is athirst come. And whosoever will, let him take the water of life freely…even so, come, Lord Jesus (kjv).

Repent, then, and turn to God, so that your sins may be wiped out, that times of refreshing may come from the Lord, and that He may send the Christ, who has been appointed for you—even Jesus. He must remain in heaven until the time comes for God to restore everything, as He promised long ago through His holy prophets.

—Acts 3:19–21

Chapter Ten

WHERE DO WE GO FROM HERE?

Isaiah 6:3 provides us a glimpse into God's throne room. As the seraphim surround Father's throne they begin to declare, "Holy, Holy, Holy is the Lord Almighty; the whole earth is full of his glory." As humans, we have a very difficult time perceiving God's kingdom, and yet it is everywhere. We have talked about God's desire for His glory to cover the earth as the waters cover the sea. (See Isaiah 6:3; Habakkuk 2:14, 3:3.) But Isaiah 6:3 tells us that all of the earth is already full of His glory. Which is it? Both! The fact is we humans don't know or understand God or His kingdom. And what we don't understand we tend to resist.

We are not as sensitive to the Holy Spirit as we need to be. The apostle tells us that a great cloud of witnesses surrounds us. Elisha asked God to open his servant's eyes so he could see the great company of angels that surrounded them. (See 2 Kings 6:17.) When clouds cover a portion of the skies above our heads, we say it is cloudy out. In fact, it is quite sunny. The sun hasn't gone anywhere. The clouds have just prevented us from seeing the full light of the sun. Enemy forces can literally block our eyes from seeing the Lord of glory in His fullness on earth. Our own strongholds, aligned with these forces, create just as much darkness for us. Christ's light dispels darkness; the darkness cannot comprehend His light. (See John 1:5.)

When darkness remains in portions of our hearts, we can be blinded from seeing God in glory upon other people and even on His creation. We tend to judge what we don't understand, further pushing away the fullness of His knowledge and presence. As we resist, the changes that He came to accomplish cannot be made. We then resist the people God uses to embody and define those changes. As a result we become unable to perceive the glory of God in areas we normally ignore. We also ignore the practical necessity for plurality in leadership and working as teams under one head, whether it is in church leadership, family or on socioeconomic levels. God's change is then short circuited by our resistant ignorance.

Because the earth is the Lord's and the fullness thereof, He has a timing for the revealing of His fullness to mankind. Each generation has brought revivals and renewals to increase our understanding of Him. Mankind has been given new technologies with each succeeding generation to help us understand Father God and His creation better.

This generation is no different. The church needs to use all the resources given it by God. We need to use all of our spiritual gifts. We must also make use of all the people God has given as gifts and all the technologies housed in the creation. God speaks from the beginning as if He already knew the end—and He does! The Bible says He is and He is to come. (See Isaiah 46:10.) Because He knows the end, we need to align ourselves in submission to His timing. When we cease from our own timing we are then able to submit to His understanding of what He reveals in this time and space within our own generation.

God in Glory Today: Who Was and Is and Is to Come

We have talked about different aspects of God manifested in glory from a Biblical and spiritual perspective. We've addressed how they relate to us as individuals, as churches and as the corporate body of Christ. While there is so very much more concerning the glory of God we have not discussed, one aspect is missing. That is how the *Shechinah* looks or manifests itself to us presently. We have talked about several physical manifestations as God has opened our eyes to see Him in the Scriptures. We have called these manifestations *theophanies*.

I realize what I am about to say is somewhat subjective, but I believe some personal observations can serve the greater good for us as brothers and sisters in Christ. I realize there are some today who say it is impossible to see the glory of God. My simple question is this: what did Peter, James and John see as Christ was transfigured? What did the 500 see before Christ ascended? What did Paul see that caused his temporary blindness when Christ appeared to him on the way to Damascus? What did John see when he was on the isle of Patmos as Christ revealed Himself?

They all saw something. While that "something" was not God Almighty sitting on the throne in glory, God wanted them to witness some aspect of Him in glory. The closest any sinner ever got to God's glory, in the New Testament, was probably Saul as He was on the Damascus road. This appearance struck him with blindness.

No doubt we will need our new resurrected bodies to be able to see or withstand the glory of God in heaven. Our earthly bodies just simply cannot hold up. But it is obvious from Biblical review that God in glory wants us to see some aspect of Him in glorious splendor. What I am about to share is only a small part of what He wanted me to see.

Personal Experiences: A Biblical Foundation

One constant throughout my many personal experiences is a combination of light and waves—something that would resemble what water does. Waves are a part of the natural world. The air around us travels in a flow or in waves. We call them streams. We have light waves, energy waves and radio waves. Our water flows

BEYOND STRONGHOLDS

in the same way. The earth, in its raw, molten form, travels as volcanic lava in waves or streams. As it builds pressure in the earth's rock, shock or energy waves are released—something we call seismic activity.

All these things produce some kind of change, either as a constant like the oceans, or as a catastrophic change as with a tornado or earthquake. Waves or streams can be manipulated to harness or change what a substance is, such as with microwaves, which change our food. Sound waves can change an atmosphere, as in a worship and praise session.

Our ancestors changed the flow of waves to harness water. In more modern times we've done it to change molecular structures to produce gas and electricity. Another example is the act of bending light and the more modern experiments conducted at the Rowland Institute for Science in Cambridge, Massachusetts by physicist Lene Vestergaard Hau. He and his team slowed down the speed of light to 38 miles per hour, instead of 186,282 miles per second (light's normal speed).[1]

The Scriptures declare that God is light, and in Him there is no darkness at all. (See John 1:5.) The book of Revelation tells us that the throne of God has what looks like a crystal sea. (See Revelation 4:6.) We're also told that the river of life flows from the throne of God and the Lamb down the middle of the great street of the city of God, the New Jerusalem. (See Revelation 22:1-2.)

It is said in many places that the sound of God's voice is as the sound of thunder—sound waves—and bolts of lightning come from the throne. (See Revelation 4:5.) Psalms 81:7 says God rescued Israel, and He answered them out of a thundercloud. John tells us that our Lord's voice was as the sound of rushing water. (See Revelation 1:15.) That is the same sound Ezekiel mentions hearing from the Almighty) and the Spirit, along with the living creatures. (See Ezekiel 1:2-4; 2:12-13.)

It is a similar sound that John hears from the heavenly chorus of believers. (See Revelation 19:6.) When the psalmist says, "Deep calls to deep in the roar of your waterfalls; all your waves and breakers have swept over me," (Ps. 42:7), we understand the depths of the Spirit of God within us that He is talking about. Nevertheless, the terms are related to either the moving seas and their surges and depths or a subterranean water supply—a place where the depth of the water creates purity. I believe this is why God comes in glory as waves, to change us.

God Is Light and Consuming Fire

God is also light. (See 1 John 1:5; James 1:17.) Light shines from the throne—incandescent, glorious and holy! As His glory-light shines, it flows throughout history, down time lines, from beginning to end. He is the Alpha and Omega. (See Revelation 1:8, 11; 22:13.) He created, and it was good. (See Genesis 1:10; 18, 21, 25.) Adam and Eve stepped into that light. They were created to be holy, and God, who is Holy light, came to rest and abide with them. As Adam and Eve rested in Him, they stepped into the light, and the light surrounded them.

Our God is a consuming fire. (See Deuteronomy 4:24; Hebrews 12:29.) Once sin was found in them, if God had not covered them with a sacrifice, that fire would have taken everything of them from the face of the earth. Nothing would have been left in this realm but ashes. Isn't that what's happening when God manifests throughout history to invade our space? The glory-light of His presence consumes and surrounds us. If it weren't for Christ's blood, we would be destroyed. So instead of us dying instantly on the spot, some of our gifts and blessings—and flesh—are consumed. We need restoration. We need the time and the uplifting of God's Word in glory to cause us to mature and to sustain us in His presence, in order to prepare us for eternity. (See Hebrews 1:3.)

We talk about a baptism of fire. I believe the baptism of fire is nothing more than God in awesome glory and light coming to us. I think either our close walk with God or our personal strongholds will determine whether that touch of God upon us is a burning baptism of fire or a light that shines through us—or both.

BEYOND STRONGHOLDS

Consecrated By Glory

Thinking back from now to my childhood, I would have to place my visual experiences with God in glory into three different classifications: glory waves, infiltrations and, for want of a better word, permeations. Standing by the altar of a church with thirty percent of the congregation in prayer and praise, a prophetess in charge of the service mentioned an anointing for those in the congregation that was about to fall for a particular purpose. The Holy Spirit told me to step back, as this anointing was only for those in the local congregation. I went back to my seat and watched as a wave literally tumbled and flowed over the folks at the altar. None of them fell down or laughed or shook. In fact, no outward physical manifestation occurred. I have since seen this on subsequent other occasions.

Other visitations of God's glory came in what I would call "infiltrations." I call it infiltration because every time I've experienced this it has been for the purpose of cleansing or kicking out enemy usurping forces, giving them no place to hide. It's as if there is a clarity of light that is indescribable. It's not just that there are no shadows visible, but a light has infiltrated every nook and cranny in the place. It reminded me of John's description of Jesus' face in Revelation 1:16.

The next experience is what I will call a "permeation." Every time I've seen this it has been in the atmosphere surrounding a believer or group of believers for the purpose of anointing them and consecrating them for works of service. It looks like a cloud. It is like a shimmering essence or light-cloud at the same time (much like what the Jews called the *Shechinah*). It also looks like a deep rolling cloud, with the feel, but not the sound, of thunder and lightning in your spirit. With it comes the experience of the awesome reality of the Lord's presence all around you (as Ezekiel, Isaiah and John experienced). To describe it, the word "hover," as the Spirit did in creation and over Mary, might be more appropriate. (See Genesis 1:2; Luke 1:35.)

The last anointing surrounding the glory of God that I've

Where Do We Go From Here?

experienced is the gold and silver "dust." I did spiritually see heavenly bronze dust once, as I was prophesying over a minister, but that one time was my only such experience. In the case of the gold and the silver "dust," while I have heard of this manifesting itself physically, I have only seen it spiritually. It was abiding on an object (church vessels), church or individual, or it was falling on a person for blessing. The Holy Ghost allowed me to see the origin of it once as a waterfall. On another occasion, He allowed me to prophesy His presence in it with a gift of prophecy over a congregation. Whether or not this "waterfall" is always present, I do not know. Psalm 42 supports this idea of the waterfalls of the Lord as deep calls to deep in our spirits. In every one of these instances, a believer or group of believers was being consecrated for works of service, along with church vessels (such as communion vessels) and church buildings.

Gifts of the Holy Spirit: Gifts of Discernment

Because each one of these experiences involved discerning what the Holy Spirit was doing for His people, I would categorize these experiences as a gift of discerning of spirits. (See 1 Corinthians 12:8–10.) In each one of these instances a gift of a word of knowledge, as well as a gift of a word of wisdom, were also involved. On two specific occasions that I can remember, these experiences also involved a gift of prophecy to a congregation. On these occasions and many others like them, they allowed God's people to know what God was doing. While God blessed me with His discernment, that discernment extended to His people as His gifts were released. I mention this because I believe that, in the coming moves of God, we will need His discernment as never before.

While all those experiences were glorious, I'm reminded of a different set of experiences.

BEYOND STRONGHOLDS

The Counterfeit

We are told in Revelation 12:15 that the dragon pursues the woman on the face of the earth, but God gives her wings of an eagle to fly to a safe place prepared for her. When the dragon cannot reach her there, he spews forth water like a river from his mouth to overcome her.

We are told that when the enemy comes in like a flood, the Spirit of the Lord will lift up a standard against him. (See Isaiah 59:19, KJV.) The NIV translates this portion of verse 19 as, "For he will come like a pent-up flood that the breath of the Lord drives along." The Masoretic Text translates this as, "For distress will come in like a flood, which the breath of the Lord drives." In my opinion, it is easiest to translate this using the verses before and after it. My own rendering of the text reads like this: "For [because] Tyre [a distressing enemy] enters by [within] a flood, the Spirit [wind-breath] 'driven'–[behold], even Yahweh with a beacon [flag fluttering] shall raise up a Standard Bearer." The emphasis then becomes more towards Yahweh, His beacon and Standard Bearer, rather than the enemy, Tyre. And it's also not clear that the flood even originates with the enemy, but that he hides within the flood. I feel the King James is the best translation in this case. That is why I reference it here. In conjunction with this, Revelation 17:15 says, "The waters you saw, where the prostitute sits, are peoples, multitudes, nations and languages."

The Word says that satan can even appear as an angel of light to some. (See 2 Corinthians 11:14.) I would so much rather talk about the wave of the Lord in glory than the counterfeit thing or how humans get involved with the counterfeit. But there is a counterfeit, and we need to be as wise as serpents, but as harmless as doves. (See Matthew 10:16; 2 Thessalonians 2:9–12.)

False Glory Waves

There have been three experiences in my life in which I have felt that I experienced a counterfeit of God's glory. When I look back

Where Do We Go From Here?

over these experiences I realized that they are representative of God's deliverance on three different levels. This is because the devil has corrupted mankind in those areas. They are on an individual basis, the creation as a whole and on a global level.

The first experience I had with false glory waves was as a young Christian. I had walked with Jesus as a child, but I backslid at age 13. At the age of 21, I was filled with the Holy Ghost. At that time the Lord made it clear to me that I was never to go into a bar. I had been a bartender during my backsliding, so obeying this word was not difficult for me.

About a year or so into my walk with Christ, I was invited to a baby shower for a fellow classmate. The party was to be held in a restaurant. I later learned that it was at a bar with a room in the back for catering purposes. I knew I had permission from the Holy Ghost to go to this affair. So you can imagine my shock when I walked into the place and realized that the bar took up the entire building! While I knew for a fact that the Spirit allowed me to go to this baby shower, I felt it would be wise to sit as far away from the bar as I could.

At one point in the event, it became necessary for me to go up to the bar to refill two or three pitchers with soft drinks to bring back to the tables. There were no alcoholic beverages being drunk, only soft drinks. It was a Saturday afternoon, and the place was closed to the public for our shower. What happened next in the spirit realm was quite new to me at that time. This was not some down and out dirty establishment. It had class. There were no outward visible signs of the demonic strongholds in the place.

Hanging on the walls from the table area to the bar and around the bar were seafaring pictures. The place had a nautical theme. The bar was located in a flood plain. In fact, a good portion of the city was located in a flood plain that was quite a problem when it rained. It also happened to be the county seat of Bergen County, NJ. A man with some political clout owned the place, or so I was told. As I approached the bar, the polished wooden planks of the floor started to slightly buckle. As I stood there, the seafaring pictures came alive. In the natural, I was not frightened or seasick. I stood there wondering what on earth was going on. I vaguely remember sort of touching the bar to place the pitchers there for a refill and stepping back. Then it happened—a wave swept over my head. The floor stopped moving, and the framed pictures became still life again.

I returned to the tables, placed the pitchers down and went to sit at my table. I said, "Lord, what on earth was that?" He said, "It had nothing on you to hold on to. That's why it passed over you and had to leave while you were there. This is why I didn't want you near a bar before this time. It was a wave of seduction that unbelievers experience. They are not able to overcome the temptation." (See John 14:30.)

Jesus tells us to overcome by the testimony of Jesus Christ and the blood of the Lamb. He exhorts the seven churches in the book of Revelation to be "overcomers." The Greek word is from a primitive word meaning "to conquer as in warfare." Many nations go to war on land and at sea as conquerors. Within six months this man was out of business in that location. I mention that coincidence simply because I have subsequently spoken to other believers who have had similar experiences and have overcome or not been affected, and the spirit was removed from that location.

It is also interesting to note that the city engineers later found a way to remove the flood waters from the streets so you could get in and out of the courthouse area in which this establishment was located. I don't mean to imply that I had anything to do with that. I simply mention it by way of coincidence, since it all took place in and around the same time. We have no idea what God decides to do, or how many other believers He uses to bring about His plans. (See Isaiah 46:8–11.) What was obvious to me was that God removed the usurping spirit and removed the business this spirit was using.

I relate this experience because it showed me as a young believer how seductive and destructive the enemy's false wave, the lie, can be. As I look back over some twenty-two years since that experience, I realize how many unbelievers, as well as believers, experience the enemy's lie as a good feeling and get trapped in so

Where Do We Go From Here?

much sin. This experience was not a good feeling for me because the Word of God dwelt in me deeply and richly. This is not the case for many, as they get caught in the enemy's false glory. Only the "Standard Bearer"—Jesus, the Word—can be lifted up to stop this onslaught.

Delivering the Creation

The next experience occurred while my husband and I were boarding our horses at a farm after we had sold our own farm. It was late when we arrived that night, around 10 P.M. As soon as we parked the car and got out, I knew a demon fled from the barn, from the area where one of my horses was located. I got the immediate impression it had been at the house where a Christian family lived, near the back of the barn, and it decided to go wandering.

I opened the door, turned on the lights and looked at our horses. They seemed fine, so I said nothing. Within half an hour one of my mares was anything but fine. She started to show signs of colic, but they were odd—not the normal signs of the condition. Furthermore, her skin started twitching as if a wave was coming out of her. I knew this was spiritual, but I called the veterinarian.

Because of the lateness of the hour, the only vet on call was an individual who had many spiritual problems of her own. I knew I could not rely on this person in the natural, and she would only complicate matters spiritually. I canceled the call and told my husband what I sensed when we first pulled up and what the outcome of my telephone call to the vet's office had been. He immediately told me he sensed the same demon fleeing the barn, and he also said nothing because the horses seemed fine.

We had taken the horse out of her stall. My husband was handwalking her in the indoor arena while I was calling the vet. I get very angry, spiritually, when the devil decides to eat my lunch for no reason at all. If there was unconfessed sin in my life or some other reason, I could understand it. But this was uncalled for. I needed to know, though, if the horse had an actual blockage in the intestine or if this was all a demonic lie. My husband is not a horse person and knew very little, at that time, about horse sicknesses. He would not have been able to understand the vision he was about to receive. As we laid hands on her and began to pray, he received a vision from the Lord of a beautiful meandering stream. I questioned him as to whether it was blocked in any way or open, and he said it was flowing fine.

That's when I knew that these "symptoms" were a lie for sure. As the word of the Lord came out of my mouth for deliverance and healing, the demonic wave of sickness came out of the horse and passed over me. Praise God, I suffered no ill effects; the Lord protected me. For a split second, I experienced the same twitchy, wave-like sensation I had watched the horse make, and then it was gone. At the same time, my husband received a vision of a wartime hospital tent, the white kind with a big red cross on it. It was out in the middle of a field flying a white banner of victory over the top of it!

The horse was fine immediately. Needless to say, we got home a little late that night. On the way home we compared notes a little more thoroughly. Both of us sensed that the demon came from the house of the Christian family who lived behind the barn. They were not home; they were at church.

Before the house had even been placed on this property, the Holy Ghost directed me to intercede for the land. Subsequently, they put a trailer there, and this family moved in. The land itself had cost the owner quite a bit of money to drain because it was located in a wet area. Furthermore, while I had no knowledge of this, I don't believe the placement of this trailer was done legally. So these people may have inadvertently moved into an illegal situation, thus giving the enemy an open door to accuse them in the spiritual realm.

The next day I shared the experience with the Christians. They admitted they sensed a presence and were struggling somewhat, financially, but otherwise were doing fine. We prayed together, and they received a deliverance and a measure of financial blessing. Unfortunately, about three or four months later this

Where Do We Go From Here?

family left the farm under a serious cloud of suspicion while the state police were called in to investigate.

Needless to say, their Christian witness was tarnished. I don't believe any charges were ever brought against them, but I do believe they were not able to fully overcome the onslaught of that demonic wave that came against them. The remainder of our stay on that farm was uneventful, and our horses suffered no more attacks. Nevertheless, the Lord opened a door for us to board elsewhere, and we took advantage of the open door.

I realize there may be some reading this experience who may question whether an animal can be traumatized by demons. The Scriptures give some examples. Obviously the serpent was infected by satan. (See Genesis 3.) Jesus allowed the pigs to be inhabited by the demons coming out of the demoniac. (See Mark 5:1–20.) They were so affected that they instantly started stampeding, thus causing their demise.

The Bible tells us that the whole creation waits in eager expectation, and it is subject to frustration and even groans for the sons of God to be revealed. (See Romans 8:19–22.) In other words, the creation is so adversely affected by Adam and Eve's sin and the subsequent results have unleashed such demonic activity that it groans. The words used here are representative of the feelings of living and breathing bodies. If they are living and breathing bodies, the spirit realm can affect them, both in a positive or negative way.

The book of Revelation talks about all the creatures in heaven, on the earth, under the earth and in the sea singing and giving praise to the Lamb who sits on the throne. (See Revelation 5:13.) Balaam's donkey was affected by God and spoke to prevent a prophet from his madness. (See Numbers 22:21–33.) If animals and even the whole of creation could be so affected within the context of both the Old and New Testaments, why would we think this could not happen now? There are other authors who function in deliverance and inner healing ministries today who have written about their experiences of delivering God's creatures.[2]

BEYOND STRONGHOLDS

Evicting the Devil

Isn't that what we're supposed to do? Kick the devil out of every area of the earth where we find him? No, Jesus did not shed His blood for an animal. But He did shed His blood for me. Early on in my walk with Him, He let me know that what affects me affects Him. If I will assume responsibility over what He gives me, then He will convey His authority to keep what I've given Him safe.

My husband and I dedicate everything to Jesus, even our animals. When they are sick we seek medical attention for them. But there are some sicknesses that only Jesus can heal. And so when I experience a problem in my life, and I've done all I know to do to be responsible for the situation and I can do no more, I have to give it to Jesus and do what He's telling me to do with it. And obviously I'm not even going to try to answer the question of whether animals have souls. I really don't think that the answer to that question matters. Whatever you personally believe on that subject is fine with me. I added this experience because it clearly shows (at least for me) the Biblical relationship between us as believers and how we can be affected on every level by the enemy, even down to the creatures God gives us.

We must recognize the lie and its relationship to sin and how that can even affect another believer in Christ. If we don't, we will not see the powerful freedom that can be ours in delivering us, the earth and creation from sin and its effects. Had God not given me and my husband discernment and authority, we may have lost a valuable broodmare, not to mention a very special animal. God wants all of us made whole on every level, even down to the jot and tittle of the creatures He gives us.

Set Free

As Christians, we do need to watch each other's back. We need to be aware, in the Holy Ghost, when to battle and when not to battle for someone. The battle is the Lord's. He trains us individually how to overcome. If we are not rooted and grounded

Where Do We Go From Here?

in the knowledge of God's Word, which will bring all of our motives, attitudes and other strongholds to the cross daily, it will be very easy for us to get trapped by our adversary. Once trapped, these strongholds can grow bitter roots and defile many, including the creation. (See Hebrews 12:15.) Without repentance the law judges us. By exposing the lie and applying the blood of Jesus to every aspect of our hearts, we can be set free. That freedom will extend to even the creation.

Experiencing the enemy's false wave of seduction is similar to being swept up in an undertow. Sometimes you can tell there are dangerous waves out there, and sometimes the water acts normal. All of a sudden you're caught up with no hope or way out. Many a boater and swimmer have learned this lesson the hard way. Having grown up around water all my life, I've had some experience with getting caught in a life-threatening wave.

I've always had a deep respect for the water, and I've never taken foolish risks. But one summer, while sitting with other people on a wading rope ten feet from shore, a wave came and swept all of us off the rope. As I came up, an undertow grabbed me and pulled my neck against the rope under the water. It felt as if I was going to panic and drown. All of a sudden, the wave released me, and I could break free to swim to the surface and breathe.

For many people, the enemy's false glory wave is like that. One minute they're enjoying life with friends and family, and the next minute they've been sucked up and away. I believe it's God in glory that sends a countercurrent to release our fellowman to help him break free from the undertow.

When Jesus called Lazarus forth from the dead, He commanded the folks standing nearby to release Lazarus from his binding burial clothes, so he could walk and function freely. Only Jesus—or the name of Jesus—can raise the dead. Lazarus was given the strength to hop up out of the tomb, but it was only those fellow believers standing by that were commanded to release him from the grave clothes. It took some effort and some willingness to put up with the stench of death for a short time, but Lazarus was set free.

BEYOND STRONGHOLDS

A Global Wave of Seduction

While the first evil wave was directed at me as an individual, and the second one was related to our brothers and sisters in Christ and how it can even affect the creation, the next wave is worldwide and far more seductive. While driving through a coastal town located on the Gulf of Mexico, I passed a billboard. I looked up and became instantly taken with the colors of the deepest blue and purple and the blackest black. They looked like they had been velvet-painted onto the billboard. Immediately a wave of happiness went through me and a seductive feeling of knowing something that no one else knew.

And then instantly it was gone. Because of the sense of happiness I felt after seeing the colors, I might have concluded that the experience came from God. It had reminded me of a time long ago when Father God allowed me to be in the fields of heaven. While that heavenly experience was totally freeing, this more recent one had a dark side. The darkness lay in the feeling that I knew something that, supposedly, no one else knew. To be honest, I didn't even know what was on the billboard or what it was advertising. I did know that the Holy Spirit was trying to show me something that grieved Him, and, by experience, I knew I had to wait for Him to speak.

The following week I had an opportunity to drive by the billboard again (by now they were springing up all over the town). It wasn't especially grand—just a picture of the earth, with the blue, purple and black background and some promotional writing for a computer company. That particular technology company was either going global or was already trading globally.

It was then that it dawned on me. For a whole generation, television was the pretty fruit the serpent had been hawking to get people to believe they will know something more. (See Daniel 12:4.) Computers and the Internet are the new toys to play with. But they are far more seductive, spreading globally quickly.

Jesus said the devil would do things in the last days that would fool even the very elect. (See Matthew 24:24; Mark 13:22.) Please

Where Do We Go From Here?

don't misunderstand me. All of the technologies created, I believe, have been given to us by God to further the gospel plan. I believe we, as Christians, should make the most of everything God gives us. But instead of using every spiritual gift and opportunity, we rely more heavily on earthly means, thus thwarting our real ability to overcome.

Instead of gaining a level of intercession in Christ on one spiritual level, we try to replace it with a new earthly avenue. The earthly is walked out after or at the same time as we overcome spiritually, not as a substitute for it.[3]

We thus put ourselves on the devil's playground, trying to play by his schoolyard rules. We try to overcome the flesh with the flesh. We do this by using some agenda or program instead of crucifying the flesh by bringing it to the cross daily, hour-by-hour and minute-by-minute. Some of our brothers and sisters get caught in the seduction of the false glory, while others of us get so busy with the earthly that we neglect our real overcoming power in the Holy Spirit.

Recognizing Deception

I mention these experiences for several reasons. In the future we will have to recognize the devil's ability to produce false glory or mimic the anointing. The devil is under the law—not grace and truth in Jesus Christ. For that reason, he can never be as powerful as we can when we move in repentance and forgiveness towards one another, by submitting to Christ and going forth with the gifts He has placed within us.

God-mandated legal authority was restored to us for the face of the earth when all authority was given to Jesus. (See Matthew 28:18.) But let's make some facts plain here. The Bible reveals that, as the prince of the kingdom of the air, the devil has one place of authority. (See Ephesians 2:2.) The Greek says he is literally the ruler of flying things. He also has another place, as the father of lies. (See John 8:44.) He puts himself forward as a god of this world. (See Luke 4:6; John 14:30, 12:31, 16:11; 2 Corinthians 4:4.)

BEYOND STRONGHOLDS

When we believe his lies we fall under his power to kill, steal and destroy. When we believe his lie that we may dethrone him, we run in circles during battle. It is only as he makes the mistake of actually engaging us here, on earth, that we have the authority to cast him off and bind his ability to function on the earth. Engaging us here, in battle on the earth will be his downfall. So he subtly lies to us so we do not recognize his strategies.

Sometimes we can get swept away by his gifts or false glory anointing and the better spiritual gift that we're supposed to have. Isn't that the same temptation with which he tempted Christ? He said, "Use your God-ordained gifts and tools to come and get me or get what you want. And in that way you'll somehow be more superior than you already are." The devil tried to tempt Jesus to misuse His divine power instead of functioning through the Holy Spirit. Jesus didn't fall into the temptation. But we do sometimes. We use God's gifts to get what we want. Because we do, we can be tempted by false prophets and false glory.

Jesus overcame satan by God's Word. (See Luke 4:1-14.) The opposite of God is not the devil. God has no opposite. He is in a class all His own! The devil has nothing of his own. Everything he has came from God originally. Have you ever wondered why worldly creativity in the arts and sciences can be so good? Who are these creators? They are people like you and me, without the benefit of the blood and the Holy Spirit-indwelled life. God gave these people gifts, but they use them for their own purposes.

Demons are then able to speak to them and influence them. But again, from where do the enemy and these unregenerate human souls get their tools? Originally, they came from God—and when they came from Him, the tools, ideas or gifts were pure and holy.

God is not an Indian giver. He does not take the gifts back. His anointing may not abide on that person, but He does not take His gifts back. (See Romans 11:29.) This is why unbelievers may see or speak truth, and why they may even prophesy. (See John 11:49-51.) This is why they may be able to experience His glory. This is why many of them can function in psychic phenomena.

Where Do We Go From Here?

Open Doors to False Glory

There are several practices I find questionable in the body of Christ that have the potential to leave us open to false glory. One is the practice of "activations." The other is the practice of having prophets stationed around the sanctuary with people being able to get words from them at any time.

Activations, as I have come to observe them, involve people going to certain locations to be "activated" in the gifts of the Holy Spirit. I want to make it clear and state that I love God's prophets and believe that God's people must be discipled in all that God has for us. I am a proponent of people being trained and raised up in the gifts of God. I believe in the laying on of hands and taught it in a foundations class once a week for many years. The laying on of hands is a foundational truth and Biblical practice from Old to New Testaments. (See Hebrew 6:1–3.) I feel the practice of activations has the potential for serious abuse and is somewhat unscriptural, in some instances.

There is no denying that God may say to someone, "Silver and gold have I none, but such as I have, I give unto you," as He had Peter pray for the lame man. Then God does the giving. But when we chase after gifts, we lose sight of the Giver. The gifts then become our central focus.

People laying hands on us becomes the central focus. We lose sight of the special relationship we may have during time and fellowship with God as He does His work in our lives and gives us gifts. God has people impart His anointing, not activate it. The difference is important. I realize there is a place where God will use another through the laying on of hands to draw out what He has already placed within us. There is nothing wrong with believers exhorting and teaching in this area. We are commanded to stir up the gifts within us. When God allows us to impart what's been given to us, we function just like Jesus did with the disciples and just like the disciples did with the rest of the world. Jesus did not activate something in them. He imparted to them.

Again, I am not saying that gifts are not transferred to people

BEYOND STRONGHOLDS

by God after He calls us to pray for them. The laying on of hands is a foundation stone of the church. It is used for the impartation of healing, the gifts of the Holy Spirit, deliverance, the baptism of the Holy Spirit and the affirmation of one another, especially by the presbyter for ordination. What I am saying is that the practice of activations has the potential for abuse, as well the potential to open the door into the psychic realm for some people.

Let me explain what I mean. Many years ago a friend invited me to a prophetic conference where they were going to do activations. I did not want to go, but the Holy Spirit gave me no excuses. I had no idea how many years it was going to take the Lord to teach me what He wanted me to learn from this conference. In this classroom-conference I was told that the attendees would be activated in their gifts. Since this was something I knew I did not need, I was going to quietly leave the classroom. As I sat there, a door to the back of the classroom opened. A beam of light came through the "open door." I turned to look behind me, thinking for sure I would see a literal door. To my shock I only saw a wall. There were no doors in the physical realm. Immediately I got the sense that a door was opened into the psychic realm. I felt no evil; I felt no good. In other words, when man opens a door into the spirit realm it can be used by anyone.

I should hasten to say that this particular organization was a wonderful group of Christian people. I knew their theology to be quite sound, even if I felt some of their practices to be a little questionable. I knew they had many successful years of training and raising up many prophetic ministers. So I was quite shocked at what I saw happen after this door had been opened. The leader of the group started to pray for those who wanted the gifts of the Holy Spirit "activated" in their lives. They would activate the gifts from one person to another in a long line of people. Up until this point I had been sitting at my table because I knew I didn't need to be in this line. Later on, the instructor made everyone get in a circle and practice prophecy from one person to the other. I tried avoiding this since I don't "practice" prophesying. Either God gives me a word or He doesn't. I watched as demons jumped on

Where Do We Go From Here?

different people in the room. Demonic activity seemed more intense near the "open door." People reacted in different ways. Some people became uncomfortable, while others, it seemed, acted like they were more "anointed." On the drive home my girlfriend and I compared notes and decided we didn't need to return. We felt it had been a learning experience, while we both got the chance to get a mini vacation.

Over the next several years I would periodically meet people that had been involved in this type of an experience. I have to say that after much conversation I began to realize their theological foundation was not strong enough to handle what spiritual experiences they were constantly seeking. I began to see a pattern after meeting several of these individuals. Again, I thought nothing of it until I happened to go out to dinner one night with a group of church people. We had all just come from a meeting with an individual who had prophesied very accurately and appropriately to many people in the church. I started to converse with him about his theology and ministerial experience. I discovered that he did activations with the same organization where I had seen the "open door" vision. I told him nothing of my prior experience years before. This person was quite sound in his theology and ministry. So I started to ask some more questions. I said, "How do you know that, during these activations, people might not get into error, or that demons may not become involved?" He replied, "Oh, we take care of that by leaving an open door for mistakes." I couldn't believe my ears. I said, "You actually open a door for mistakes?" He said, "Yes." I said, "How do you know satan won't use your open door?" He said, "Because we pray God will take care of any mistakes we make, and we plead the blood of Jesus over them." I knew if I pressed the issue it would just cause dissension, so I dropped it.

I began to realize that we can get slightly off in some of our practices. In this way we create strongholds because we refuse to change our "correct" practices. We forget that as humans we have power in a spiritual realm. If we go into that realm by some of our good ideas, the enemy is able to use it, no matter how much "blood" we plead over it. Mistakes need to be repented of and then never repeated again. The blood of Jesus is powerful enough to stop demons in their tracks. But if we misuse it consistently, we trample it under foot. (See Exodus 12:7; Hebrews 6:6.) Someone in this group had to understand their door was really open into the psychic realm, where we are commanded never to go. (See Deuteronomy 18:10–12.) The blood of Jesus is not a magic wand to be used so we don't have to change our ideas and repent of some of our stronghold practices. Repentance means change. Just because we see results doesn't mean they were achieved by God.

Prophets Ready to Give Words

The second problem is similar to the last one. Again, I have no problem with prophets prophesying in the sanctuary. But when we station them around the church every week so they can give "words," we set up Christian idols. People go to them instead of seeking God for themselves. In the Old Testament they could get away with this because the Holy Spirit was not poured out on all. In the New Testament, Christ was offered up so the Holy Spirit and His gifts could be given to His body as He sees fit, not as we demand.

If God is not giving someone a word, my past experience is that there are usually good reasons for this. I have found that there are good reasons why God has not released some people to function in their gifts. Many times, when I get around pastoral ministries, the shepherding gifts become more pronounced in my life. I've never had a time when I've gone to a healing crusade and I didn't come home with gifts of healing far more pronounced than when I left. I'm not suggesting that God doesn't use people to transfer blessings by the laying on of hands, through the revelatory gifts or gifts of prophecy. He does. And when it's done according to Scripture, it's holy. I've been blessed by God's people releasing the gifts of the Spirit to me, and I've been blessed by releasing many of the Holy Spirit's gifts to God's people. But we need to be careful and discern if our central focus and attention has become the gifts or the Giver. Everyone says the focus is on the Giver, but I have noticed, over time, in these meetings and within the congregations that encourage such practices that they become subtle idols.

Love Covers a Multitude of Sins

Many times, in our zeal to implement the fullness of the gospel, we don't realize that we have let some subtle attitude, practice or habit creep into our lives. If we can be patient with each other and willing to learn, we can set up an environment where we can all be willing to change. I'm not trying to correct things. All I can do is share what I believe God is showing me. Let me share an experience I had with a young man who had been involved in many of our modern-day prophetic church practices, and how the love of Jesus can restore us.

A number of years ago we had two young men in their early twenties to whom we were ministering Christ in the church. One came from a broken home but was attempting to walk with Christ by following His Word. The other young man was a struggling homosexual who had at one time functioned in a church with a prophetic call on his life. I was in the church one day as they both were in the sanctuary. The young man from the broken home had a brain injury. As a result he was having a hard time reading God's Word. The Lord asked me to pray for his healing. As I prayed for the young man's healing, a ball of light came from heaven and touched him. I said nothing. There was no need to. By faith I just knew it was done. The other young man, we'll call his name Charles, was sitting nearby watching. Charles had been on fire for the Lord at one time. He was now struggling with sexual addictions. He talked a good Christian talk and knew the Scriptures quite well. He had been "activated" in some prophetic gifts.

Charles said to me, "How did you do that?" I said, "Do what?" He explained that he had seen the light come from heaven. I said, "I did nothing. God gave him a gift of healing so he could read His Word." He said again, "I know that, but how did you do that?" I replied with the same answer, and he asked me the same

BEYOND STRONGHOLDS

question one more time. It finally dawned on me that Charles had a demonic spirit. This spirit was using his gift of prophetic insight. He was seeing accurately, but the demon wanted the gift for its own use, to use it through him. It was similar to what Paul experienced with the soothsaying damsel and what Peter and John experienced with Simon wanting to purchase God's gifts. (See Acts 16:16–18; 8:18–20.)

Since Charles had been around some other prophetic ministry in the past, he expected me to teach and activate him further in his "gift." I knew I had to get through to him and ignore the devils. He needed to stop using his gifts, come in line with the Word of God in his heart, repent and then the demons could be cast out. So I explained that God is the one who gives gifts. I told him that when you study His Word, fast, pray, repent and obey God in every area of your life, He can bless other people around you. Of course this explanation didn't satisfy the devil, but Charles did ponder what I said. He eventually did get delivered. The enemy kept trying to use his gifts, and they appeared very impressive. He tries to do the same with Spirit-filled Christians. Suppose I got it backwards and started to teach Charles something other than what God said he needed then, which was salvation and deliverance? He would not have been set free at that time. All we have to do is be slightly off with God's gifts and not willing to repent. We can then function in false glory.

We have the gifts of the Holy Spirit because the Holy Spirit is alive in us. The gifts flow through us like water. They are poured in and then poured out. We can stir them up, and someone else may draw them out. When we speak of "activating" the gifts, it sounds like something mechanical. As a result, sometimes our attitude surrounding the gifts may also become mechanical. As this subtle attitude shift takes place, we may substitute mechanical activations for the moving of the Holy Spirit. This is the same type of mistake the children of Israel made when they drove the Ark of the Covenant on a cart being pulled by oxen rather than carrying it on their shoulders.

Where Do We Go From Here?

Stealing Holy Gifts

The devil has nothing of his own. All he can do is take godly ideas, tools and gifts, and pervert and corrupt them. In that way he can try to change them into something they were never intended by God to be. The simple fact, though, is we have the same tools and gifts given to us by God. But the devil does not have our calling or authority on the earth. This is why he must use our own strongholds to pervert God's witness. It is through our lack of vision and knowledge that the purity and the use of God's gifts are lost to us, along with the people God gives us as gifts.

The devil needs us. He has no legal right to come to earth except that we give it to him. And frankly, we have no legal right to pull him down from the place in the air in which God lets him stay for now. The devil knows this. When this occurs, we ignore pulling down our own stronghold ideas that we have lifted up higher than God's Word. So we wind up in trouble on two fronts. We're in disobedience to God in our lives individually because these strongholds are sin, and we're trying to fight the devil in places in which we are not designed to fight him. (See Revelation 12:7–8.) Our real place of authority is the earth. The devil does not want to fight us where we can win. So he convinces us to try to bind satanic principalities in the air. I'm not saying that there is never a time for principalities in the air to be captured. I feel the angels of God do a better job at that than we ever could. It is our job to be obedient and kick them off of the earth first.

Some make a big deal of the devil's title as "the prince of the power of the air." I need to ask a question. Is that air you're breathing or the Word of God? Both! The Bible says that God created all things by the word of His mouth. (See John 1:3; Isaiah 55:11.) The Word says that His Word sustains all things. (See Hebrews 1:3.) The Word is Jesus Christ. It is in Him we live and move and have our being. (See Acts 17:28.) God's Word created the very air we breathe. The very air that holds even the prince of the air up is upheld by God's Word. It is an ever-expanding word that constantly drives chaos out to create something out of nothing. When we move with His Word, think with His Word and mind, have His knowledge, do not resist His presence or name and we become His totally whole people, that Word will no longer hold satan in his place as the prince of the air. It will be right on God's time schedule because of the Word He has already spoken over satan so that he'll be cast for all eternity into the lake of fire. When we come in agreement with God's Word as God's people for Planet Earth, our strongholds will no longer give satan a place to hawk his wares. It is our sin, as God's people, that keeps the earth bound.

The Effects of Our Strongholds: Separation and Captivity

The reality of this truth hit me hard many years ago when the Holy Spirit showed me something out of the Scriptures that grieved me, because of our sin. However, it also made me realize all does not need to be lost because of that sin.

The colors of heaven are magnificent—nothing here on earth compares. They are so filled with glorious color that trying to describe, let's say the color green, by saying deeper than deep green cannot do the color justice when you see it from heaven's eyes. When God had Moses build the tabernacle or tent of meeting, color schemes figured prominently into its building and coverings. God is a colorful God. After all, light holds within it all the spectrum of color the world knows. One of the most colorful places in the tabernacle—and the subsequent temples—was the veil or covering that covered the opening to the holy of holies.

Blue, purple and scarlet, mixed with the artistic handiwork of ornamental cherubs, are seen. (See Exodus 26:1.) These, of course, are not the only colors we see. There are gold, silver, bronze; deep, dark, blood red; browns, blacks, and the shadings in between, and pure white. There are two other places where a covering of different colors was symbolic and important. It had no direct connection with God's covenant, the temple, its

Where Do We Go From Here?

worship, its vessels, or priestly servants. Those places are Genesis 37 and 2 Samuel 13.

In Genesis, the story is Joseph's coat of many colors. In 2 Samuel it is Tamar's coat of many colors. Most people know of Joseph's story, but Tamar's sometimes gets lost or forgotten. The Hebrew words for these coats are the exact same words. The two closest concepts we see, while not employing the same words, are the outer garment of the high priest and Christ's "coat," which was seamless. (See John 19:23.) The two words used in Genesis and in 2 Samuel to describe these garments are not used together in any other place in the Scriptures to describe such a garment except in these two places. While the literal meaning for the word *pas* is no longer really known, when we put it together with the other word, *kethoneth*, they are translated to mean "a coat or long-sleeved tunic of wide breadth and/or many colorations (possibly also pleated), symbolic of what royalty might wear."

Coats of Many Colors

These facts fueled my interest to study these stories more closely. We all understand Joseph's coat as symbolic of the love of his father, with an understanding of the coloration being symbolic of God's favor or anointing (especially in glory). In Tamar's case, her coat was worn for the same exact reasons. While Joseph's is special because he is the only son to receive this coat, Tamar's is special because she and her sisters, as the virgin daughters of King David, would be the only individuals as a unit or team to receive these robes or coats.

Tamar's represented her individual purity while being a part of a whole. Joseph's was symbolic of the purity of his individual relationship with his father, while being a part of a family unit. For all these reasons, we can look at these two individuals as representing our special relationship with our heavenly Father and His glory that rests upon us.

As we remain in spiritual virginal purity to Him, we may wear this glory. It sets us apart and clothes us. There are times when this symbol of Father's love and the spiritual purity we have from Him cause jealousy, acts of violence or murder, control and manipulation to come forth from our brothers and sisters.

In Tamar's case, her half-brother Amnon desires this purity for himself, without wanting to pay the price for its upkeep. Our willingness to walk in Father's purity in glory will cost us something. Redeeming us, so that we may experience it, didn't come cheaply for Him; why should it for us? Amnon was the firstborn son of King David. Wanting Tamar sexually was a clear violation of God's Word in Leviticus 18:9. Many of the rabbinical teachings during Christ's time would have forbidden such a marriage.[4] Even asking such a thing may have been seen as trying to seal his right to eventually ascend the throne. (See 2 Samuel 16:21–22; 1 Kings 1:2–3, 2:13–2.3.) It is Tamar's response that we should note.

Tamar lived these experiences and speaks directly to us concerning what her father's attitude might have been had Amnon only desired to be upright and honorable toward her. (See 2 Samuel 13:13.) Rape is never about sex. Jesus made that clear. (See Matthew 5:27–28.) It is about sinful areas of our hearts that wish to control and manipulate—to rebel and be stubborn. It is wanting to have what another has and getting it for ourselves, never asking our heavenly Father for His desires on an issue in our lives. When we walk in a place of special relationship or understanding of Father God that others desire for themselves, they become glory snatchers. The outcome of this sad story had devastating consequences for Israel as a nation. It was like a silent bomb went off in that bedchamber and rippled down the corridors of David's time on the throne.

It causes Absalom, Tamar's full brother, to secretly plot Amnon's death. Once Absalom kills Amnon, he flees the country. This fuels an already vicious cycle within Absalom to eventually garner David's throne. While God spares David and the throne, the nation goes through a civil war. Many blame David's sin with Bathsheba as the source. God forgave David for this sin once David repented. Nevertheless, the effects of sin must also be dealt with. It is not enough to just recognize our strongholds, but we must root out the behavior patterns that support them.

David needed to deal with Amnon and counsel Absalom and Tamar. Had he diligently attended this situation, the bomb may have had far less damaging long-term effects. We are never told that he did. In fact, what we are told is that after Amnon had raped Tamar he hated her more than he had originally "loved" her. He throws her out of his house, and she throws dust on her head and tears the robe. We are told she lived desolate in her brother's house all the days of her life. The term used here, in conjunction with Tamar's name being listed with the king's sons in 2 Chronicles 3:9, would prove that she never married.[5]

This story continues to grieve us to this day. It's because of the devastating consequences that our strongholds produce, that they affect an entire nation. In this story we see all the strongholds reviewed in this book and their horrible effects: control, manipulation, violation of God's Word, substituting our own knowledge, the lack of God's presence and judgment against women. The sad reality is that once we become defiled, and that defilement is not removed, the symbol of the glory of God is torn. We end up sitting in ashes in the house of our brothers and sisters, never again becoming active participants in the kingdom.

Joseph's Coat of Many Colors

While Joseph's story is just as sad as Tamar's, it ends far more gloriously and for a very predictable reason. We all know the story. Joseph's brothers desired to kill him because of jealousy. He's got something given to him by God that they do not have, and they become filled with jealousy.

Unfortunately, this is so typical even in the church. Their response is murder. There are two dissenting voices in the group. One wishes for total restoration (Reuben), the other, not quite wanting Joseph back, but not wanting to be blamed for his murder either (Judah).

What is done with Joseph's coat was what caught my

attention. In Tamar's case, she rips it in hopelessness. Joseph is never given the chance—thank God. We read that a goat is sacrificed, and the garment is dipped in blood. While the brothers do this to hide their ruse, God uses this symbolism to display Christ and, hence, restoration.

We are never specifically told here that they tore the garment. From Jacob's response when he sees the coat, we assume that the brothers probably did. We read in Genesis 37:23 that the brothers stripped the coat off Joseph. While a shade of this word can mean to flay, it means just what it says: something was taken from someone by force. This same word is used here and elsewhere to describe the same action. It is used in Numbers 20:28 when Moses strips Aaron of his high priestly attire before Aaron dies, thus symbolizing the anointing being taken away from him. We see this same thought repeated later when Job cries out that God has stripped him of his glory. (See Job 19:9.)

And that's my point. This coat, as in Tamar's case, carried a sense of royalty with it. Because it probably carried the color white in it, this meant that Joseph would not have been required to work as hard or in the same manner as his other ten half-brothers.[6] He would have been set apart as a "prince" by his father. So when this particular word "stripped" is used, it could possibly mean that they tore it. The more meaningful implication is that they forcibly took the coat off of him and, by doing so, desired to strip, separate or flay away from Joseph that symbol of glorious anointing and princely position given him by the father.

We can be thankful for the blood of Christ when those around us act jealously because of the anointing Christ gives. This leads me to another thought. Christ's garments were divided among the four soldiers stationed at the cross. But his coat was seamless, and they did not wish to tear it. So they cast lots for it.[7] (See John 19:23–24.)

Since Joseph symbolizes Christ in many other respects, it would not surprise me if the coat had not been torn, but because of the blood, Jacob, in his anguished state, simply assumes that Joseph has been torn to pieces.

For many years the brothers look good in their father's house,

Where Do We Go From Here?

while Joseph is a slave elsewhere. All of this would be a sad story indeed if the ending were not given to us. We know Joseph winds up being a high official in Egypt, second in command to Pharaoh. (See Genesis 41:38–46.) Joseph's brothers go before Joseph to purchase food because of a regional famine. At this point, it is Joseph's turn to resist the temptations of his own personal strongholds. When he does, he delivers a nation.

In the cases of both Tamar and Joseph, their families, the same children of their father, want for themselves the symbol of that glory-anointing that their respective coats represented. In both cases, they must resist the stronghold temptations within them to see their nation delivered from strife, war and starvation. They must deal with the effects of these strongholds within. It's not enough to just repent of them. They must deal with the results that sin causes and remove the roots that cause sin.

Taking Up Our Crosses

We are told to daily take up our crosses and follow Christ. (See Matthew 16:24.) Every day, we must bring to the cross those areas in our hearts that hinder God's plan. These are the things that resist the Lord of Glory when He shows up to rest and abide. When we, like Joseph, walk in forgiveness and wisdom, God can do something with us. If not, the effect of this stubbornness is desolate solitude in our Father's house.

Brothers and sisters, as we studied in chapter 8, the effect of these stronghold resistances is separation. As I look at church history and see all the separation that has taken place, I fear that if we do not look at these issues of our hearts, we will be in danger of separating the body of our Lord even further when the next move of glory appears.

Many claim the different denominations within Christendom have been God's plan all along. I have no argument against that. But I do not think it's because that was what was needed. Jesus told the Pharisees that God allowed Moses to write a bill of divorcement because of the hardness of their hearts. I see nowhere in Scripture where God's perfect desire for His people is division among them. But I do see many times where He allows division to show us something about our sin or to pass judgment on our sin.

If we can respect our individual Christian beliefs and pull down our own strongholds, the importance of reaching the lost will unify us. While we may still have some differences, we will be a far more united force in the world, and will represent Christ more clearly. We will then be able to represent Christ in government, commerce, industry and the sciences, instead of relegating those areas to the unsaved. If we would exchange our unhealthy stronghold attitudes for Christ's attitude, I believe the Lord would anoint us to bring the *rhema* and *logos* words of God to bless and renew the unsaved who work within these groups. We will be able to expose the strongholds the enemy has used to entrench himself within those systems.

Change or Stay in the Wilderness: What's at Stake?

The Next Generation

When God wanted to deliver Israel from Egypt, He used a representative from Israel—Moses—to do so. When God wanted to save Israel within her Babylonian captivity, He used a woman—Esther—to do so. He needed a man in Moses and a woman in Esther because of the principalities or satanic strongholds that bound His people in those areas. These satanic strongholds come in agreement with our human strongholds and reproduce some of their ideas and personalities in us, as humans. This is why government, industry, commerce and the sciences have been bound. God's men and women need their voices restored in these areas so they can be faithful end-time witnesses to people bound in these systems. If we do not examine these strongholds in us as God's people, satanic strongholds will continue to gain strength. As we give these satanic rulers footholds, we don't realize that we cover them and give them authority, which is what they crave. It takes someone—a representative who will die to these strongholds

Where Do We Go From Here?

from within—to go forth in Father God's image and give Him the worship, homage and all the glory.

This is why Christ, the God-man, was needed to take back and restore the captive earth. Adam and Eve came in agreement with the enemy concerning God's Word. Israel of Christ's time came in agreement with Rome. God used this scenario to offer Christ as the sacrifice for Adam and Eve's sin. This is why His bride, the church in unity in her God-ordained place on the earth, must learn how to come in total agreement with God's desires. Not partial agreement, but total death to the flesh is required to complete the restoration of the earth.

For many of our brethren it is just too much effort to pull up these strongholds from within or to pull these attitudes down from the lofty places in which we put them. Pulling down strongholds from the heavens seems more palatable. When we stay in God's Word, these strongholds become obvious and exposed. But we neglect the reading of His Word. Even this neglect has to do with our resistance to the Lord of Glory. We don't see our belief systems and attitudes as resistances, but they are. Let me be clear and state unequivocally that what's at stake here is the ability for every blood-washed, born again, Holy Ghost filled believer to be a glory filled, bondage-breaking miracle conductor! And that kind of glory will pass to the next generation.

Companies of Believers

There are entire companies of believers being formed by God quietly on the sidelines, waiting to be unleashed to counter the devil's lies and false glory. Examples of these are fivefold ministry; Joseph-Daniel-Esther ministries; Elijah-Isaiah-Ezekiel companies of believers, and Jonathan to Davidic pastoral mantles. But what kind of church climate and church leadership will they encounter? Is the very environment to which they need to retreat full of the hypocrisy of our resistances to the very glorious presence of God? It is that presence that we so desperately need to keep the fire going.

BEYOND STRONGHOLDS

Ten books could be written about these different groups of believers and their unique gifts and callings from God. Am I trying to say they shouldn't experience hardship? No. David had to encounter the bear and the lion before Goliath could be brought down. Many of these types of leaders are going to be very different from the sweet-faced cherubs we want saints to be. They will have to be different. That is because they are called to go into different areas of politics, science, sports, media, education and the arts, and then they must network there and start ministries within those worldly fortresses.

In some cases it will take teams of apostles, prophets, pastors, evangelists and teachers to disciple them. This can be a headache, and far too time consuming for conventional pastors without the benefit of other fivefold ministers. They must also learn submission and appropriate God-ordained hierarchy. They must learn how to overcome in the face of enemy attack. Every one of us must learn how to overcome in light of suffering and pain. We all have resistant strongholds that need to be crucified on the cross. Jesus said we would have trouble in this world, but we need to be of good cheer; He overcame the world. How are we to overcome? By the blood and the testimony. (See Revelation 12:11.) When Christ overcame, the glory infused His human body, and He was raised with a new body. He became the firstfruit of many brethren. Are we willing to give up our church building practices and Christian business marketing plans to build bodies of believers to take back Planet Earth?

In some churches the blood is no longer preached. In other churches the testimony of Jesus Christ, which is the very Spirit of prophecy, is so controlled and even denied that people must get permission to move in a gift of prophecy. Is it any wonder that the patterns of resistance to the God of glory are left unremoved and unrepented? Will God have to purge us as He did Israel by removing the leaders? Does He have to allow persecution and judgment like Israel experienced?

Some could argue that God is totally sovereign, and these issues will work themselves out. God is totally sovereign, and yet

Where Do We Go From Here?

we as humans are given total responsibility. These two thoughts are equally true and, when taken together as a whole, go against the law of our human reasoning. I take nothing away from either. You cannot see the fullness of divine sovereignty until you see your responsibility as a human. Conversely, you cannot truly see your responsibility as a human until you see the total sovereignty of God. Because of this, an alarm needs to sound throughout the body—an alarm of wooing and calling. There must be a wake-up call to search out the depths of our beings and expose everything before the Holy Ghost.

The Church Triumphant

What will it take for us to create an environment that is so healthy that God's people are released into the world as a powerful force? God's people should be able to walk into the food markets, the discount stores, the hospitals or the auto shops and see people delivered and set free, because God in glory worked through them mightily. It's going to take more than one generation doing it all. It takes both mothers and fathers to create a healthy household. It takes all the diverse people of this planet to make up the world's nations. It is going to take the church moving as a triumphant force under the banner of God in glory.

Adam and Eve fell because they relied on something other than God's Word. His knowledge was no longer their source. They exchanged His presence and His identity for their own control, their own way of doing things. We haven't changed much as people. We rely on everything else but His Word. Healing services, prayer meetings, teaching, preaching and even prophesying—I'm not against any of these things, nor do I believe we shouldn't do these things. But has there been a subtle shift in the depths of our beings, so that those things sustain us, instead of His Word? (See Psalm 12:1-6.)

As I've shared before, I believe God wants to infiltrate us in glory. But do we want to insult Him by having Him fill us when the Holy Spirit and God's Word are not sustaining us? For most of us, our paychecks sustain us. For most churches it's their meetings that bring in sustenance. Isn't that why we're supposed to fast? It's an act of worship that says that nothing, not even food, sustains me. Only you, Jesus! Only you, Father! Only you, Holy Spirit!

Suppose we fast our own way of doing things and say, "It's not the signs, the wonders or the prophecy. It's not even that we are a quiet church. It's nothing but you, Jesus." Isn't that what's going on around the throne of God in the heavenlies—Pure, undiluted worship? It is worship that says absolutely nothing but God Almighty sustains and holds up all in all. When we live in that kind of worship, Father God will alight on the sacrifice.

Clear the Wilderness of Our Own Hearts

Before Jesus came the first time, God sent a prophet as a voice of one calling from the wilderness to make straight the way of the Lord, clearing a highway for Christ to come. (See John 1:19–23.) Each one of us has a desert place or wilderness place in our own hearts. Dealing with the effects of these sinful strongholds will clear our paths, making stony places smooth and giving our Lord a highway on which to come and walk. Each generation has Jesus coming to it. One day a specific generation will see His literal Second Coming. My heart yearns for that to be the generation in which I live. But if it is not, our desire should be to expose the lie of the enemy that captures our hearts and covers our paths. We must straighten the crooked and stony paths before mankind stands at Father God's throne to be judged. We must be saved and healed. As God's people are healed, healing flows to the nations. Judgment must begin in the house of God. (See 1 Peter 4:17.)

The last move of the God of glory restored our understanding of God as Father. As we laughed and shook and fell down before His mighty presence, we rose back up with a new understanding of what it means to be resurrected with Christ. This next move of the God of glory will restore an understanding to us of God, the eternal judge. Whole churches and people groups will start to cry and grieve for their sins and the sins of those around them. We will learn how to move in words of proclamation. As a result, when the bride speaks, God will accomplish it, and entire people groups will be saved and set free!

But He will not give that kind of power to a stronghold-filled bride. If we do not judge and bring these strongholds to the cross quickly, judgment will indeed fall on some houses. This is a transition period. These two understandings of Father and eternal judge will, to some degree, overlap each other in our transitional period of time. They will overlap each other also as God manifests Himself to us in different churches.

"See My Glory!"

I had an experience with the Lord a number of years ago. It made me realize that each church should take a long, hard look at its theological foundation and the overriding mandate given them by our Lord. This is to express Christ to their own neighborhoods. And they should take a long, hard look at where they are in the building process.

God revealed to me that explosive ministry is coming to our churches. One day as I was near my office, walking down the aisle way, I heard Father God say, "Let Me preach." I stood back, and I heard Him move through congregations, making proclamations and changing worship leaders in one service to express something in song differently. I saw Him use different people groups to turn around and minister to others as a prophetic anointing flowed through them.

I heard these words: "Why should the intercessors be off in a room somewhere? Why aren't they in the midst bringing to birth? Where are the deliverance and inner healing teams?" I saw ushers—both men and women—being used, as Aaron and Hur, to hold people up under God's anointing, so those people could be used to lay hands on others. I saw children being brought in to serve communion and lay hands on the sick. I heard angels on assignments and peals of thunder-fire and glory.

Then, with a grieving, groaning and pent-up anguish from the

BEYOND STRONGHOLDS

Spirit that I cannot describe, I felt Elisha strike the waters and say, "Where is the God of Elijah?" Then silence. And as His awesome presence surrounded me, I heard Him say, "Stand Up Church! See My Glory!"

That's when it dawned on me that all the marvelous miracles and all the wonderful promises of God cannot come close to revealing who He is until we actually say, "Where are You, O Lord?"

That is why I still feel compelled to say, before we ask for Father in glory, let us ask to be holy. Before we ask for the manifestations of Him in glory, let us ask for manifested humility. Before we ask for outward signs and wonders, let us ask for the wonder of a pure heart before God and towards one another.

It is in that environment that God's people can be all He has planned for them to be. It is in that environment that the sinner cries out for God, and the demons flee from God. It is in that environment that we go beyond our strongholds and allow Father God to infiltrate us with all that He is, so that He, in glory, is what shines through us, dispelling the darkness on the earth. And individually, as we walk in that glory one-by-one, His glory shall cover the earth as the waters cover the sea. (See Habakkuk 2:14.)

Notes

Introduction

1. Edersheim, Alfred. *The Temple: Its Ministry and Services.* Peabody, MA: Hendrickson Publishers, Inc., 1994, p. 17.
2. Edersheim, *The Temple,* pp. 17-18.

Chapter 1–Beyond Strongholds

1. For those who wish to research God coming in manifested glory during our modern church experience, there are three good books I could recommend. One is *The Eternal Church*, by Dr. Bill Hamon, Christian International Publishers, Phoenix, AZ, 1981. In it the author catalogs the historical times of these revivals and the corresponding inventions that were created for the furtherance of the Gospel. Another excellent work on the subject of church history is by Earl E. Cairns, entitled *Christianity Through the Centuries*, Zondervan Publishing House, Grand Rapids, MI, 1981. This textbook documents the different historical milestones throughout the whole of church history. For those who do not have the time to devote to reading a large volume like this but would like to research modern historical movements of God in a shorter, but still quite comprehensive way, there is a work by Charles P. Schmitt called *Floods Upon the Dry Ground*, Destiny Image Publishers, Inc., Shippensburg, PA, 1998.
2. No doubt many human ideas are influenced by the lies of demons, principalities and powers. Why else would people believe that homosexuality can be an "alternative" lifestyle or that alcoholism is a genetic sickness? Other examples of demonically influenced human ideas include Hinduism, Buddhism, cults and occult activities and their teachings that can permeate our society.
3. Fox, Everett, "The Five Books of Moses," *The Schocken Bible,* Volume 1, Schocken Books, Inc., a registered trademark of Random House, Inc., New York, 1995, pp. 497-498.
4. Until our Lord's literal Second Coming, we can all agree that Paul is speaking of our spirits being seated with Christ, not our physical bodies. I am mentioning this plain distinction so there is no mistake as to what position in prayer and action I am referring to. We pray in total faith, knowing that our Lord is right next to us and hears our every word. As a result, we should respond with actions of repentance and humility framed in positive, overcoming power (faith) because of what Christ promises and gives us. Not as some have used these scriptures to command celestial beings above us, good or evil. Not even the archangel Michael dared to bring an accusation against the devil (see Jude 8,9). Our Lord gave us authority here on the earth. It is here on the earth that we may bind enemy attackers. See also *Needless Casualties of War,* by John Paul Jackson. Fort Worth, TX: Streams Publications, 1999.
5. Cairns, Earle E., *Christianity Through the Centuries.* Grand Rapids, MI: Zondervan Publishing House, 1981. See also *Rees Howells Intercessor*, by Norman Grubb. Fort Washington, PA: Christian Literature Crusade, 1987.

Chapter 2–Recognizing the Time of Our Visitation

1. Read John 14-16; note John 15:26.
2. John 14:10-14; note verses 13-14.
3. I might also point out here that Samuel himself, just like Ezekiel, was a transitional prophet, speaking to the nation on how to change politically, both in religious leadership and secular leadership.
4. Everett Fox, *Give Us A King,* Schocken Books, Inc., a Registered Trademark of Random House, Inc., New York, 1999, p 72.
5. I am not against DNA Blood-typing, nor the other positive scientific and technological discoveries I believe God has given us. I believe we should use every tool He gives us for mankind's betterment and the furtherance of the gospel. I am against the abuse to which those discoveries are sometimes subjected.

BEYOND STRONGHOLDS

6. I am not espousing lawlessness here, nor encouraging anyone to throw out his or her Social Security cards. I am speaking about spiritually knowing and recognizing godly order as opposed to entrenching ourselves in manmade rules, regulations and ideas, which eventually have an unhealthy effect on the body of Christ.

Chapter 3—The Word

1. This is not to be confused with the Hebrew word *bohow*, which is used in the same sentence of Genesis 1:1. As we study Genesis for our purposes of studying strongholds set up against God's Word, I would like to mention that we will not be discussing creation theology or eschatology (the study of the church in end-time events) in this book. For no matter what your belief system is concerning such issues, although quite important, those beliefs are not essential in dealing with personal strongholds.
2. English concordances cite the word as *dabar*. It is pronounced *davar*. This is because the bet has no daghes (dot) in the middle of it. For the purposes of this book, we shall spell out the Hebrew as it should be pronounced. Weingreen, J., M.A., Ph.D., *A Practical Grammar for Classical Hebrew*. Second Edition, London, UK: Oxford University Press, 1959, pp. 3,5,14.
3. Wagner, C. Peter, *Churches that Pray*. Ventura, CA: Regal Books, 1993, p. 137.
4. Edersheim, Alfred. *Sketches of Jewish Social Life*. Peabody, MA: Hendrickson Publishers, Inc., 1994. pp. 136-139.

Chapter 4—The Word in His Prophets

1. Funk & Wagnalls Encyclopedia. 1972, Volume 19, p 55.
2. *Eerdmans' Handbook To The World's Religions*. Grand Rapids, MI. William B. Eerdmans Publishing Company, 1994, pp. 42.
3. Cairns, Earle E. *Christianity Through The Centuries*. Grand Rapids, MI: Zondervan Publishing House, 1981. pp. 61-121.
4. Ibid., pp. 121-133.
5. Ibid., pp. 151-156.
6. Ibid., pp. 165-171.
7. Woodward, Kenneth L. "When Saints Go Marching In." *Newsweek Magazine* 4 Sept. 2000.
8. *The Oxford English Dictionary*. London, UK: Oxford University Press, Amen House, 1961. Volume IV, p. 343.

Chapter 5—His Knowledge

1. Sandford, John, and Mark Sandford. *A Comprehensive Guide to Deliverance and Inner Healing*. Grand Rapids, MI: Chosen Books, Fleming H. Revell, a division of Baker Book House Company, 1992. p. 53.
2. Ibid., pp. 18-19.
3. Ibid., pp. 53-54.
4. Ibid., p. 57.
5. Ibid., pp. 55-60.
6. Webster's Deluxe Unabridged Dictionary, Second Edition. New York, NY: Simon and Schuster, 1979, p. 1733.
7. Sanford. A Comprehensive Guide to Deliverance and Inner Healing. pp. 59-60.
8. Fox, John. *Fox's Book of Martyrs*. Grand Rapids, MI: Zondervan Publishing House, 1926.
9. There are those who date Daniel 9-10 in the same year. Theologian Edward Reese dates it as 537 B.C. and 539 B.C., a two-year difference. However one dates these events, it is obvious that some period of time elapsed between Daniel 9 and Daniel 10. And, obviously, 21 days elapsed during Daniel's fast (Dan. 10:2). Reese, Edward. *The Reese Chronological Bible*. Minneapolis, MN: Bethany House Publishers, 1977, pp. 1158, 1164.

Chapter 6—His Presence

1. I do not include the symbolism of the Jewish practice of the cup and loaf at Passover, nor the "Elijah chair" in some synagogues simply because these symbolize

Notes

      Messiah coming for the first time to our Jewish brethren. God's witness is that Messiah, Jesus Christ, has already come in the flesh, been sacrificed, buried and has risen again to sit at the right hand of God. (See 1 Peter 3:21-22.)

2. Reese, Edward. *The Reese Chronological Bible*. Minneapolis, MN: Bethany House Publishers, 1977, pp. 422, 423-431.
3. Ibid. Reese states that the theologian Frank Klassen has the ark leaving Israel in 1036 B.C.
4. The reason why many of the early scholars don't count this son of Gideon as a God-ordained judge is because he was born of a concubine, and not an Israeli one, but one from Shechem. But more importantly, he does not meet with the criterion of peace and rest for Israel from their enemies that the Scriptures give for the judges, since he murdered 69 of his father's sons; thus precipitating God sending an evil spirit to take him out. (See Judges 2:16; 9:23.)
5. Hartill, J. Edwin, D.D. *Principles of Biblical Hermeneutics*. Grand Rapids, MI: Zondervan Publishing House, 1947, p. 119.
6. Ibid.
7. Reese. *Chronological Bible*. p. 430.
8. Ezekiel 14 gives us a good example of this principle. It's here that we understand that when we put up stronghold stumbling blocks in our own hearts to God's way of doing things that He allows His presence to fall even on a false prophet to prophesy. It's in that place that even an accurate word can come from the mouth of a false prophet.
9. Edersheim, Alfred. *The Temple: Its Ministry and Services*. Peabody, Mass: Hendrickson Publishers, Inc., 1994, pp. 300 (quoting from the Mishnah).
10. Ibid., pp. 299.
11. Pamphilus, Eusebius. *Eusebius' Ecclesiastical History; Popular Edition*. Grand Rapids, MI: Baker Book House, 1955, pp. 49.
12. Edersheim. The Temple, pp. 298-299.
13. Ibid., pp. 299-300.
14. Ibid., p. 294.
15. *Eusebius. Ecclesiastical History*. pp. 104-106.
16. It would seem that Paul refers to something similar concerning unbelievers in 2 Thessalonians 2:11 where false prophecies, signs and wonders are being displayed.
17. Reese, *Chronological Bible*. Index pp. vii-viii; from D, Josiah to H, Ezekiel's prophecies after Jerusalem's fall. This covers pp. 962-1115.

Chapter 7—The Name

1. From Jesus to Christ, the First Christians. Frontline. Producer and writer, Marilyn Mellowes. Senior producer and director, William Cran. A four-part education video. WGBH Educational Foundation, Distributed by PBS Home Video, a department of the Public Broadcasting System, 1998.
2. Ibid., Part 1.
3. From Jesus to Christ. Frontline. Holand L. Hendrix, President, Union Theological Seminary.
4. Ibid., Part 1.
5. Edersheim, Alfred. *Sketches of Jewish Social Life*. Hendrickson Publishers, Inc., 1994, pp. 112, 117-118.
6. Ibid. pp. 167-194.
7. Edersheim. Sketches. pp. 111-113, 221-222.
8. From Jesus. Frontline. Prof. Paula Fredrickson. Boston University.
9. Young, H. Brad. *Jesus the Jewish Theologian*. Peabody, MA: Hendrickson Publishers, Inc., 1997, pp. 14-16.
10. From Jesus. Frontline.
11. Ibid., Prof. Michael White, University of Texas, Austin.
12. Ibid.
13. Ibid.
14. Fox, John. *Fox's Book of Martyrs*. Grand Rapids, MI: Zondervan Publishing House, 1926.

BEYOND STRONGHOLDS

Chapter 8—His Image in His People

1. See footnote 3 from chapter one.
2. Schmitt, Charles P. *Floods Upon the Dry Ground.* Shippensburg, PA: Revival Press, an imprint of Destiny Image Publishers, Inc., 1998, pp. 186-190.
3. Schmitt, Charles P. *Floods Upon the Dry Ground.* Shippensburg, PA: Revival Press, an imprint of Destiny Image Publishers, Inc., 1998, pp. 201, 203.
4. Schmitt, Charles P. *Floods Upon the Dry Ground.* Shippensburg, PA: Revival Press, an imprint of Destiny Image Publishers, Inc., 1998, pp. 190-195.
5. Ibid., p. 181.
6. Ibid., p. 189.
7. Schmitt. *Floods.* p. 211.
8. Ibid.
9. Sandford, John and Mark Sandford. *A Comprehensive Guide to Deliverance and Inner Healing.* Grand Rapids, MI: Chosen Books, Fleming H. Revell, a division of Baker Book House Company 1992, pp. 285-286.
10. Thieves of Time. Native American Rights Fund. PBS Documentary. WSRE-TV, Pensacola, FL.

Chapter 9—His People in His Image

1. Bickle, Mike with E. Michael Sullivan. *Growing in the Prophetic.* Creation House, pp. 178-180.
2. Edersheim, Alfred. *Sketches of Jewish Social Life.* Hendrickson Publishers, Inc., 1994, pp. 107-111. See also pp. 109-111 concerning Lois and Eunice.
3. Bickle, *Growing.* pp. 179-180.
4. Edersheim. *Sketches.* pp. 115-116, 123-124.
5. While God likens a husband's headship to Christ, we need to realize we are not to act like we are God in heaven, to be obeyed no matter what we do. Likewise, while the bride of Christ is perfect and spotless, we need to realize we are not always perfect and spotless in our human flesh.
6. Gaus, Andy. The Unvarnished New Testament. Grand Rapids, MI: Phanes Press, 1991, pp. 222-223.
7. Coates-Markle, Linda, with Emily Kilby, "Choosing to Survive." Equus Magazine, September 1996, 231: 34-41.
8. Ephesians 4:8 says the word "men." But the Greek is the word *antropos*, meaning "humans or mankind." It is not gender specific. The word "men" could be easily translated as "world." So it would read, "When He ascended on high He led captives in His train and gave gifts to the world."

Chapter 10—Where Do We Go From Here?

1. Rodgers, Adam. "Going Faster Than Light?" *Newsweek Magazine*, March 1, 1999, 61.
2. Sandford, John, and Mark Sandford. *A Comprehensive Guide to Deliverance and Inner Healing.* Grand Rapids, MI: Chosen Books, , Fleming H. Revell, a division of Baker Book House Company, 1992, pp. 231-240.
3. While Paul tells the Corinthians that the earthly came first and then the spiritual (1 Cor. 15:46), he is talking about our new, resurrected bodies. He makes it quite clear that those of the flesh live according to the flesh, and those of heaven live after the Man from heaven (verses 48-49).
4. Edersheim, Alfred. *Sketches of Jewish Social Life.* Hendrickson Publishers, Inc., 1994, pp. 143, 144.
5. Ibid., pp. 138, 146.
6. Meyer, F.B. Joseph. *Christian Literature Crusade*, Fort Washington, PA: Christian Literature Crusade, 1982, p 12.
7. Edersheim, Alfred. *The Temple: It's Ministry and Services.* Hendrickson Publishers, 1994, Inc. See p. 68 for the priestly implication of the word "coat" or "vesture."